KU-532-625

LEEDS BECKETT UNIVERSITY
LIBRARY
DISCARDED

71 0019331 4

THE GUINNESS GUIDE TO
BALLET

THE GUINNESS GUIDE TO
BALLET

Oleg Kerensky

GUINNESS SUPERLATIVES LIMITED 2 CECIL COURT, LONDON ROAD, ENFIELD, MIDDLESEX

710 019331 4

LEEDS POLYTECHNIC

453364

A V

50653

26.5.83

792.8

Editor: Alex Reid
Design and layout: David Roberts

©Oleg Kerensky and Guinness Superlatives Ltd 1981

Published in Great Britain by
Guinness Superlatives Limited,
2 Cecil Court, London Road,
Enfield, Middlesex EN2 6DJ

Colour separation by Culver Graphic, High Wycombe, Bucks.
Typeset in Great Britain by Sprint, Beckenham, Kent
Printed and Bound in Yugoslavia by Mladinska Knjiga, Ljubljana

‘Guinness’ is a registered trade mark of Guinness Superlatives Ltd.

British Library Cataloguing in Publication Data:

Kerensky, Oleg
    Guinness guide to ballet
    I. Ballet
    I. Title
    792.8   GV1787

ISBN 0-85112-226-4

Contents

Acknowledgements

Anyone who writes on ballet today can rely heavily for factual information on two dictionaries: *The Concise Oxford Dictionary of Ballet* by Horst Koegler and *A Dictionary of Ballet* by G.B.L. Wilson. Writers on the standard repertory have long relied on the descriptions provided in C.W. Beaumont's *Complete Book of Ballets* and its various supplements. I gratefully confess my debt to all these books. I also confess my use of my own book, *Ballet Scene*, which is now out of print. For recent news and opinions of the ballet world, I have frequently consulted the principal magazines: *The Dancing Times* and *Dance and Dancers* in Britain, and *Dance Magazine*, *Dance News* and *Ballet News* in the United States. I am grateful to the unique research facilities of New York public library's dance collection at Lincoln Center, to my friends and colleagues—especially Jack Anderson, Robert Baker, Clive Barnes, Patricia Barnes, George Dorris, John Percival and Freda Pitt—who lent me books or cuttings and good-naturedly answered my questions, and to the press representatives of various ballet companies who provided me with information and with tickets for their performances at times when I was more concerned with writing this book than with immediate reviewing. I have tried to make the text as 'objective' as possible, but even the selection of material is inevitably a personal choice and my tastes and opinions must necessarily intrude. For these, and for any mistakes of omission or commission, I must accept full responsibility.

The author and publishers would like to thank the following organisations and individuals for their assistance in supplying illustrations as follows: BBC Hulton Picture Library, *p. 9, 11 right, 12, 15, 33, 40 right, 58, 71 upper and centre, 73, 76, 83 left, 129, 142, 148, 186, 189*; Danish Tourist Board, *p. 100*; Lois Franhine, *p. 97*; Institute of Choreology, *p. 46 right*; Museum of London, *p. 3*; New York Public Library, *p. 85, 86, 95, 97*; Popperfoto, *p. 65*; Raymond Mander and Joe Mitchenson Theatre Collection, *p. 10, 11 left, 40 left, 46 left, 70 left, 71 right, 140*; Royal College of Music, *p. 50, 51*; Sovfoto, *p. 11 upper, 102 left*; Martha Swope, *p. 194*. All other illustrations are the copyright of the Mike Davis Studio and our sincere thanks go to Jesse Davis for his very great assistance and support in this project.

Preface

More and more people all over the world have discovered the appeal of ballet in recent years. What was once a minority art, for a sophisticated and élite audience, is now performed to packed houses in almost every city of the civilized world. Two or three ballet companies often appear simultaneously in London or New York. Ballet is constantly seen on television, is featured in commercial musicals and even in advertisements, and has been included in several successful films. *The Turning Point,* a film about ballet dancers which incorporated a great deal of dancing, was a big success. Star dancers like Margot Fonteyn, Rudolf Nureyev and Mikhail Baryshnikov have become household names. Ballet can no longer be dismissed as dated, or as too expensive an activity for the modern world. Despite inflation and other economic worries, it is booming.

What is it' eal? The secret of its success is that it has man) ufferent appeals. It is an art, which can involve great music and painting as well as dancing skill. It is also an entertainment, spectacular, exciting, and sometimes amusing too. Many ballets make ideal family outings and provide young children with the best possible introduction to the magic of the live theatre. Major companies like the Royal Ballet and New York City Ballet now give regular special performances for schoolchildren, who are introduced to ballet as part of their normal education. Ballet can be as thrilling as a sporting event; dancers train like athletes and achieve amazing feats of speed, balance and elevation. These feats are all the more exciting and effective for being precisely timed, for being executed simultaneously by a group of people, and for being performed to music.

Many ballets, with their old-fashioned fairy-tale stories, provide a welcome escape from the problems of modern life. Others deliberately try to depict or comment on real life. They may have complex psychological themes, depict key moments from birth to death, or suggest emotions like love, jealousy, loneliness or despair. Ballet can be laughter-provoking or tear-jerking, it can be intellectually stimulating or provide mindless pleasure. It can have as many styles and subjects as any other theatrical form.

There are still those, however, who are frightened of ballet. They may think it too 'highbrow' or too 'soppy'. They may suspect that they don't know enough about it to understand it. Some people find the spectacle of men in ballet tights to be faintly ridiculous or even effeminate; some music-lovers resent the distraction of watching while they are listening. There will always be some who prefer opera, or plays, or musicals, or who do not like the theatre at all. But there are many more who once were wary of ballet but were quickly converted when they tried it. Often they get 'hooked', as on a drug, wanting to see more and more. It is not necessary to 'understand' ballet, or to know much about it, in order to enjoy it. It can be enjoyed instantly, with a spontaneous gut reaction. Then it can be appreciated more deeply as more is learned about its past, about how it is done, and about the differences between various styles, dancers and ballets.

This guide introduces ballet to those who do not yet know it and tries to help those who already love it to extend their knowledge and appreciation. It is a guide to ballet today, looking at the past so far as it affects the present and gazing a little speculatively into the future. There was a time, not many years ago, when a book of this kind would have described every ballet company, every ballet and every important dancer in the world. That is now impossible. Britain and the United States alone have more ballet than could be fully chronicled in a single book. So this guide points to many of the most interesting things happening in the world of ballet today and to the people who are doing those things. It also indicates where readers may discover more for themselves.

1
A brief history

PREPARING *for a* MASQUERADE.

The traditional Harlequin in the Italian *commedia
dell'arte*, one of modern ballet's ancestors. From
Italy, the stream of ballet flowed through France to
Denmark and Russia, then back to France and
England. It now flourishes in almost every country
of the world

The earliest British entertainments resembling ballets were the Elizabethan masques. Then, John Weaver (1673–1760) staged *The Loves of Mars and Venus* at Drury Lane Theatre in London in 1717. This was a story told without spoken words, using dance and mime. But this type of theatre did not take root in England, and ballet did not really flourish in London till the twentieth century. The main stream of ballet had its source in Italy, enlarged considerably in France, flowed strongly through Denmark and Russia, and then returned to western Europe from Russia. Thence it spread to the United States and subsequently to the rest of the world.

Dance was part of theatre from the earliest times. It featured prominently in Greek comedy. Something like ballet was involved in the Italian harlequinade (*commedia dell'arte*) which flourished from the sixteenth to the eighteenth centuries. (This old style of pantomime can still be seen at the open-air theatre in Tivoli Gardens, Copenhagen.) Harlequinades were exported from Italy to France in the eighteenth century for the entertainment of King Louis XIV. The King appointed a royal dancing master, danced in court entertainments himself, and encouraged Molière to include balletic interludes in his plays. He also founded the National Academy of Music and Dance, which is now the official school of the Paris Opéra Ballet.

The Academy taught the five positions of the legs and feet and the importance of 'turn-out'—turning the leg out sideways from the thigh—which remain the basic elements of classical ballet training to this day. The eighteenth-century French ballerina Camargo shortened her skirts to reveal her ankles and to make possible delicate little

Jean-Georges Noverre, the 18th-century French theorist who laid down early principles establishing ballet as a serious art

steps and jumps, the 'footwork' which is still a test of a true ballerina.

The first great theorist of ballet was also French. Jean-Georges Noverre (1727–1810) created ballets in Paris and Stuttgart, and also laid down written principles intended to make ballet more coherent and artistic. These principles were revived in this century, in a more sophisticated form, by the Russian ballet master Mikhail Fokine (1880–1942). Both Noverre and Fokine believed that ballet should be a blend of various ingredients—music, décor, drama and dance—linked by a definite theme. This idea helped to raise ballet's status from mere entertainment to recognition as a serious art. Nowadays, however, ballets do not conform to any particular principles. Many of the most successful works today have no story and no décor; some even have no music. What they must have—if they are really ballets—is theatrical dancing, though even that principle is sometimes ignored.

At least two nineteenth-century French ballets—*Giselle* and *Coppélia*—survive in something like their original forms and have found popular and permanent places in the international repertoire. Two others—*La Sylphide* and *Sylvia*—are sometimes revived though the first is much better known in Bournonville's slightly later Danish version and the second is scarcely known at all, despite its Delibes score and Ashton's attempt to give it a new lease of life. An even earlier French ballet, *La Fille mal Gardée,* first performed in Bordeaux in 1789, has now been given worldwide popularity by Ashton's new version.

Italian and French ballet masters were responsible for launching ballet in Denmark. The pioneer work was done by Vincenzo Galeotti (1733–1816), whose charming little work, *The Whims of Cupid and the Ballet Master* (1786), is still performed by the Royal Danish Ballet and is the oldest work to survive in the present-day repertoire. Galeotti was followed by Antoine Bournonville, whose main claim to fame is as the father of August Bournonville (1805–1879). It was August who created *La Sylphide* and many other ballets which remain the nucleus and pride of the Danish repertoire, and which enabled ballet to flourish in Copenhagen from the nineteenth century till now. The Danish ballet was only discovered by the rest of the world in the 1950s. Until then, Bournonville's works were unknown elsewhere; now some of them are standard items in the international repertoire, though not as popular or as frequently performed as the great Russian classics.

It was another Frenchman who started ballet in Russia. Marius Petipa (1818–1910) created some of the most famous ballets of all time—*The Sleeping Beauty, The Nutcracker* and *Swan Lake.* Some of his other works, like *Raymonda* and *La Bayadère*, have recently come back into favour. Under his guidance, Russian ballet developed extremely high technical standards of dancing and produced big spectacular works at the Imperial Maryinsky Theatre, now the Kirov, in St Petersburg, now Leningrad. Tchaikovsky, Glazunov and other composers wrote specially for Petipa, producing some of the best ballet music of all time. This Russian tradition has been continued in the twentieth century by Prokofiev and Stravinsky.

Petipa's assistant, Lev Ivanov (1834–1901), is now known to have been responsible for much of the actual dancing—the choreography—in Petipa's ballets. In particular, he devised the dances for *The Nutcracker* and for two acts of *Swan Lake,* including the most famous section, the lake-side scene. He created a more lyrical, less obviously brilliant, style of dancing which in its turn influenced the work of Fokine, the Russian choreographer who brought ballet back to France.

Russian ballet burst on Paris, where the art had fallen into neglect, in 1909. It was brought there under the management and guidance of Serge Diaghilev (1872–1929), a great organizer, fund-raiser and innovator, with the ability to find and bring together great artists from various spheres

Marius Petipa, the French choreographer who settled in Russia and made the famous Tchaikovsky classics

and with the taste to supervise and guide their work. His first season of ballet in Paris had not merely Fokine but also some of the greatest dancers of all time—Pavlova, Karsavina and Nijinsky. Their

Above: *Serge Diaghilev, who brought Russian ballet to the West and started its present popularity:* **right:** *Karsavina and Nijinsky, two of Diaghilev's greatest stars, in* Le Spectre de la Rose *at Covent Garden, 1911*

Above: *Colonel de Basil, who continued Diaghilev's work with his Ballets Russes;* **right:** *La Fille mal Gardée, one of the oldest surviving ballets, in Sir Frederick Ashton's immensely popular version for the Royal Ballet with Brenda Last as Lise and Desmond Kelly as Colas*

work was a sensational revelation. From then till his death, Diaghilev introduced a dazzling series of dancers and ballets, composers and designers, to the western world, having his biggest successes in Paris and London. The whole subsequent flowering of ballet in the West can be traced directly to his influence. His artists subsequently split up, settled all over the world and helped to launch a large number of new ballet companies. These include the British Royal Ballet, American Ballet Theatre, New York City Ballet, and even the Paris Opéra Ballet, which was reorganized and revitalized by Serge Lifar (b. 1905), one of Diaghilev's last stars.

The other equally great influence on western ballet was Anna Pavlova (1881–1931), the most famous ballerina of all time, who left Diaghilev to form her own company which toured to almost every corner of the globe. Everyone who saw her was captivated, and many were inspired to take up ballet as a career. Members of her company set up

schools in different parts of the world. Many people who later became leading figures in the world of ballet—including Sir Frederick Ashton (b. 1904), the British choreographer, and Sir Robert Helpmann (b. 1909), the Australian dancer-choreographer, got their first inspiration from her.

After Diaghilev's death, Russian ballet continued to tour in the West, during the 1930s, under various names which generally included the words 'Ballets Russes'. Colonel de Basil was Diaghilev's immediate successor and Monte Carlo became Russian ballet's home. During the 1940s, 'Ballets Russes' were toured in the United States by Sergei Denham. More influential, in the long run, was the work done by members of Diaghilev's company who settled permanently in England and the United States. In London, Marie Rambert (who was Polish, b. 1888), and Ninette de Valois (who is Irish, b. 1898), both founded ballet schools and companies. Rambert, who had helped Nijinsky to stage his *Rite of Spring* for Diaghilev, nurtured many of the brightest talents in British ballet and the company that bears her name still survives. De Valois, who danced with the Diaghilev ballet from 1923 to 1926, was encouraged by Lilian Baylis to form a company at the Old Vic, a company which has grown to become the Royal Ballet. George Balanchine (a Georgian b. 1904), who worked with Diaghilev from 1925 onwards, settled in New York where he became a founder and the principal choreographer of New York City Ballet. The Royal Ballet and New York City Ballet are now two of the greatest companies in the world; some people would say they are *the* greatest.

Other ballet companies in the western world today are mostly off-shoots of one of these companies. Balanchine has influenced styles of choreography all over the world, especially in the United States where numerous companies outside New York are modelled on his, often using dancers trained in the School of American Ballet, the official school of New York City Ballet. Dancers trained at the Royal Ballet School or in the Royal Ballet have gone abroad to found or direct companies in Australia, Canada, South Africa, Germany, Italy, Norway, Sweden, Turkey, Iran and many other countries. In particular, John Cranko (1927–1973), the South African choreographer who had his early experience with the Royal Ballet, launched the Stuttgart Ballet on its international career. Partly in consequence, almost every city in western Germany, a country with no previous ballet tradition, now has its own company.

Other notable 'exports' from Britain have been Celia Franca, who went to Toronto to found and direct the National Ballet of Canada, and Peggy van Praagh who did the same thing in Australia. Some British dancers even 'invaded' the United States, founding or directing regional companies in Houston, Texas; Baltimore, Maryland; and Buffalo, New York. There was also a reverse exchange, when the American modern dancer Robert Cohan became the first director of the London Contemporary Dance Theatre.

Ballet has also flourished in eastern Europe. In the Soviet Union, the tradition founded by the Tsars and the methods of training developed in St Petersburg continued and expanded. The Soviet Government transferred the main ballet company from Leningrad to Moscow, but the best training continued to be at the old school. New ballet companies were encouraged in provincial cities, notably Kiev, Novosibirsk and Perm, and second companies of a more experimental nature were also set up in both Moscow and Leningrad. There are now about forty Soviet companies. After the Second World War, when the Soviet Union took control of Eastern Europe, companies were set up in the satellite countries, most successfully in Budapest, Hungary.

The Soviet Union, the United States, and Britain have all taken shares, separately, in training dancers and encouraging ballet in Japan. The Japanese have now learned this Western skill with the same ease and speed as they have learned other Western techniques. Japanese companies tour the world and give technically impeccable performances of Western classical ballets.

In the United States, black dancers have achieved similar success. Arthur Mitchell's Dance Theatre of Harlem, an all-black company, has mounted various standard works, ranging from those of Petipa to those of Balanchine, and has toured with them to England and the rest of Europe.

These developments do raise some aesthetic, dramatic and social questions. Ballets are designed for particular dancers, with specific facial and bodily characteristics. The nature of the ballet inevitably changes when the cast changes. The change is even greater when a white cast is replaced by an oriental or black one. Westerners find Japanese faces less expressive than European ones. Black dancers have different physiques and look different, even when performing the same steps. When Dance Theatre of Harlem staged *Swan Lake,* they felt that the traditional white costumes would make too great a contrast with the dancers' bodies, and dressed them instead in pale blue.

The Russian nineteenth century classics were primarily vehicles for ballerinas, and the ballerinas of those days were extremely petite. Today's dancers tend to be much taller, which alters the appearance of the movements, particularly when the ballerina is lifted in the air. The female *corps de ballet* in those works was intended to be uniform.

Ballet companies used to insist on their ladies all being roughly the same height and build, and even sometimes all having the same coloured hair. Nowadays much greater diversity is generally accepted, and is indeed welcomed by some companies and audiences.

In many ways it is still easier for an audience to accept an all-white, all-oriental, or all-black company than a racially mixed one. The principal Western ballet companies are mainly or exclusively white. However political and social considerations increasingly dictate racial integration, and this is gradually becoming accepted.

When Jerome Robbins originally cast a black male dancer opposite a white woman in his version of *Afternoon of a Faun* in 1959, British audiences thought the ballet must be making some sort of racial statement. This was not intended. Nowadays audiences are learning to ignore such differences. Nevertheless, there is a problem, shared with drama and opera. Quite apart from aesthetic considerations, there is the question of dramatic verisimilitude. Should audiences be prepared to accept black parents of a white child, or vice versa? These are all questions which are still to be resolved, and their resolution will depend on the evolution of our society in general.

Right: *A famous poster advertising the Diaghilev ballet in Paris, 1913*

Left: *Pavlova in her dressing-room during her company's season at the Théâtre des Champs-Elysées, Paris, in 1924*

2
The language
of ballet

Students of the Royal Ballet School, Caroldene
Horne and Peter Fairweather, doing the difficult
'fish-dive' which ends the Aurora *pas de deux* in
The Sleeping Beauty. Most technical terms in ballet
are still in French, but 'fish-dive' has generally
replaced *'temps de poisson'* in Britain and the
United States

It is difficult to talk or write about ballet without using words and phrases which have acquired specialized meanings. For example, ballets themselves are commonly divided into different categories, such as *classical, romantic, ballet blanc, neo-classical, abstract, dramatic,* and *full-length.*

Classical and *romantic* are opposites in art history, with the classical period preceding the romantic. In ballet, romantic came before classical, but the distinction between the two is in any case very blurred. *Giselle* and *La Sylphide* are classics which can also be called romantic. It is common usage to describe all ballets which have survived from the nineteenth century as classical, and now there are also twentieth-century classics, works which seem to have taken a permanent place in the international repertoire.

The romantic ballets tell stories, usually about fantasy creatures—fairies, sylphs, witches and the like. Their heroines are scarcely flesh-and-blood women but are idealized creatures, remote from everyday life. Even Giselle, who starts off the ballet as an apparently ordinary peasant girl, soon reveals herself to be highly strung, naive, over-fond of danc-

The romantic in ballet: a Festival Ballet production of Les Sylphides

The classical in ballet: Lesley Collier dancing Aurora in the Royal Ballet production of The Sleeping Beauty

ing. She commits suicide or dies of a broken heart (depending on the production and the ballerina) and in the second act she has become a ghost, a wili.

A romantic ballerina wears an ankle-, or calf-length dress (the 'romantic tutu') and specializes in being light, ethereal, unworldly. She prefers to create a mood and move us with emotion rather than to perform virtuoso steps and excite us by sheer brilliance. Most of the great ballerinas have been romantic, from Taglioni through Pavlova, Markova, Fonteyn, and Ulanova to Makarova. They had the technique which conceals technique, a higher type of artistry than showing off technical feats for their own sake. Romantic ballerinas are often accused of being technically weak, but this is usually a deception. All the ballerinas named actually had very strong techniques, even if they neither could nor wanted to balance as long or jump as high as some other dancers. However several of them were also able to go on appearing successfully in middle-age, when they had to rely increasingly on style and interpretative skill rather than on dancing.

A purely classical ballet, on the other hand, depends on its dancing. The thin pretence of a story is mainly an excuse for brilliant dancing, lavish spectacle and attractive, melodious music. *The Nutcracker* and *The Sleeping Beauty* are essentially ballets of this type, despite some recent attempts to make them more dramatic and 'romantic'. The classical ballerina wears a short tutu, designed to reveal as much of her body as is considered decent and to give her the maximum freedom to execute complex steps. She makes her effects, not through acting or emotion, but by seemingly effortless performance of brilliant solos and duets.

Some of the oldest classics are neither 'romantic' nor 'classical'. They are folk-tales, with peasants, toy-makers, fishermen and other real people as their characters. *La Fille mal Gardée, Coppélia* and most of Bournonville's ballets are of this type. These ballets also have their own special brand of ballerina, the 'soubrette,' who is usually good at being saucy, humorous and charming, rather than an airy sylph or a cool technician.

All these categories of ballets and dancers overlap. Petipa liked to mix all these styles in his full-length ballets (see below), most notably in *Don Quixote*. Similarly most great ballerinas have been successful in classical, romantic *and* soubrette roles. Despite the general rule that the romantic ballerinas achieve the most fame, the American ballerinas Rosella Hightower and Maria Tallchief, and many of the principals of New York City Ballet, could be regarded as mainly classical, while Lopoukhova, Danilova and the Soviet ballerina Lepeshinskaya achieved their biggest successes in soubrette roles.

In modern times, Balanchine has created a vogue for 'neo-classical' ballets. These are abstract displays of pure dancing, totally without story and often without costumes or décor. A few of these ballets, like *Serenade,* do hint at a 'romantic' mood or at human relationships between the dancers. Some claim that no work performed by human beings can be entirely abstract, that even cold aloofness is a mood of a kind. However it certainly is difficult to detect any mood or emotion in many modern 'abstract' ballets. Some choreographers have gone even further to eliminate hints of humanity by enclosing the dancers in sacks or other disguises, making them look more like mobile sculptures or efficient automata than human beings.

Full-length means a work in more than one act—two, as in *Giselle, La Fille mal Gardée* or *The Nutcracker,* three as in *Coppélia* or *Romeo and Juliet,* or four as in *Swan Lake* or *The Sleeping Beauty.* In another sense, any complete ballet, even if it lasts only ten minutes, is of course 'full-length'. But *full-length* has come to mean a ballet occupying a whole evening's programme on its own, though even that is not always the case. *Giselle* and

Coppélia, though 'full-length', are sometimes performed with one or even two other short ballets.

A programme consisting of several short ballets is now generally described, in Britain anyway, as 'a triple bill'. This is accurate enough when the convention of performing three ballets in one programme is observed, but there has on occasion even been publicity describing programmes with four ballets as 'a triple bill'!

A *'divertissement'*, originally a 'diversion' included in an opera or play at the French Court, is now a series of short dances, in contrasting styles, usually occurring as part of a celebration in a classical ballet—the wedding in *The Sleeping Beauty* or the birthday party in *Swan Lake.* The *divertissement* was the excuse for a choreographer like Petipa to stage pseudo-national dances as well as one or two virtuoso danced duets, or *pas de deux. Divertissements* can also consist of a wide variety of different dances, by different choreographers, performed by a galaxy of star dancers at a charity gala or company anniversary. A *divertissement* can even be performed without star dancers, though that is usually less satisfactory.

A dance for two people is normally still called a *pas de deux.* The original French vocabulary of dance survived in pre-revolutionary Russia, where French was in any case the language spoken at court and by the educated classes. French remains the commonly accepted language for dancers of all nationalities. Attempts are constantly being made in Britain and the United States to anglicize the language of ballet, but the results are often awkward. 'Duet' is sometimes used instead of *'pas de deux'*; the trouble is that it suggests musical instruments or singing voices rather than danced steps. The *'pas de trois'* is not usually translated as 'trio', nor the *'pas de quatre'* as 'quartet'.

It used to be thought that the *pas de deux* was inevitably an expression of love, stylized and formalized, between the two performers. The classic Petipa *pas de deux* normally celebrated flirtation, love or betrothal. It had a standard form: the actual *pas de deux,* including slow turns and balances for the ballerina, supported by her partner, followed by solos ('variations') for the man and the woman, concluding with the fast, breath-taking finale ('coda') for the two together, working the audience up to a fever pitch of excitement. Later choreographers devised *pas de deux* in much freer, less formal styles.

When choreographers started creating *pas de deux* for two men, or two women, this logically suggested homosexual love. In some cases, such as Nijinska's *Les Biches,* this is indeed the case; in other cases, such as Hans van Manen's *Four Schumann Pieces,* there is ambiguity and un-

Merle Park and Rudolf Nureyev in a pas de deux *from Nureyev's Royal Ballet production of* The Nutcracker

certainty, probably deliberate. But there are plenty of *pas de deux* in which no erotic or romantic content whatever is intended or even remotely suggested. Many of Balanchine's *pas de deux,* for example, are as abstract as the remainder of the ballets in which they feature.

The *choreographer* is the person who devises the actual steps of a ballet, showing the dancers what to do. Normally the choreographer also devises the whole ballet, choosing or writing the story and selecting the music and décor. The verb 'to choreograph' is cumbersome; writers do not like having to refer to someone 'choreographing' a work. This difficulty has led some critics to describe choreographers as 'writing' a ballet, and even to refer to the 'text' of a ballet. This is misleading, suggesting that a ballet is written down by its creator, like a book or a musical score. Ballets *can* now be written down in various systems of notation, but they are not created in that way. They are created by choreographers in the studio, trying out steps, patterns and groupings on live dancers.

The *ballerina* is the leading female dancer in the classics. This is one of the few examples of the

Students of the Royal Danish Ballet School practising
pliés (above) *and* demi-pliés (below)

earlier Italian terminology surviving the French *danseuse*. Traditionally the leading ballerina of a Russian company was known as the *prima ballerina assoluta,* or in France as the *première danseuse étoile.* The Royal Ballet revived the term *prima ballerina assoluta* for Dame Margot Fonteyn, but only about the time she retired from dancing! It has become common practice to describe any female dancer in classical ballet as a ballerina but strictly speaking 'ballerina' should only apply to the interpreters of the leading classic roles: Aurora, Giselle, Odette-Odile, Swanilda, and so forth. It can be argued whether every interpreter of these roles is entitled to call herself a ballerina; it makes perfect sense to say 'she may be dancing Giselle, but she is not a real ballerina, only a soloist'. It makes sense, but it is of course a subjective judgement about the quality of the dancer.

Soloists are the next rank of dancers. As their title implies, they dance solos, as distinct from the leading roles. The term *'coryphée'* used to describe the third rank, the women who appeared together in groups of three or four, as distinct from the *corps de ballet,* the chorus which provided the background for the classic ballets. Recently the Royal Ballet appropriated *coryphée* to apply to both men and women of a certain seniority, regardless of what roles they danced.

In these egalitarian times it is becoming increasingly common for companies to list their dancers alphabetically, without giving them distinctive ranks or titles. The Royal Ballet, followed by London Festival Ballet, took to calling all their dancers *artists,* distinguishing between *'principal artists, solo artists* and mere *artists*—in other words, the *corps de ballet.* Festival Ballet even had *senior artists.* American companies now generally list their dancers in two or three separate groups, without giving them any titles.

The leading male dancer was traditionally called the *premier danseur* or, if he was the romantic, aristocratic type, the *danseur noble.* These terms have largely gone out of use. (Some people would say caustically that there are no more dancers justifying the 'noble' description!) The distinction between purely classical dancers, *character* dancers and *demi-caractère* (the translation, 'half-character', is never used) has also become blurred and is virtually extinct. The purely classical female dancer dances on the points of her feet, and is more concerned with dancing than with acting; similarly the male is concerned mainly with partnering and with virtuoso jumps and spins. The character dancer specializes in mime and national folk dances rather than in classical technique, while a *demi-caractère* dancer uses classical technique in roles of a less romantic or noble kind, roles which require comic or other strong characterization. Massine specialized in creating such roles, and so did Antony Tudor. Alain in Ashton's *La Fille mal Gardée* is *demi-caractère,* while Widow Simone is full 'character'.

Dancers are judged for a number of qualities, not merely for technical virtuosity. Technical terms for some of these qualities are *plié, turn-out* and *line. Pliés* are exercises done at the beginning of every daily class—bending the knees to go all the way down into a full crouching position, keeping the back upright, or bending half-way (*demi-plié*). A dancer with good *plié* will find it easier to jump and to land softly, without a heavy thud.

Turn-out is achieved through years of training. The feet and legs are increasingly turned out sideways from the thigh, so that eventually the foot can be placed sideways at an angle of 90 degrees. Dancers can often be distinguished by their habit of standing around in this position, even off stage. A very turned-out walk looks artificial and stagey, and 'modern' choreographers have reacted against it, sometimes insisting on deliberately 'turned-in' positions. But without good turn-out, the dancer cannot do the complex leg and foot movements required in ballet. This is one of the main reasons why training has to start young.

Line is a very elusive concept. When a dancer stands and moves with his head, torso, arms and legs always forming a harmonious and attractive pattern, then the dancer is said to have good line. It is partly a matter of physical proportions, partly a matter of instinct, and partly a matter of training. A dancer must constantly look in the mirror to check line. A dancer with short arms or legs, out of proportion to the rest of the body, or an unusually short or long neck, will find it difficult to achieve. Long legs can 'get in the way' and look ungainly, especially when a dancer is jumping or being lifted in the air. It is sometimes suggested that it does not matter what dancers look like as long as they have good technique. But audiences do not want to watch ugly or mis-shapen dancers. Elegance is an essential of good dancing. Audiences may not be aware of line as such, but they will instinctively feel that something is wrong when a dancer's line is ugly or awkward.

Line is also important when two or more are dancing together. Very often they must 'mirror' each other, holding their arms or legs in parallel, or else they must provide a contrast with each other, combining to form an interesting pattern. Traditionally a contrast was expected between a man and woman dancing together, but choreographers today often prefer to give them identical movements, dancing in parallel with each other. They also create similar effects with unisex groups of men or women.

Dancers are sometimes divided into those who are primarily *terre à terre* and those who excel in *élévation. Terre à terre* (literally, ground to ground) applies to dancers who are good at steps on the floor of the stage but do not have a very high jump. *Elévation* is the ability to jump high and look graceful while doing it. *Ballon* is also used to describe a quality of lightness and bounciness in a dancer, like a balloon. The ideal dancer, needless to say, would be good at everything, but in practice all dancers have their strengths and their weaknesses. Many great ballerinas have not been notable for their *elévation.* Equally, many dancers with good jumps have still failed to be great dancers.

Some dancers are easy to lift; others may look easy but may almost be breaking the backs of their partners. The skill of the partner can often conceal the difficulty of the '*lift*'. Choreographers are constantly inventing new and more complicated lifts and different positions in which the dancer can be held aloft. Soviet choreographers developed a number of spectacular lifts in which the man holds his partner high in the air, supporting her with only one hand while stretching the free arm confidently out into the air. Modern Western choreographers have developed lifts for men, as well as the traditional ones for women.

Attempts to describe complicated steps in technical words usually become misleading. There is no exact agreement about which term describes which step; even dancers and teachers often disagree about the correct description. However there are certain standard steps which it is useful to recognize by name. A *jeté* is a jump from one foot to the other—*grands jetés* are those big scissor-like jumps which can bring dancers diagonally across a stage at rapid speed. The *entrechat,* usually performed by men, is a vertical jump with the legs and feet criss-crossing. If neatly done, with a high jump, it is one of the most exciting steps in ballet and it is included in the male solos in all the most famous classical *pas de deux. Tours en l'air* are perhaps even more exciting, especially when performed by a dancer circling the stage at speed, and spinning in the air while holding a fixed pose.

One of the standard virtuosic ways of ending a *pas de deux* is the *fish-dive.* The ballerina jumps towards her partner, who catches her with one arm with her head down, almost touching the stage. This requires really skilful partnering; some male dancers prefer not to risk it. The *pirouette,* which can be performed by men and women, is a spin on one foot, with the other foot raised. The *fouetté* is a particular type of *pirouette,* usually performed by women—most notably in *Swan Lake* and *Don Quixote*—in which the raised leg is 'whipped' round the

other knee in a circular movement while the dancer spins on the supporting leg.

Some of the most difficult and exciting footwork is grouped together as *battements*, which range from small beats of the foot just off the ground to large beats in big jumps like the *cabriole*.

Bourrée is the term used to describe the steps used by a female dancer moving across the stage in small, silent steps on her points. There are various posed positions on the stage, of which the best known is the *arabesque* in which the body is balanced on one leg, with the other leg stretched out behind and the arms also outstretched to give balancing line.

A final word about vocabulary: it has long been customary in Britain to call dancers 'girls' and 'boys', regardless of their age. Some people now feel this to be demeaning and some newspapers object to their critics using these words. 'Men' and 'women' are gradually becoming more frequently used, the modern equivalent of the courteous, old-fashioned 'ladies' and 'gentlemen' of the ballet.

Bournonville style: Eva Evdokimova doing a pirouette in Napoli (above) *and a typical 'Danish' jeté* (below)

3
The making of a dancer

Children at the Royal Danish Ballet School doing
exercises at the *barre*. Work at the *barre* begins
every ballet class and is a daily routine for even the
greatest dancers

need a certain body to be in ballet (and specific

Over the years, a complex system of training has been evolved for classical ballet dancers. The system varies a bit between different countries and between different schools, and new methods and exercises are sometimes evolved. For example, teaching in the Soviet Union is now based on exercises developed by Agrippina Vaganova, who taught in Leningrad in the 1920s and 1930s; the school there is now named after her. Her methods helped to produce the more acrobatic style which is typical of modern Soviet dancers, and which has influenced dancing all over the world. Another famous teacher, Vera Volkova, influenced classical technique in the West, especially in Copenhagen where she moved the training away from the traditional Bournonville classes into something more like the Russian tradition.

Whatever the school or the teacher, however, the fundamentals of ballet training remain the same. Formal training usually begins between the ages of nine and eleven, though children may have taken simple dancing lessons before then. The Royal Ballet School, the leading school in Britain, starts children at eleven, and does not particularly want them to have had any previous training. They look for lively, likeable personalities, with musicality and the right physical attributes.

The girls must be well proportioned, slim, with a well-shaped neck and not too large a head, with loose leg extensions and good feet. Height prediction tests are normally made, as girls ideally should grow to at least 5ft 3in. Until recently, 5ft 6in was regarded as about the maximum desirable height, but dancers are getting taller all the time—like the rest of the population. There have always been some unusually small ballerinas and some exceptionally tall ones. Ballerinas in the nineteenth century were petite, and classical choreography tends to look better with shorter dancers. Tall girls often look awkward in classical lifts, and also have dif-

ficulty in finding sufficiently tall partners to lift them without strain. Some tall ballerinas have even had to give up their careers prematurely for this reason.

On the other hand, tall girls can bring extra authority to roles like the Queen of the Wilis in *Giselle* and the Lilac Fairy in *The Sleeping Beauty,* and often have a very graceful line. Balanchine has a notorious liking for tall, long-legged ballerinas, and the average height of the girls in New York City Ballet is noticeably greater than in the Royal Ballet.

Boys should have a good athletic frame and physique, a good jump, plenty of vitality, and should grow to about 5ft 8in or more. Very short male dancers, like Wayne Sleep of the Royal Ballet or Jean-Pierre Frohlich of New York City Ballet, usually find themselves restricted to character parts, like jesters. In recent years there have been some experiments with drugs to make young dance students grow taller, but both the efficiency and the morality of such treatment remain debatable.

All ballet schools rightly emphasize the tough, athletic qualities needed for classical ballet, especially for the boys. It is generally considered desirable for young boys and girls to be taught separately, whenever possible, and for them to have teachers of their own sex. It certainly seems to be true that the greatest ballerinas have been trained by former ballerinas and the male stars by male teachers. Several retired ballerinas of the Imperial Russian Ballet taught with great success in Paris after the Russian Revolution, and a new generation of retired ballerinas—such as Danilova and Dubrovska—contributed their experience and expertise to the teaching at the School of American Ballet in New York into the 1980s.

Teachers are always dancers or ex-dancers. Some dancers have no desire or aptitude for teaching; others have become just as famous as teachers as they were as dancers. Some teach mainly

Children at the Royal Ballet School (White Lodge) doing arabesques. Balances of this kind are practised daily in centre work

by verbal explanations and give only the slightest physical demonstrations of what they require; others give what are almost complete performances in front of their classes! The most distinguished ballerinas and former ballerinas usually reserve their teaching for the most advanced students, and for dancers who are already members of a company.

The reason for keeping the sexes separate, at least with young students, is that in classical ballet the men are supposed to appear virile and strong and to be contrasted with the gentle, feminine qualities of the women. The students model themselves on their teachers, and can get the best advice from teachers who have developed the very qualities they are trying to impart. The distinction between the sexes has become blurred in many modern-style works, which are often deliberately 'unisex' in style.

There used to be a strong prejudice against ballet training for boys, especially in countries like Britain and the United States, where there was no ballet tradition. (In Russia and Denmark, ballet has long been recognized as an honourable and manly occupation, which is one reason those countries have always found it easier to produce good male dancers.) Dancing was thought of as effeminate, and male ballet dancers as homosexuals. As in all the arts, the proportion of homosexuals in ballet *is* higher than in the community as a whole. Some of the most famous male dancers—technically and athletically strong—*have* been homosexual. Nijinsky was bisexual. On the other hand, many famous male dancers have been notoriously heterosexual, enjoying reputations for being a menace to the ladies of the *corps de ballet!* The dancers who may seem effeminate on the stage are not necessarily those who are homosexual offstage. In any case, the prejudice against male dancers has decreased, as has the prejudice against homosexuals.

Television, giving wide exposure to the tough physical feats achieved by dancers, has done a great deal to destroy the prejudice. So have male superstars like Nureyev and Baryshnikov, who have proved that a male dancer can become as rich and famous as a ballerina.

One of the attractions of ballet training, for many parents, is that both boys and girls must submit to a strict routine and must learn considerable self-discipline. These are features, not just of ballet training, but of a dancer's entire life. The training is probably as good, in terms of character-building, as any education available. Many people remain grateful for the physical and mental disciplines they learned, even if they do not go on to use them in careers in ballet. Margot Fonteyn once said that many young people are discontented because they do not know what to do with themselves. She was

grateful for never having had that problem—she always knew she was due at class, rehearsal, or performance!

A corresponding disadvantage of ballet training is that it often leaves the students undereducated. So much time must be devoted to the physical demands of ballet, that there is never enough time for reading and for general education. The schools attached to major established companies, like the leading Soviet companies, the Royal Danish Ballet and the British Royal Ballet, provide full-time tuition, with most of the younger pupils living in. Obviously they try to balance the needs of specialist ballet training and of all-round general education, but the latter rarely reaches a very high level. In Britain, even the dancers' knowledge of the history of their own art, and their understanding of the allied arts of music and painting, are usually surprisingly limited. Schools which provide only ballet training, like the School of American Ballet, have to leave time for their pupils to get their general education elsewhere, but that system is not likely to be any more satisfactory, and there can be an awkward conflict between the requirements of the two schools.

Another disadvantage of embarking on a ballet training is that there can be no guarantee of success at the end. At any time during the training, the student may develop an injury, may grow too tall, or may simply fail to develop the technique or personality judged necessary by the school. It is kinder to the student to terminate the training as soon as this happens, rather than continue to build on false hopes. Even when the training is satisfactorily completed, there is still no guarantee of a job in a ballet company, except for the most outstanding students.

It is often assumed that the very first thing a girl must do on entering ballet school is to learn to balance on the tips of her toes, her *pointes* or *points.* This is not the case, though unfortunately it is the way that ballet was sometimes taught. Too early a start on *pointes* is painful and harmful, and often causes permanent damage to the feet, sometimes preventing a dancing career. Girls should not start till they are 12; at the Royal Ballet School, point-work is sometimes left as late as 15. Unfortunately some smaller schools, often under pressure from over-ambitious mothers, still allow very young girls to start dancing on their *pointes.*

Men are not taught to dance on *pointes,* though some can do so. Certain choreographers have exploited this gift for specific purposes, for example the solo Nijinska made for Dolin in *Les Fâcheux* and Ashton's solo for Alexander Grant as Bottom in *The Dream.* The cossacks of Russia appear to dance on *pointes* in soft boots, but these folk-dances are actually performed on the knuckles of the toes.

Exercises to strengthen the arches of the feet, and the use of the thigh, knees and ankles, are essential to every ballet class. Girls soon learn also to darn the ends of their point shoes, and sew on the ribbons which tie around the ankles—tasks which are still performed personally by even the most famous ballerinas. Darning the ends is the best way of helping to get a good grip on the stage when on point.

But dancing is not all a matter of legs and feet. The dancer has to learn disciplined use of the whole body. The ideal dancer would have an expressive face, lyrical, soft arm movements, a supple back, good posture, balance, speed, elevation, and precision as well as quick, strong footwork. The effort to acquire all these physical qualities is endless; obviously no dancer is equally gifted with them all.

Apart from physical techniques, dancers should learn about make-up, mime and acting, and something of the history of their own art and the different styles of ballet. Above all, they must imbibe music from an early age. Some children are naturally musical, synchronizing their movements to it perfectly. Others have to learn, while some otherwise good dancers remain unmusical throughout their careers, 'counting' under their breaths to keep in time with even the most obvious melodies and never really 'feeling' the music.

Classes are normally accompanied by a live pianist, though small schools may have to be content with recorded music. The pianist becomes adept at improvising phrases, often taken from well-known ballets, to suit the steps and speeds required by the teacher. The teacher becomes equally adept at inventing new combinations of steps (*enchaînements*) to test the pupils in new ways; some teachers create quite interesting choreography in class! One of the things the dancers learn from an early age, is to memorize and repeat steps very quickly, immediately after they are set by the teacher. This helps them later, when they have to learn a large number of roles in the repertoire of whatever company they join.

Classes always begin with work at the *barre,* a horizontal wooden bar fixed to the wall of the studio and used by the dancers for slight support. The first exercises are usually *pliés* and various other stretching exercises for the arms and legs. The dancers exercise one arm and leg, resting the other arm or foot on the *barre,* then switch to the other side. Each exercise at the *barre* has to be repeated on both the right and left side. At least one wall of a ballet studio is lined with mirrors, so that the dancers can watch themselves all the time, noticing everything from the position of their arms and legs to their facial expressions.

Work at the *barre* usually takes up about half the class. It is followed by *centre work,* in the middle of the studio. The dancers in a large class split into smaller groups to take turns in practising running jumps and other virtuosic steps and, as they grow older, partnering or *double work* as it is sometimes called.

All exercises and ballet steps begin and end in one of the basic *five positions.* These are essentially positions of the legs and feet, though there are

Right: *Point-work. First two pictures show* échappés, *the feet moving from a closed to a more open position; third picture shows dancer poised on point and the last shows the feet crossing when she* bourrées *across the stage*

Below: *The basic* five positions *of the feet, which begin and end all steps in classical ballet. Note the right-angled turn-out of the feet in all positions*

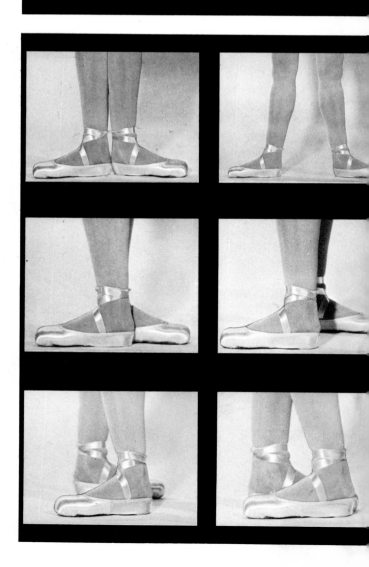

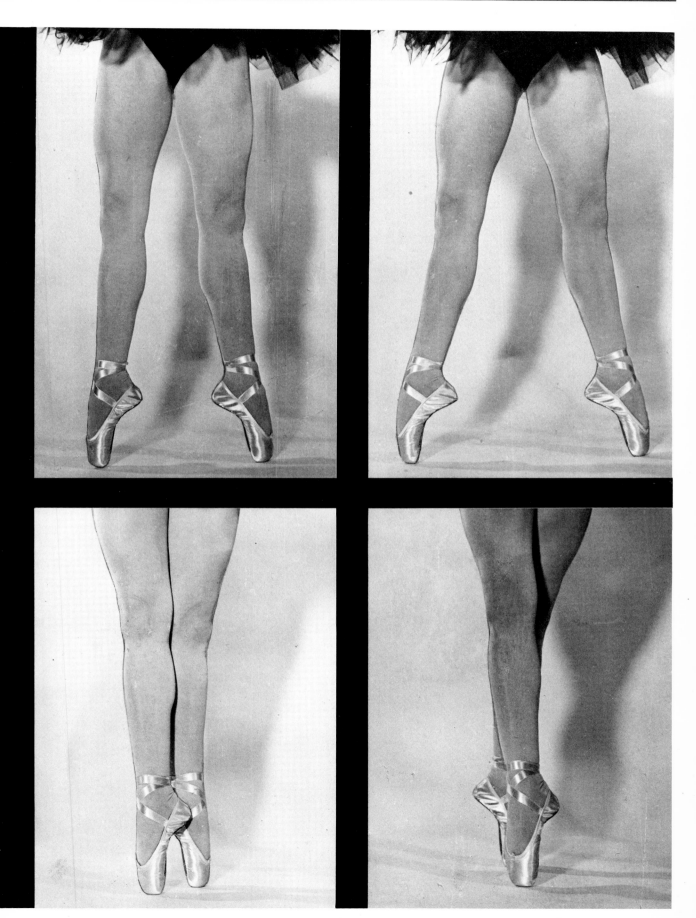

various standard arm positions to go with them. Even when taking up these positions, the dancers must also pay attention to the rest of their bodies—the graceful and appropriate positioning of the head and torso.

After the energetic centre work, most classes end with some quiet exercises, possibly with *pliés* again, and often with the dancers practising *révérences*—the formal bows and curtseys, with which the dancers respond to audience applause at the end of a performance. Very often the dancers also applaud the teacher.

The Royal Ballet School is divided into two sections, junior and senior. Students come to the senior school at 16 years of age from other schools, in Britain and abroad, to perfect their ballet training, joining those who graduate directly from the junior school at White Lodge, a beautiful building in Richmond Park. The senior school in Baron's Court is only a few miles from, and is on a direct underground line to, the Royal Opera House, Covent Garden, where many of the students hope to perform.

In the final years at a school attached to a major ballet company, the students learn the repertory and specific style required by that company. They begin to appear with the company in small walk-on parts. Indeed they may already have walked on as children, in such ballets as *The Nutcracker*. New York City Ballet and the Royal Danish Ballet regularly use children in many of their productions. Senior students will be learning major roles in the repertory; some of them will get an immediate chance to dance these roles in the school's graduation performance.

Schools attached to big companies often give annual public performances. The Royal Ballet School has for several years given a single annual performance at Covent Garden, usually followed by a week or two of performances in a London suburban theatre at Wimbledon or Richmond. In 1981, these performances were given at Sadler's Wells Theatre for the first time. These are fully staged performances, complete with scenery and costumes. Either a full-length ballet or three short ballets are usually performed, so that the programme is identical with one that might be given by the Royal Ballet itself. Sometimes the quality of the dancing is just as good too!

The School of American Ballet, attached to New York City Ballet, gives two or three performances annually in the theatre of the Juilliard School, where the SAB is housed. The programmes usually consist of short ballets and extracts, sometimes including ballets specially created for the students by their teachers and by young dancers of the company. There is an orchestra, but no scenery, and the whole atmosphere is less formal than the Royal Ballet School's performance. The standard of dancing, however, is just as high.

The practice of giving such performances is spreading. It was always the tradition in Russia, and recently the Paris Opéra began to do the same thing. Dancers who do well in class sometimes do less well in public performances, and vice versa. So these graduation performances give companies a better opportunity of judging which dancers they may want to recruit. They also give critics and devoted audiences an exciting opportunity to discover the stars of tomorrow.

White Lodge, Richmond Park, the elegant home of the Royal Ballet's junior school since 1955

4
Ballet as a career

Injury can put a sudden end to a ballet career at any
time. Dancers must take great care of their bones
and muscles. Photo shows pupils of the Royal Ballet
School receiving attention to hands and ankles

When school is finished, around the age of eighteen, there is the problem of getting a job. Far more highly proficient ballet dancers are now trained than can possibly be assimilated in ballet companies. Many of them will have to be content with jobs as teachers, dancing in commercial shows on stage or television, or ending up with jobs quite unconnected with dance, despite all the training. The major ballet companies mostly recruit their dancers from their own schools, but can only take a small proportion of the dancers those schools produce. Some important companies, like London Festival Ballet, do not have their own schools, and must recruit elsewhere. Graduates from the leading British and American ballet schools can often get jobs in other countries, either in Europe, Asia or Latin America. Many British dancers, for example, have made successful careers in Germany and the Netherlands.

The Royal Ballet recruits mainly from its own school. Students from all over the world attend the school, and if they are citizens of the European Common Market they are of course eligible to work in Britain without formality. The Royal Ballet used to recruit many dancers from Commonwealth countries, but this became more difficult with the new immigration and work permit laws. The company has not so far recruited black dancers, even if they are British. Other British companies recruit from all the main schools, usually by audition.

Promotion to soloist rank is usually within a company, dancers working their way up gradually from the *corps de ballet*. It is most unusual for a new entrant, straight from school, to be given solos immediately. Even the most talented young dancers, who have danced leading roles at school performances, normally have to sink back into the anonymity of the corps, at least for a time. There are exceptions to this, however, particularly in the smaller companies and in those which do a lot of touring, where opportunities may occur much more quickly.

London Festival Ballet and Scottish Ballet sometimes recruit principal dancers from outside the company, particularly from abroad. In recent years there has been quite a considerable exchange of dancers between British companies, especially between the Royal Ballet and London Festival. This seems likely to continue, especially as the two most recent directors of Festival both came from the Royal, and Norman Morrice, the most recent director of the Royal, came from Ballet Rambert.

When dancers join a company, they are by no means finished with classes. Indeed every professional ballet dancer, even the most famous and successful, attends class every morning of the working week. This is essential, to keep the body in supple shape, to correct mistakes and weaknesses as they occur, and to develop new strengths and technical achievements. All companies hold their own daily classes, and dancers who are not permanently attached to a company normally pay for private classes with a teacher of their choice.

It must be admitted that ballet is a risky, tiring and in many ways unrewarding career. Rates of pay do not compare favourably with those in commercial shows and on television, where the work is less arduous. Star dancers can earn a great deal of money with guest appearances, especially in the United States, and with television and film work. But even ballet stars rarely make as much money as opera stars, pop singers, or famous football players. In some countries they do not earn as much as lawyers, doctors or dentists. On the other hand, dancers in a company do at least have regular, and not just occasional, employment, and more and more companies are now introducing pension schemes, and special funds to assist dancers who are incapacitated by injury.

In addition to going to daily class, ballet dancers must spend most of every day rehearsing new roles or new ballets, and warming up for the actual performances. Members of the *corps de ballet* and all the members of small companies usually have to do eight performances a week, though principal dancers do considerably fewer.

Before each performance there is a stretching and warm-up period on stage. If the dancers are on tour, they will need to space out their movements and groupings differently on each new stage, and get the feel of each new auditorium, finding some object out front on which to focus or 'spot', when they turn, and judging how big their gestures and expressions must be to project in that particular house.

Touring imposes its own strains, but also has its rewards. Constant travelling, often on the one free day of the week, is time-consuming and tiring. Family life is almost impossible. Many dancers give up their careers rather than abandon the comfort of a permanent 'home' like Covent Garden or the New York State Theatre. But only a select group of the world's leading companies, and those attached to opera companies, have permanent homes. Most companies are constantly on the move. Some dancers actually prefer the touring life, with its opportunities for seeing new places, making new friends, and the constant challenge of winning over new audiences. Wherever they go, dancers are usually invited to parties and lavishly entertained.

The risks of illness and physical injury, which plague every dancer's career, are perhaps even greater with an arduous touring schedule. A tired dancer is more prone to injury, and in some places

Above *and* **below:** *Professional dancers studying at Rosella Hightower's school, the Centre de Danse Classique, in Cannes, France. Famous dancers from all over the world come to this school to perfect their technique*

on tour it may be difficult to get first-rate medical attention. Even in the comparatively sheltered environment of an opera-house or other permanent home, a misjudged landing from a jump or a sudden fall can end a career in a moment. Knee injuries, torn Achilles tendons, and arthritis in the toes are especially common dancers' ailments. So are crippling leg cramps, which can cause a dancer to abandon a performance suddenly. Members of the audience would enjoy performances much less if they realized how often the dancers are in pain, sometimes only able to perform with the aid of pain-killing drugs.

Even if a dancer escapes disastrous injury, a career in ballet is still remarkably short. For every Margot Fonteyn or Alicia Alonso who dances to the age of 60 (and it is hard to think of any other examples among ballerinas), there are countless legions who have to give up in early middle-age. That is the normal thing. Men must nearly always abandon virtuoso leading roles around the age of 40. Mime and character roles can be taken at any age, but there are not enough of these roles for all the dancers needing them, and many dancers have neither the talent nor the temperament for them. It is sometimes said that there are more opportunities for men than for women to continue in ballet as administrators, teachers or choreographers, and that many of the women naturally leave when they marry and start families. With increasing equality of opportunities and status between the sexes, the opportunities in ballet will presumably also become more equal.

However that may be, the need to give up dancing and find a new occupation in one's late 30s or early 40s can be acutely demoralizing and traumatic. Most dancers have dedicated themselves entirely to their art, have not learned any other skills, and have not prepared themselves for the inevitable. Some very successfully launch new careers: others are less fortunate.

Dancers must therefore be very dedicated and very devoted to their art and work. Many dancers say they felt the urge to dance from a very early age. This applies particularly to men, who still have to overcome considerable prejudice against their work, especially when they are young boys. Many male stars say they only feel truly satisfied when they dance, and it was the awareness of that satisfaction which gave them the strength and the determination to pursue their training against the objections of their families and the ridicule of their friends. Girls are more likely to be put into ballet schools by fond parents, and some ballerinas admit that they had no particular desire to dance when they started training. In many cases the training was prescribed as a treatment for some physical weakness or ailment. The enthusiasm and dedication for dance came later. Without that enthusiasm and dedication, a career in ballet is unlikely to last long. With it, a dancer can achieve an exhilaration and a feeling transcending mortal existence which makes all the hard work and physical suffering worthwhile.

5
Stars

Anna Pavlova, one of the greatest stars of all time, whose name became a household word. Only Nijinsky, Fonteyn and Nureyev, have been as famous. Stars like these win new audiences and attract new talents to ballet

It should be fairly easy for an expert to know a good dancer. Steps are either performed correctly or incorrectly—as Martha Graham remarked in her memorable film *A Dancer's World,* 'a foot is either pointed or it is not'. Technical skill is measurable—a balance can be held longer, a jump can be higher, the number of spins in the air or while balancing on one foot can be greater. Yet there is a surprising amount of disagreement even about these things. Critics often differ about the technical ability of a dancer, sometimes saying diametrically opposite things. Part of the explanation is that different observers look for different qualities in a dancer. One critic may be so impressed by high jumps that he ignores imprecise footwork, or vice versa.

Another part of the explanation is that there are many intangible and subjective factors which influence our judgement of a dancer. Otherwise, every technically brilliant dancer would be a star, and every star would be technically brilliant. Neither of these things is the case.

One of these intangible factors is musicality. Musicality in dancers does not necessarily mean a deep interest in music, or great knowledge of it. Fonteyn, one of the most musical of all ballerinas, rarely went to concerts or listened to music outside ballet. But she had an instinctive feel for movement to music, developed in the early days of her career with the help of Constant Lambert, then musical director of the Sadler's Wells Ballet. Lambert used to be amazed at the way Fonteyn always arrived at the right spot on the stage, without any sign of haste or anxiety, at precisely the right musical moment.

Some dancers always seem to be slightly out of time with the music, or the effort of keeping in time shows, as they are counting out the beats to themselves. A musical dancer 'feels' the music, which admittedly is not always possible with unmelodic modern scores or with abstract electronic sounds. That is why a truly musical dancer, like Pavlova or Fonteyn, tends to be happier with more conventional, melodius, 'danceable' scores.

Not that musical dancing is a matter of slavishly following the music. Sometimes the dancer can be almost imperceptibly ahead of the music, deliberately giving an impression of stimulating it by dancing, rather than the reverse. Just as opera singers sometimes hold notes extra long to achieve an effect, some great dancers may hold poses or balances, demanding that the music follows them. In certain display pieces, the conductor must follow the dancer, not the other way round. Ideally there is a collaboration between dancers and the conductor about this: the conductor will say when the music cannot be adjusted and when it can.

Great Russian dancers, in particular, have tended to pull the music about to suit their purposes. This sometimes leads to accusations that they are unmusical, a taunt frequently levelled at the great present-day ballerina Natalia Makarova. But a great artist can get away with things, and indeed benefit from them, which a lesser artist would be ill-advised to attempt.

What makes a great dancer? It is largely a matter of personality and acting ability, over and above technique. Some dancers, like Nureyev or Alexander Godunov, rivet an audience's attention the moment they come on stage, before they dance a step. They have magnetism, charisma, call it what you will. Some dancers can make you believe that the character they are playing is a real person, with a real mind and feelings. This ability is what distinguishes a great Giselle, as danced by Ulanova, Markova or Makarova, from a merely competent one. Christopher Gable was not one of the greatest virtuosos in British ballet, but those who saw his Romeo, his artist in *The Two Pigeons* or his young boy in *The Invitation*, were deeply moved and will always remember those performances in preference to many other interpretations which were technically more brilliant. The same is true of the Canadian ballerina Lynn Seymour, whose Juliet and Giselle had the same intensely-felt and dramatic quality.

These qualities are not the same as glamour or sex appeal, though those can of course help a dancer too. Moira Shearer's success was at least as much based on her glamour as on her dancing. Yet most of the world's great ballerinas have not been famous beauties; some of them have actually been quite plain, though obviously they had the well-proportioned bodies required for classical ballet.

It used to be considered bad form to mention sex appeal when discussing classical dancers. That inhibition—like so many others—has largely disappeared in recent years. Some ballet-goers are so serious in their approach to the art that they genuinely blind themselves to the sex appeal, or lack of it, of the dancers they are watching. Yet in the past ballet was often a display of pretty girls for tired businessmen or rich aristocrats. A present-day ballet audience also contains many people who go to ballet partly for the sensual thrill of seeing good-looking young people doing athletic movements in brief, tight-fitting costumes.

It is very difficult to resist a dancer one finds sexually attractive. On the other hand a dancer blatantly flaunting sex appeal can be irritating and vulgar, especially if the appeal is not the kind that attracts. There is no doubt that the sharply different estimates of certain dancers by different critics is sometimes the result of the critic's sexual or gut reaction.

Needless to say, this is not just a matter of men reacting to pretty girls. Most people respond to some extent to the sex appeal of both sexes, whether they consciously recognize this or not. In addition, ballet attracts many homosexuals, who will obviously be more susceptible to the attractions of their own sex.

This sexual element in dancing accounts for much of the prejudice against male dancers. Ballerinas in the romantic classics were essentially remote, demure creatures, scarcely real women at all. It has even been suggested, by the American writer Arlene Croce, that this accounts for their appeal to male homosexuals. It was only in the lighter ballets, and in *soubrette* roles, that ballerinas flaunted their sex appeal. In any case it was generally considered legitimate for women to do that.

Men in ballet, on the other hand, have often showed off their physiques and their magnetic personalities. This was traditionally considered slightly indecent, just as it used to be considered bad form for men to use perfume or make up, or dye their hair.

Nijinsky's appeal was partly due to his magnetic personality, as well as to his remarkable dancing. He constantly scandalized audiences with his brief costumes, and indeed was dismissed from the Imperial Ballet in St Petersburg for revealing too much of himself. Later stars of the Diaghilev ballet, like Massine and Lifar, were sensationally good-looking and appeared in scanty costumes which exploited the fact. In our own day, the screams of teenage girls for various male dancers have as much to do with their sex appeal as with their dancing. The British critic Richard Buckle once suggested that Nureyev's fans might well have been chanting: 'We want Rudi, preferably in the nudi!'

Nevertheless, personality and strength of will are more important to a dancer's success than any amount of physical appeal or glamour. They are also more important than sheer technical skill. Ballerinas who rely mainly on personality and interpretative ability tend to excel in romantic roles—while those with perfect leg and foot techniques, and maybe less personality, prefer purely classical roles. The romantic roles rely more on lightness, facial expression, and stylish interpretation. In Russia and Denmark, ballerinas were traditionally type-cast as 'classical' *or* 'romantic'; those who danced *Giselle* and *La Sylphide* rarely danced *Swan Lake* and *The Sleeping Beauty*, and vice versa. In Britain and the United States, on the other hand,

Rudolf Nureyev and Erik Bruhn, considered the greatest male dancers in the world in the 1960s, were close friends and studied together at Rosella Hightower's school

a ballerina has generally been expected to dance all the leading roles. The motto here might be a paraphrase of Gertrude Stein—a ballerina is a ballerina is a ballerina.

Fonteyn, though strong in personality and despite weak feet, was better known for most of her career as Aurora and Odette than as Giselle. Later, when her technique began to slip, she specialized in Giselle; her partnership with Nureyev in this ballet was world-famous. She was a good example of the importance of will-power. She was not naturally gifted with a strong technique, suffered considerably with her feet, and was often in pain. But she was always determined that anything she did should be well done and she was always prepared to make a fresh effort. Some ballerinas, when they encounter difficulty doing a particular step, simply abandon it, so that their range becomes smaller and smaller. Fonteyn never admitted defeat, struggling in class to overcome any problem.

Nureyev, the first of the many ballet defectors from the Soviet Union, had to show enormous willpower to get into ballet at all, to stay in Leningrad once he had been trained, and to grasp the opportunity to escape at the Paris airport. He is a perfectionist, often irritating his colleagues by

Left: *Fonteyn and Nureyev in* Le Corsaire pas de deux, *staged by Nureyev and danced successfully by these artists all over the world.* **Above:** *Natalia Makarova, the great Russian ballerina, as Giselle, one of her most famous roles with the Kirov Ballet. Makarova was generally acknowledged to be the greatest classical and romantic ballerina of the 1970s*

his demands for the very highest standards of performance.

Sometimes dancers can achieve even greater success with a lasting partnership than they can on their own. Markova and Dolin, Fonteyn and Nureyev, Carla Fracci and Erik Bruhn, and Antoinette Sibley and Anthony Dowell, were more famous together than they had previously been separately. A special sort of chemistry can develop in a great partnership, a *rapport* between the two dancers which audiences feel but cannot explain.

It is sometimes suggested that another quality making a great dancer is a specific, individual style of movement. Many great dancers have specific steps which will always be associated with them, and which they tend to insert in almost every role they dance. The Anglo-American critic Clive Barnes once wrote that the difference between a good dancer and a great one is that the latter has a specific, recognizable movement style.

Certainly we all remember star dancers for particular things—special jumps or arm movements, a particular way of curving the body, a way of walking, a smile or an expressive use of the eyes. The dancers we remember, and recognize, and want to see again and again, are the true stars.

'Star' is regarded in some circles as a term of abuse. Companies without stars try to make a virtue of necessity by singing the praises of the *ensemble*. Indeed a star-less ensemble, working as a team, can be marvellous to watch. Some people dislike the cult of personality, and think that stars—stealing the limelight and often 'doing their own thing'—are bad for the art of ballet. Many modern ballets, created for an ensemble, can be unbalanced by a star personality. But the classics need stars, especially in the ballerina roles, if they are to make their full effect.

Choreographers also need star dancers to stimulate their creative juices. Several choreographers have been inspired by particular dancers, with special movement styles and qualities of personality. Equally dancers benefit by working with a choreographer, who develops unsuspected sides of their abilities. A great dancer *can* work without a choreographer, as did Pavlova and as most dancers have to do at times. Makarova's successes have mostly been in standard roles, not specifically created for her. Many of Fonteyn's, on the other hand, were in roles tailor-made for her by Ashton. Some other ballet dancers might have developed into stars if they had had choreographers to inspire them.

Stars are of course invaluable at the box-office. A Fonteyn or Makarova, a Nureyev or Baryshnikov, can sell out a performance regardless of what they dance. They can attract an audience for new works which might otherwise play to empty houses. Many companies try to avoid reliance on stars, and some of them—like New York City Ballet—do not advertise in advance which dancers will appear on a particular night. But audiences tend to adopt dancers and make them into stars, whether the managements of the companies like it or not. And managements do like it in the end. At times the Royal Ballet has charged extra high prices when big stars are appearing.

Ballerinas and their male partners are not the only stars. Dancers with sufficient personality may become stars in acting or character dancing. There have been star mimes, like Sir Robert Helpmann, and star character dancers like Léonide Massine and Alexander Grant. Stars make something so special of their roles that they stand out above any other interpreters.

The same is true in modern dance. Most modern dance companies were created by dancer-choreographers, essentially making works for themselves. Isadora Duncan, Ruth St Denis, Martha Graham, and more recently José Limon, Merce Cunningham and Paul Taylor were stars. Their works undoubtedly lost a great deal when they ceased to appear in them. Indeed it is doubtful if a Duncan or Graham work can ever reveal its full quality without its creator. In that sense, 'modern' works are even more dependent on stars than are the classic ballets.

6
What is a choreographer?

Dame Ninette de Valois teaching at the Royal
Ballet School. As well as being the founder and
guiding spirit of the Royal Ballet, she was a
choreographer who provided British ballet with
some of its earliest and most enduring works —
The Rake's Progress, Checkmate, and *Job*

The choreographer is the creator of a ballet. There can be a ballet without music, décor, costumes or plot, but unless someone tells the dancers what to do there is no ballet. (There could be some improvised movements, but those do not constitute a ballet; if the improvised movements are memorized and repeated, then the ballet has been choreographed by the dancers themselves.)

The actual term *choreographer* only came into general use during this century. Literally, according to its derivation from the Greek, it means 'dance writer', and at one time the term was used to describe a person who tried to write down dance steps in some form of notation. Nowadays, the terms for that job are *dance notator* or *choreologist*. The choreographer does not write down steps; he creates them for the dancers.

Normally he also does much more than that. He is the person in charge of a new ballet. He chooses the composer and designer, he selects or even writes the story, he rehearses the work and supervises every aspect of production, including the lighting. He may write a scenario, or choose an existing one, commission a writer or decide to make a purely abstract ballet. He may select existing music,

Above: *Nijinsky in his celebrated role of the Golden Slave in Fokine's* Schéhérazade, *with the Diaghilev ballet in 1910.* **Left:** *Michel Fokine, the choreographer, dancing in his* Le Dieu Bleu *with Tamara Karsavina. Fokine and Nijinsky are among the few choreographers who were also great dancers*

Choreographers at work: Kenneth MacMillan rehearsing his Elite Syncopations *with the Royal Ballet* **(top left)**, *George Balanchine rehearsing New York City Ballet in* Union Jack **(top right)**, *and Sir Frederick Ashton supervising a Royal Ballet rehearsal* **(below)**

or commission a new score. He may later reject the music or décor he has commissioned. In any case he will probably work closely with the designer and composer, giving them specific instructions.

This procedure is not inevitable. Diaghilev often engaged a composer or designer before he selected a choreographer. He often decided on the scenario, and then offered it to a choreographer. But artistic directors like Diaghilev do not seem to exist nowadays. An artistic director may still veto the work of a choreographer, or make constructive suggestions, but even that amount of supervision or interference is rare.

Theoretically there is no reason why a separate director should not be engaged to stage a ballet choreographed by someone else. It has often been suggested that a distinguished stage or operatic producer might be the right person to supervise the revival of a classic ballet, as they might supervise a Shakespeare or Verdi revival. There have been some experiments along these lines, but none has been notably successful. Nearly always, the choreographer is the director.

Choreographers are either dancers or former dancers. It is virtually impossible for a person who has not trained as a dancer to create dances. It is sometimes said that choreographers are failed dancers, and this is sometimes true. Very often dancers who are not doing too well, for one reason or another, decide to try their hand at choreography. Sometimes dancers switch to choreography as their dancing days come to an end. Busy and successful dancers have not usually time to think about choreography, which is a lengthy creative process.

Some great dancers, however, were also great choreographers: Fokine, Nijinsky and Massine are the most obvious examples. Neither Sir Frederick Ashton nor George Balanchine made great reputations as dancers, nor did John Cranko or Kenneth MacMillan. On the other hand, Makarova, Nureyev and Baryshnikov all choreographed from time to time while still dancing, but none produced an undisputed masterpiece to make their choreography as famous as their dancing.

Nowadays most ballet companies do everything possible to encourage their dancers to try their hand at choreography. They hold choreographic workshops, at which new works are tried out. The great majority of these works are imitative and undistinguished. Some dancers are not even capable of creating interesting groupings or steps, or of setting them to appropriate music. Many others are quite good at producing competent pastiches, works which look like imitation Ashton, Balanchine or Robbins, but which have no originality and no lasting value.

A real talent for choreography usually becomes apparent very early in a dancer's career. Some reveal this talent while they are still at school. Dancers with dominant personalities, with intellectual interests or creative flair soon get discontented with simply performing steps set by other people, and start creating their own.

Not that choreography is entirely a one-way process. Many great choreographers, including Ashton and Balanchine, get inspiration and stimulation from their dancers. A step or position is suggested to the dancer, the dancer suggests another, or tries it in different ways, and the choreographer chooses. On the other hand some choreographers arrive in the studio with an exact idea of what they want, and proceed to instruct the dancers in its execution.

There is no system of training choreographers. Diaghilev deliberately trained Massine, introducing him to composers and artists, taking him to art exhibitions and concerts, and guiding his reading and travel. Massine chose to believe that choreography could be taught by rules and by his own special system of written notation. He taught his system of choreography for a time at the Royal Ballet School, with no success.

In creating a ballet, the choreographer may be seeking a way of telling a story in dance and mime, or of interpreting a piece of music or a mood. He may be arranging various steps in different ways to achieve his purpose, or he may consciously be trying to invent new steps, new lifts, new groupings. This is comparatively rare. After all, there must be a limit to the number of steps a dancer can achieve, though it is amazing how often new ones appear to be invented. They may simply *look* new, from the way the choreographer uses them or strings them together. Recently choreographers have been particularly inventive in creating new 'lifts', new ways in which dancers can be carried, raised and lowered.

Some writers on ballet have claimed that the only truly valuable and original choreography is the creation of new steps and movements to suit specific characters. Fokine condemned 'the combination of ready-made and established dance steps', and in many of his ballets he did create new styles and new movements, as did Nijinsky and Massine. But his condemnation would dismiss Petipa (as he intended it to) and most of the work by such modern masters as Ashton and Balanchine. Ironically, audiences today prefer ballets by Petipa, Ashton and Balanchine to those by Fokine, Nijinsky and Massine.

John Cranko once told me that he regarded the invention of new movements as the essence of choreography. Most choreographers, however, probably attach at least as much importance to the seemingly inevitable way they arrange existing steps, suiting dancers and music, and to the way they discover new talents in dancers, bringing out aspects of their techniques and personalities that they did not themselves know they possessed.

Choreographers vary greatly in the way they go about their work. Ashton generally started by falling in love with a piece of music, listening to it over and over again until it became a part of him. Then he developed a theme to suit it, and some ideas about dances and dancers. In some cases he had a mental scenario which was not made explicit in the ballet. He thought of *Monotones*, for example, as an exercise in weightlessness, as men move in outer space, but he left it to audiences to interpret as they wished. Antony Tudor often said that his semi-abstract ballets, like *Shadowplay*, had very specific stories. But he refused to explain what these were. He rarely explained much to the dancers about why they were doing what they were doing, though at the last stage of rehearsal he would suddenly surprise them by giving them some psychological motivation. When asked by critics or members of the audience if a ballet had a certain meaning, he would generally agree with whatever meaning they proposed!

Balanchine's method of creation was very similar to Ashton's. Sometimes, however, both choreographers would start with a specific idea or theme, and then search for music and a choreographic method of interpreting the idea. For many years Ashton toyed with the idea of a ballet based on Alexandre Dumas' *La Dame aux Camélias*. At various times he considered different possible musical scores, and it was a long time before Humphrey Searle was finally commissioned to orchestrate Liszt's Piano Sonata in B minor and produce the score for *Marguerite and Armand*, a very successful vehicle for Fonteyn and Nureyev. In the case of *Enigma Variations*, it was Julia Trevelyan Oman, the designer, who suggested the scenario about Elgar and his friends, though her scenario was simplified and adapted by Ashton. When Ashton decided to make a ballet based on Turgenev's play *A Month in the Country*, it was the Oxford philosopher Sir Isaiah Berlin who suggested that Chopin would be the most suitable composer.

Sometimes a piece of music is stored in a choreographer's mind, awaiting a suitable treatment. Antony Tudor had wanted to use Richard Strauss's incidental music for Molière's play *Le Bourgeois Gentilhomme* for a long time before he actually used it for his ballet *Knight Errant*.

Choreographers cannot always wait for inspiration. Resident choreographers with a ballet company are expected to produce new works fairly regularly. Balanchine was very prolific in his output for his New York City Ballet; inevitably, some of his ballets were more successful than others, and not all of them have survived. Ashton or Balanchine could always produce a perfectly acceptable ballet for a special occasion or for a specific dancer, even if the ballet produced to order was not always a masterpiece. The directors of German ballet companies, where the audience consist mainly of subscribers who constantly expect new works, have to produce two or three new ballets per season. John Cranko in Stuttgart and John Neumeier in Hamburg were particularly skilful in doing this.

Some distinguished choreographers, however, are much less prolific and find it difficult to work to order. The least prolific of all the great choreographers of our time has been Antony Tudor, whose total output is very small, and who had long periods of non-creativity. Nijinsky was a very slow worker and produced only four ballets before he went mad.

The way in which choreographers use music varies enormously. It may be a precise setting of steps to the beat of the music, which can look very attractive and 'musical', but can also look drearily literal. Balanchine often got round this problem by making his dancers move a tiny fraction ahead of the music, so that the music appeared to be flowing from the dancer, rather than the other way round. Balanchine also varied the effect by using groups of dancers, repeating a step or a movement successively, instead of all together, so that the dance seemed contrapuntal to the music, the two offsetting each other.

Fokine, Ashton and Cranko were inclined to set their dancers moving *through* rather than exactly *with* the music, using the music more as background than as an exact literal accompaniment to the steps. That is why their works can often be labelled *romantic* rather than *classical*.

These choreographers, however, did not go as far in that direction as many self-consciously 'modern' choreographers, who use music entirely as atmospheric background, bearing no discernible relation to the dancing. Choreographers like Maurice Béjart, Glen Tetley and Merce Cunningham sometimes rehearse their works with one piece of music, and then substitute another for the performance, or else use no music at all. It has become a trademark of 'modern' ballets that they often start in silence, or that the dancing continues even when the music stops. Moreover the 'music' may consist of recorded sound effects, electronic noises, or human speech, either on tape or spoken by the dancers.

It is this endless variety of possible choreographic styles that causes dancers and critics to be constantly looking hopefully for new choreographers. It might be thought that there are quite enough good ballets in existence by now to provide a satisfying repertory for every company and every audience, even if no new works were created at all. Indeed there are. The need for new ballets can easily be exaggerated. It is unreasonable to expect the constant creation of new works which can compete with established masterpieces, any more than we expect the frequent creation of new classic novels, paintings, symphonies or operas.

The example of opera is particularly apt. The most recent operas to have become widely popular, those by Richard Strauss and Puccini, are about as old as Fokine's ballets. New operas are rare events. Ballet is far more up-to-date than that. A substantial part of every major repertory has been created in the lifetime of the present dancers, and new works are added regularly. The middle of the twentieth century has probably been the most creative period in the whole history of ballet, because of the vast number of ballet companies, dancers, and choreographers or would-be choreographers.

Many of the new ballets are speedily forgotten; some should never have been produced in the first place. But there is no tried and trusted way of sifting the chaff from the grain in the process of creation. Even Diaghilev could not always do so. Artistic directors of companies are rightly nervous of stifling original talent at birth, and often fear that their judgement or taste will turn out to be outmoded, or wrong. A ballet is not really tested until it is performed before an audience.

People sometimes sneer at ballet because so many of the works performed are old, with corny or naive plots, 'irrelevant' to the present-day world. But dancers and their audiences need the great works of the past, if only to set standards of judgement and comparison. The dancers need the challenge of attempting the classic, difficult roles that have been done by their predecessors. Audiences love comparing different interpretations of the leading roles. Indeed that is one of the main attractions of regular ballet-going. Dancers also need the stimulus of new works, created especially for them. The ideal repertoire blends the old and trusted with the new and experimental. That is what virtually all of the world's main companies do, or try to do.

7
Ballets preserved

Dame Marie Rambert watching a class at her school
being taught the Benesh system of notation. This
system is now used by most British and West
European ballet companies, but few dancers or
choreographers can write or read it. Modern
methods of notation have made the recording and
reproduction of ballets much more accurate than
ever before

Traditionally, ballets survive by being handed down from generation to generation of dancers. Dancers teach their younger colleagues their roles. Inevitably the interpretations and the steps become altered gradually, as new dancers want to do things in their own way. If the choreographers are still around, they frequently alter their own ballets to suit new casts, or their own changed tastes. If a ballet was dropped from the repertoire for several years, it used to be virtually impossible to revive it. Many old ballets have been 'lost' in this way, notably many of Bournonville's full-length works which were abandoned in Copenhagen in the earlier years of this century. Nijinsky's *Faune* disappeared for a long time, and was only restored with great difficulty by Ballet Rambert, under the personal guidance of Dame Marie Rambert who had worked with Nijinsky. Similarly the veteran ballerina Tamara Karsavina helped to recreate Fokine's ballet *Le Spectre de la Rose*, which had not been performed in London for many years.

There are various systems of notation for writing down ballets; some of these systems have existed for a long time. The full-length Russian classics were notated in the *Stepanov* system. Some of these notations were taken from Russia in 1918 by Nicolai Sergeyev, who had been a director at the Maryinsky Theatre in St Petersburg. These notations became the basis of the famous British stag-ings of the classics. Massine's system was adapted from Stepanov's.

The best-known systems of notation today are *Labanotation*, based on a method originally suggested by Rudolf von Laban, a pioneer of central European modern dance in the early years of this century, and *Benesh Notation*, developed in London in the 1950s and 1960s by Rudolf Benesh and his wife Joan, a former ballet dancer. Large claims are made for both systems, and there is an intense rivalry between them. Benesh, administered from the Institute of Choreology in London, supplies *choreologists* to most British and many other West European and Commonwealth ballet companies. These companies now generally notate new ballets as they are created, and revive them, or mount works from other repertoires, with the aid of the choreologist and the notation. Even if the choreographer is available in person, and there are still dancers who remember the ballet, the notation is a useful memory-aid.

Labanotation is more complex, requiring more writing, than Benesh. Its supporters claim that it is also more precise and thorough, giving more complete details of every movement and expression. Its headquarters are at the Dance Notation Bureau in New York. More than 200 ballets have been recorded in Labanotation, mainly in the United States.

An engraving of Kellom Tomlinson, one of the earliest dance notators

FAIRY OF THE ENCHANTED GARDEN

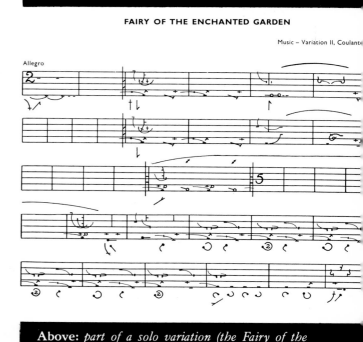

Above: *part of a solo variation (the Fairy of the Enchanted Garden) from Petipa's* The Sleeping Beauty, *in Benesh notation.* **Right:** *Joan Benesh with some of her pupils*

Both systems are difficult to learn, and it takes a long time to record a complete ballet in either system. Most choreographers and dancers are incapable of reading or writing notation, though the Benesh system is now taught at the Royal Ballet School. Few pupils really master it, any more than children who learn foreign languages at school can really speak them.

The advantages of notating a ballet are fairly obvious. If Petipa's and Bournonville's ballets had all been notated in one of the modern systems, we should be able to revive the forgotten ones now. On the other hand, accurate notation might have inhibited people from making changes, and we might be left with dated and uninteresting versions of the classics, by comparison with the ones we now do have. Tastes change from generation to generation, and so do the technical abilities of the dancers.

Some people argue that the principle of natural selection has worked well in ballet:—the bad ballets have been forgotten and the good ones have evolved as they were handed down from dancer to dancer. On the other hand, some ballets are ahead of their time. It would be wonderful to be able to revive the three lost Nijinsky ballets, which might be better received now than they were in his time.

If ballets are to be notated, it is obviously important that changes made in them by the choreographer for various subsequent productions should also be notated. This has not always been the case. Living choreographers alter their ballets considerably. Balanchine is the most extreme example of this; recently he even shortened his 'classic' *Apollo*, removing the birth at the beginning and the ascent to heaven at the end, and making it an even more abstract ballet. More subtly, he also changes the actual choreography in his ballets. Sometimes, when a ballet is to be revived without the choreographer's personal supervision, an argument develops between the choreologist and the dancers who remember how they used to do it. It may be that the notation score is inaccurate; it may be that the ballet was altered by the choreographer at a time when no choreologist was present; and of course the dancers' memories could be at fault. That is the least likely explanation, as dancers have very good memories for the ballets they have danced, much better than the choreographers, who are usually so immersed in their latest works that they have quite forgotten what they did before.

Of course choreographers, ballet masters and dancers can still alter ballets which exist in precise notation. But then it requires a conscious decision to alter something which has acquired a degree of permanence merely by being written down. Without notation, it is possible to alter a ballet semi-consciously, imagining that it is not being altered at all. This is psychologically easier. But it would be a pity if the script of a ballet came to be regarded as sacrosanct; a ballet is not the same as a piece of music, a play or a book.

The fact that living interpreters are involved in executing the choreography means that it must inevitably change as new dancers take over the roles. It may be true that no two musicians play an instrument in exactly the same way, but at least they can play exactly the same notes. Dancers' instruments are their own bodies, and no two bodies are the same. The same step looks different when danced by different dancers, and may no longer be so suitable or effective in a particular ballet.

Ballets can also be preserved on film or video tape. Massine regularly used old films of his ballets, in addition to his notation, when reviving his works. Many companies now regularly film their productions, and of course many of them are taped for television. But films can only show a ballet from one angle at a time, are two-dimensional, and often only show a small part of the stage and the action. If they are shot in close-up, general patterns and groupings are lost; if from a distance, detail and facial expressions are lost. These are among the disadvantages of ballet in the cinema or on television. It is almost impossible to stage a ballet entirely from a film or videotape record.

Notation and film are useful aids to a choreographer or ballet master in reviving a ballet, but most people now agree that they are not enough. A ballet mounted entirely from notation is likely to lack some authentic details and is also likely to lack vitality, to seem more like a museum piece than a living work. This is partly because a ballet needs to be adapted to its dancers, and to some extent perhaps to the changing tastes of its audience. Dame Ninette de Valois put the relationship between the notation and the choreographer or producer of a ballet very well when she compared the notation to an orchestral score and the person staging the ballet to the conductor. The score needs a conductor to bring it to life, and no two conductors will play the same piece of music in quite the same way.

8
Music

John Lanchbery rehearsing the orchestra at the
Royal Opera House, Covent Garden. Lanchbery is
one of the exclusive band of specialist British ballet
conductors whose services are now in demand all
over the world

However care is taken for the music not to dwarf the ballet... The music needs to be suitable for the dancing

Music plays a crucial part in the success or failure of a ballet. The Petipa-Ivanov works with music by Tchaikovsky are better known and more frequently performed than the ones with music by Minkus, or even Glazunov. Many modern abstract works are performed more because of their music by Stravinsky or Prokofiev than because of their choreography. However, good ballet music is not the same as good concert music. Adam's score for *Giselle* or Delibes' *Coppélia* are not played as complete works in the concert hall but are both admirable ballet scores—tuneful and with clear rhythms which are easy to dance, yet with recurring themes linked to the drama. On the other hand, serious symphonic music, when used for ballet, often appears to be too interesting in its own right and to distract from or dwarf the dancing.

It used to be fashionable to sneer at the 'hack' ballet composers of the nineteenth century—such as Lumbye, Minkus and Drigo. Recently they have come to be appreciated for what they were, and today we sometimes wish that ballet companies had equally competent and understanding composers working for them regularly. Minkus and Drigo were employed as official ballet composers in Imperial Russia; nobody is employed in that way anywhere today.

Tchaikovsky even wrote ballet music to order for Petipa, being given exact instructions by the choreographer about the duration of the music, the tempo and the mood. Most serious composers would be unlikely to agree to anything like that today. Few serious composers now write ballet music, though Prokofiev and Stravinsky of course did.

Prokofiev's ballet music is in the Tchaikovsky

Piotr Ilyich Tchaikovsky, the most famous and successful ballet composer of all time

tradition—melodious, rhythmic and atmospherically appropriate to the dramatic action. His scores for *Romeo and Juliet* and *Cinderella* even contain 'hummable' tunes, which are popular with dancers and audiences alike.

Stravinsky's early ballet scores, notably *Petrouchka* and *The Firebird*, were colourful and atmospheric, with considerable touches of Russian folk-melody. His *Rite of Spring* is a loud, over-powering work, exciting in its own right and often more interesting than the choreography set to it. His later ballet scores tended to be percussive and bitty, rather than melodic. Balanchine specialized in setting these scores, devising a new jerky style of choreography for scores like *Agon*. Balanchine also took numerous concert pieces by Stravinsky and used them as ballet scores. There was a close friendship and collaboration between the two men and Stravinsky became the most performed composer in the New York City Ballet repertory. He came to be regarded by many of the company's followers as the greatest ballet composer of the twentieth century. His music is, however, an acquired taste. Many dancers prefer to perform to tunes which they can respond to instinctively, rather than having to count complicated measures to themselves.

Balanchine's musical versatility is such that he has choreographed successfully to every sort of music, from the corniest and most banal to the most sophisticated. His composers range from Bach and Mozart, through Tchaikovsky and Verdi, to Hindemith and Webern. Nor does he forget American composers. Some of his most successful works use music by the neglected Charles Ives, by the popular march-writer John Philip Sousa, and by the contemporary orchestrator of popular and folk-tunes, Hershy Kay. Other modern American composers have preferred to write for 'modern' or 'folk' ballets. Aaron Copland composed for Martha Graham and for Agnes de Mille's *Rodeo*, Leonard Bernstein for Jerome Robbins's *Fancy Free*, *Age of Anxiety*, and *Dybbuk Variations*, to say nothing of the dance-musical *West Side Story*.

Many great composers wrote occasional ballet music. Even Beethoven wrote a ballet—*The Creatures of Prometheus*—but unfortunately the scenario has consistently defeated choreographers, and the music is seldom heard. In our own times, something similar has happened with Benjamin Britten's admirably atmospheric and danceable full-length score for *The Prince of the Pagodas*. Opera composers working for the Paris Opéra in the nineteenth century had to include ballets in their works. Verdi's ballet-music for that theatre, long neglected, has recently been rediscovered and used by numerous choreographers, including Balanchine, MacMillan and Robbins.

In recent times choreographers have become more daring and ingenious in their choice of music. Léonide Massine achieved a kind of revolution in the 1930s with his 'symphonic' ballets, using symphonies by Brahms and Tchaikovsky. This use of music was derided in the 1940s and 1950s, but taste has now gone full circle. Choreographers now think nothing of using symphonies, oratorios, song cycles, or concerti as accompaniments to their works.

They also adapt music from operas, having it re-orchestrated, or patch together scores from different pieces by the same composer. Tchaikovsky's non-ballet music is the most regularly used for such purposes.

Music critics and regular concert-goers are often surprised to 'discover' unfamiliar music when they visit the ballet. Even Tchaikovsky's Second Piano Concerto was for years much more familiar to ballet-goers, as the score for Balanchine's *Ballet Imperial*, than it was to concert-goers who often only knew his First Piano Concerto. Ashton unearthed music by Satie which at that time was scarcely known to the music-going public for his *Monotones*, and the same is even more true of Charles Koechlin's music used by Antony Tudor for his *Shadowplay*. Barry Moreland's *Prodigal Son (in Ragtime)* anticipated the popularity of Scott Joplin and his contemporary ragtime composers. In their search for new and interesting scores, present-day choreographers have unearthed music ancient and modern, including the electronic and the *avant-garde*, which is not performed at concerts and would not be sufficiently well-known to attract an audience if it were.

In Britain, a number of distinguished and successful scores have been specially written for modern dramatic ballets. Ninette de Valois' classics, *The Rake's Progress* and *Checkmate*, both owe part of their success to their music, by Gavin Gordon and Arthur Bliss respectively. Gordon was not known as a concert composer, while Bliss was one of the most important serious composers of his generation, but both their scores serve the ballets equally well.

Ballet music is not necessarily dance music. Sometimes it is—matched exactly to the steps. Sometimes instead the music provides an atmospheric or dramatic background, or serves as a source of emotional inspiration to dancers and audience.

One of the difficulties about using distinguished concert music for ballet is that it is not often possible to achieve standards of performance in the theatre to equal those normally taken for granted in the concert hall. The orchestras which play for ballet are not symphony orchestras, though some opera-houses do have orchestras of symphonic quality. Top concert soloists—singers, pianists, violinists—are not normally prepared to perform for ballet except on special gala occasions.

It is also difficult to get top-ranking conductors to appear at ballet performances. Conducting opera is more prestigious, partly because the conductor is in charge of the singers as well as the orchestra. In ballet, the dancers are usually unwilling to take direction from the conductor, and in some cases the conductor is obliged to follow the dancers, rather than the other way round.

A conductor once told me that whereas opera singers often wait after a performance to hear what the conductor has to say about them, dancers wait to tell the conductor what they think of him!

There can be no simple rule about whether dancers should follow the conductor, or vice versa. In symphonic works, the conductor can usually insist on his own interpretation and *tempi*, but when the dancers are doing difficult steps, involving jumps, balances or turns, the conductor normally has to adapt his *tempi* to their physical capabilities. Tall dancers generally do turns slower than small dancers, and some dancers balance longer than others.

There is a well-established tradition of dancers adapting *tempi* to suit themselves, much as opera singers hold a high note. Purists often object to such practices, but the public expects and adores it. A great artist, like Pavlova in the past or Makarova today, can adapt musical *tempi* to her own requirements while making the result seem artistic and almost inevitable.

Igor Stravinsky, regarded by many — including Balanchine — as the greatest composer of ballet music in the 20th-century

Conducting for ballet is a specialized task, requiring great understanding and sympathy for the dancers. Regular ballet conductors attend rehearsals, and work out *tempi* jointly with the dancers. It is this co-operative aspect of the work which particularly appeals to some conductors. Like ballet critics, conductors have to be in love with ballet, because they have to conduct the same scores over and over again. They can greatly enhance or seriously mar a performance, giving the music the life and the dancers the secure support they need, or making the dancers uncomfortable and the ballet dreary and slow. Their contribution is not easily appreciated by the audience, or by most ballet critics, who rarely find space to discuss the quality of the music or of the conducting.

In recent years, Britain has produced a remarkable crop of specialist ballet conductors. Robert Irving and John Lanchbery, who were each, at different times, principal conductors of the Royal Ballet, both went abroad—Irving to become musical director of New York City Ballet and Lanchbery to fill the same position with the Australian Ballet, and later with American Ballet Theatre. This meant that at the end of the 1970s, both the leading American ballet companies had British musical directors. Terence Kern of Festival Ballet and Scottish Ballet also conducted a great deal in the United States, and became musical director of the Joffrey Ballet in 1980. Patrick Flynn, who emigrated from Britain to New Zealand, was a conductor for American Ballet Theatre for a time from 1976 and conducted the Chicago dance festivals in 1977 and 1978. James Slater, originally a pianist at the Royal Ballet School and then with Festival Ballet, was persuaded by Beryl Grey to start conducting. He went to Houston, Texas, in 1978, becoming music director of the Houston Ballet.

Other British ballet conductors have thrived in Germany, a country famous for producing its own symphonic conductors. Ashley Lawrence conducted the ballet regularly in Stuttgart and Berlin before returning to London to succeed Lanchbery with the Royal Ballet. Stewart Kershaw, David Coleman and Francis Rainey also conducted ballet regularly in Germany; in 1980, Kershaw went to the United States to become a regular conductor with American Ballet Theatre.

One of the ballet conductor's problems is to avoid boredom, both in himself and in his orchestra. Lanchbery, Lawrence and Kern have varied the routine of conducting by arranging musical scores for new ballets. Lanchbery's arrangement of music by Hérold and other composers for Ashton's *La Fille mal Gardée* has become a 'classic' score. Charles Mackerras, who used to conduct ballet before he switched to opera, performed a similar service for Cranko's *Pineapple Poll* and *The Lady and the Fool*.

Orchestras usually respond enthusiastically to a new conductor, but eventually familiarity begins to 'breed contempt', and the standard of performance falls. This has been noted regularly at Covent Garden. There might be something to be said for regular exchanges between companies and indeed in recent years Irving and Lanchbery returned to Covent Garden as guests.

The problems facing conductor and orchestra are immense. It is not only a question of having to adjust *tempi* to a point where the actual sound of the music suffers. Frequently dancers have to appear in a ballet at short notice, without orchestral rehearsal, and the conductor has to be quick to adapt himself. There are even times when whole ballets are performed without orchestral rehearsals.

It might be thought that many of these problems could be solved by using recorded music. Modern stereophonic high-fidelity recording and reproduction of a first-rate performance often sounds better than a live performance by second-rate artists. On the other hand, there is something deadening in the theatre about recorded sound—a loss of atmosphere and a loss of the sense of occasion. Moreover it is obviously impossible for a recording to be adapted to the needs of different dancers, or to be adjusted to meet any sudden crises which may happen on the stage. A conductor can often 'cover' a late entry, or the awkward gap when a dancer falls.

In any case, the British Musicians Union normally forbids the use of recorded music, at any rate in theatres which have facilities for live musicians. Visiting companies with complicated recorded scores have sometimes had to cancel visits to Britain because they could not find, or afford, a live orchestra capable of producing a similar sound. Many Continental and American companies do regularly use recorded sound. Even at large theatres in New York, like the City Center, recorded sound is common. This enables companies who would not otherwise be able to afford New York seasons to do so. Something could perhaps be done to allow similar use of recorded sound in Britain.

A ballerina compares notes with the conductor during a rehearsal

9
Décor
and costume

Doreen Wells, now Marchioness of Londonderry, the
Sadler's Wells ballerina, seen here at Gamba's the
famous London shoe shop

53

Costumes and scenery are vital ingredients of many ballets though they can be changed without necessarily changing the whole nature of the work. Change the choreography or the music, and you no longer have the same ballet, though there have been some experiments in presenting the same choreography to different music. Change the design of the costumes and scenery, and although you change the appearance of the ballet, there is a sense in which the ballet itself remains the same. The classic ballets are constantly redesigned, and in recent years some modern ballets too have been redesigned within a short time of their creation.

The nineteenth-century classics created at the Paris Opéra and the Maryinsky Theatre, St Petersburg, were as much visual spectacles as musical or choreographic events. They invariably had realistic and elaborate sets, with painted backdrops and solid objects—houses, trees and so forth—on the stage. The settings may not have been authentic, in the sense of depicting the place or the period where the action of the ballet was supposed to be taking place. *Don Quixote* did not look truly Spanish or *La Bayadère* very Indian. But they were pretty and eye-catching. The settings for Bournonville's ballets in Copenhagen were more authentic.

Fokine's revolution was partly a revolt against the traditional approach to décor. The costumes and sets of his ballets, and of his successors with Diaghilev, were intended to be integral parts of the works. Whereas the older classics are not permanently linked with any particular designer, most of Fokine's works are. When we think of *Le Spectre de la Rose, Carnaval, Schéhérazade* or *L'Après-midi d'un Faune*, we think of Léon Bakst's designs at least as much as we think of Fokine's or Nijinsky's choreography. The designs tended to be simpler and more economical, often suggesting a place or a mood rather than actually depicting it, and leaving more stage space for dancing. The same is true of Alexandre Benois' designs for *Petrouchka* and *Les Sylphides*, though this last ballet has frequently been re-designed, while nearly always retaining the original Corot inspiration.

Diaghilev commissioned many of the best painters of his time to design ballets for his company. One was André Derain, who designed Massine's famous *La Boutique Fantasque* in 1919 and who was still designing for Massine thirty years later—*Mam'zelle Angot* (1947) and a revival of *The Good-Humoured Ladies* (originally designed by Bakst) in 1949. The most famous of all Diaghilev's designers was Picasso, whose décors for Massine's *Parade* (1917) and *Le Tricorne* (1919) have become classics. The fantastic cubist costumes for *Parade* were the main reason for the ballet's revival by the City Center Joffrey Ballet in the United States and by London Festival Ballet in the 1970s. (In 1981, the Metropolitan Opera, New York, courageously staged a totally new version of this ballet, David Hockney replacing Picasso as its designer.)

Since Diaghilev's day, décor for modern ballets tended to get even sparser, partly because of a modern taste for simplicity and partly for reasons of economy. Backdrops are often plain or have only a simple abstract pattern. Sets may consist of a few sculptural objects, or a few ropes, or the 'décor' may be achieved with film or photo projections, or entirely by lighting effects. Diaghilev, who generally supervised the lighting of his productions himself, staged an experiment in 'multi-media' effects in *Ode* (1928), choreographed by Massine with décor by Pavel Tchelitchev and Pierre Charbonnier. In the United States, Alwin Nikolais pioneered elaborate lighting and film effects, making them vital parts of his modern dance works. 'Multi-media' of all kinds has now become commonplace.

The importance of varied and interesting lighting, often as a substitute for any other décor, has been increasingly recognized in recent years. Jean Rosenthal became famous for her lighting designs for New York City Ballet, at a time when the company scarcely used any décor, and now many ballet companies employ lighting 'designers'.

One of the most successful combinations of realistic painted scenery with photo projections was achieved by the German opera designer Günther Schneider-Siemmssen in his designs for Panov's ambitious ballet version of *The Idiot*. Rapidly changing photos were used, for example, to provide backgrounds for Rogozhin's pursuit of Myshkin through the streets.

As choreographers and ballet producers have become increasingly aware of the importance of design as a vital factor in the success or failure of their work, they have insisted on specific designers to work with them wherever they go. Several specialists in ballet design have emerged in Britain in recent years, and have travelled the world to work with the choreographers who discovered them in Britain.

Nicholas Georgiadis and Barry Kay have designed most of the spectacular full-length works choreographed or produced by Kenneth MacMillan and Rudolf Nureyev, Peter Farmer has done the same for Peter Wright, becoming an acknowledged specialist in designing *Giselle*, and Peter Docherty has collaborated equally regularly with Ronald Hynd. Both Farmer and Docherty have also designed the sparser, more abstract sets required for many modern ballets. Nadine Baylis has also specialized in this field, working particularly with

Norman Morrice and Glen Tetley. All these designers are better known for their work in ballet than in any other field.

Occasionally choreographers and dancers decide to do their own designing. Ashton designed the costumes for his *Monotones* (1965), most notably the distinctive close-fitting head-dresses, and he even designed the décor for *Rhapsody* (1980). Anthony Dowell designed the costumes for some of the *divertissements* he and others danced with the Royal Ballet, and has toyed with the idea of becoming a designer when he has to give up dancing.

In the Netherlands, Toer van Schayk combined the roles of choreographer and designer, doing sculptural sets for ballets by Rudi van Dantzig as well as for his own works. Jean-Paul Vroom has become well-known as the designer for Hans van Manen's abstract ballets, even designing an ingenious variety of brief underwear for the male dancers!

In the United States, Rouben Ter-Arutunian has done attractive semi-realistic sets for such Balanchine ballets as required them. Balanchine's abstract ballets were almost invariably costumed by Karinska, in a wide variety of tunics and simple frocks and tights based on practice dress. Two designers of Italian origin, both specializing in more elaborate, spectacular decors, have recently had successes in the United States: Santo Loquasto, who did Baryshnikov's production of *Don Quixote*, and Pier Luigi Samaritani, who did Makarova's *La Bayadère*, both for American Ballet Theatre, which for many years had Oliver Smith, himself a designer, as one of its co-directors.

Just as Fokine's works are permanently linked with their designers, so are some of the standard modern works in the British Royal Ballet's repertoire. Sophie Fedorovitch's geometric backdrop and costumes for Ashton's abstract masterpiece, *Symphonic Variations*, have been generally accepted as a vital ingredient in the ballet's success. Her simple but evocative set suggesting the outside terrace of a country house played an equally important part in creating the atmosphere of Andrée Howard's *La Fête Étrange*. Ninette de Valois' *The Rake's Progress* depends heavily on Rex Whistler's authentic recreation of Hogarth's prints and her *Checkmate* will always be associated with the 1930s poster-art style of E. McKnight Kauffer, an American born artist who successfully brought chess figures to the stage.

Most people would probably agree that Osbert Lancaster's humorous but realistic sets are an essential part of Ashton's *La Fille mal Gardée*, and they have been reproduced wherever this version of the ballet has been staged. Some critics, however, would prefer the final scene without cut-out animals hanging from the ceiling. It is also perfectly possible to imagine Ashton's ballet being equally successful, as the nineteenth-century classics are, with different designs. On the other hand it would be hard to improve on Jacques Dupont's airy studio, immediately evoking Paris, and the swift transformation he devised from the caravans at the gypsy camp, for Ashton's *The Two Pigeons*.

Ashton's *Cinderella* acquired a different feeling when the décor was changed from Jean-Denis Malclès' original light fantasy sets to much more conventional realistic ones by Henry Bardon. The Royal Ballet's 1968 production of *The Sleeping Beauty* would probably have had a longer life if people had liked the long pseudo-medieval dresses designed by Lila de Nobili. Everyone pined for the old ones with their shorter-length tutus, designed by Oliver Messel. On the other hand, the very long run of *The Sleeping Beauty* in Paris in 1960 was due largely to the popularity of the spectacular costumes designed for the Cuevas company by Raimundo de Larrain. These costumes struck many British visitors as too flippant and too reminiscent of a night-club revue, but they were regarded by the French as the ultimate in fashionable chic.

Many of the best fashion designers and painters have regularly worked for ballet in France, where new ballets often seem to be more about décor and costumes than about dancing. André Levasseur, a designer who started his career with Dior, also did costumes for Ashton and Balanchine. Roland Petit's works were always notable for their designs, especially by Wakhévitch, Bérard, Clavé and Beaurepaire.

In Germany, the best-known designer of recent years is Jurgen Rose, who designed regularly for Cranko in Stuttgart and more recently for Neumeier in Hamburg.

Sometimes designers have second thoughts about their own works, seizing a further chance to make improvements or to do things which were not possible originally. Georgiadis made his *Romeo and Juliet* for the Royal Ballet even more elaborate and spectacular once the ballet had established itself in the repertoire and Leslie Hurry did several versions of the company's *Swan Lake*.

Sometimes too, the designer can collaborate with the choreographer in the actual staging of the ballet. Many modern ballets feature a change of drop-curtain or of lighting, or the movements of some abstract objects, as part of the ballet. Decorative changes of this kind usually suggest some dramatic or emotional change of mood, or some dramatic development, though this change or development is by no means always reflected in the choreography. In that case, the result is to leave the

Sketch by the famous designer Alexandre Benois for Dr Drosselmeyer, the fantastic magician in The Nutcracker

Balanchine did not rename his *Apollo* in 1979 when he revived it without the step-ladder which had previously served as a birth-place at the beginning and a stairway to paradise at the end. The ballet, which was always semi-abstract, became even more so in its new incarnation.

In England, Kenneth MacMillan has also experimented with changing designs for his ballets. *Solitaire* originally had a backdrop and costumes by Desmond Heeley suggesting, in fantasy style, a wasteland occupied by scaffolding and street kids. When redesigned in 1978 by Barry Kay, it seemed to become a ballet about a Degas girl and a troupe of clowns in a strange fairy-land, which caused many people to revise their opinions of the whole ballet, liking it more or, in most cases, less.

When MacMillan's *The Four Seasons* was first staged, at Covent Garden in 1975, it had a design by Peter Rice which suggested the facade of a busy inn or brothel. When redesigned by Barry Kay for the Paris Opera in 1978 it became a very elaborate affair, suggesting the old Empire music-hall in London, with chariots, helmets, and spangles among the accessories on the stage. An obvious attempt to please the French taste for spectacle, it was an immediate disaster, mostly because of the décor. Back at Covent Garden in 1980, the ballet was presented without décor, as an abstract work, and found much greater favour with the critics than before.

A change of costumes can also seriously affect the success and popularity of a ballet, as has been noted in the cases of *Ballet Imperial* and *The Sleeping Beauty*. Audiences accustomed to brief and revealing costumes, which are now the fashion, often resent any attempt to turn back the clock, as Lila de Nobili did when she re-introduced slightly longer tutus for the ladies in *The Sleeping Beauty*, in an attempt to provide a more 'period' style.

The history of ballet costumes is in fact partly the history of the gradual reduction of the amount worn by the principal dancers in classic ballets. It is also a history of a series of 'uniforms' which have at various times been accepted as standard dress for ballerinas and their partners.

Until the 1730s, the dresses worn by lady dancers still reached to the ground, making any intricate foot and leg movements difficult and invisible. Then La Camargo raised her skirts to her ankles so that people could see her ankles crisscrossing in *entrechats*. The principal male dancers at that time wore tunics based on those worn under their armour by medieval knights. Neither the male nor the female costumes varied much, no matter what role or what work was being danced.

In the 1830s, Marie Taglioni started the fashion for the *romantic tutu* which was to become the 'uniform' for most nineteenth-century

audience wondering what the change 'means'.

Choreographers can also have second thoughts about their ballets and about how they want them to look. Balanchine loves altering his own and other people's ballets, and in recent years has preferred to strip them of their décor and make them more abstract. The New York City Ballet even staged *Les Sylphides* in practice dress, calling it *Chopiniana* and making it look more like Balanchine than Fokine. (It also sounded like a different ballet, as it went back to Chopin's original piano music instead of using an orchestration, as Fokine did.)

When Balanchine decided to abandon décor for his *Ballet Imperial*, he recognized the change in the nature of the ballet by actually changing its title. At various times the ballet had been designed by Doboujinsky, Berman and Ter-Arutunian, always suggesting the aristocratic splendour of the Russian Imperial Court. In 1973, it was produced on a bare stage, in costumes more like practice dress than the formal tutus of nineteenth-century ballet, and was re-christened simply *Piano Concerto No 2*, the Tchaikovsky music to which it is danced.

Above, *Benois's designs of accessories for* The Nutcracker

Right, *De Valois'* The Rake's Progress *with Margaret Barbieri. One of the costumes and the set by Rex Whistler, based on Hogarth's paintings*

Below: *Robert Helpmann as the Red King and Beryl Grey as the Black Queen in de Valois'* Checkmate, *showing the striking costumes and décor by E. McKnight Kauffer*

Marie Taglioni in La Gitana, *a ballet created for her by her father, Filippo Taglioni, providing her with one of her most popular roles*

La Camargo, the 18th-century ballerina who first shortened her skirts to reveal her ankles. She was also one of the first to wear drawers when dancing (Painting by Nicholas Lancret)

ballerinas and which we still see, somewhat modified, in ballets like *Giselle* and *La Sylphide*. A tight-fitting bodice topped a long flowing tarlatan skirt, reaching half way down the calves and swirling in the air in high jumps. The romantic tutu was nearly always white, and the ballerina usually wore jewellery. Sometimes her head and bodice were decorated with ornaments to suggest the country or the period where the action of the ballet was supposedly taking place. The non-dancing characters, courtiers, huntsmen and older people—usually wore more realistic costumes; only the dancers appeared in ballet 'uniform'.

After the *romantic*, came the *classical tutu* jutting out horizontally just above the ballerina's knees. This was introduced by the Italian ballerina Virginia Zucchi in the 1880s, and became standard in all the great Petipa-Ivanov classics.

The romantic and classical tutus still remain the uniform for ballerinas in the nineteenth-century ballets and are also worn in many of the present day abstract ballets. The tutus have, however, tended to get shorter and flimsier. Less material is used, so that more of the ballerina's leg is visible when it is raised; frequently her underwear is visible too. Similarly men's jackets have got shorter, now generally only coming down to the waist, and male dancers no longer wear outer garments over the tops of their tights. Frequently their underwear can be seen through their tights. Things have come a long way since Nijinsky was sacked from the Maryinsky Theatre in 1911 for wearing too short a jacket, causing members of the audience to get out their lorgnettes and opera glasses for a closer look at the famous dancer!

Within the past twenty years it has become usual for both men and women to appear in modern ballets in body-fitting, all-over tights, plain or patterned, opaque or semi-transparent. The advantage of this new 'uniform' is that practically every muscle of the dancers' bodies can be clearly seen, and their line is uninterrupted by any costume. Not all dancers benefit from so much exposure. Oddly enough, despite revealing the exact shape of the body, this uniform often has the effect of reducing the difference between the sexes, making both men and women seem somewhat androgynous and sex-less, which suits the 'unisex' fashions and sexual equality of our age and the equally 'unisex' choreography which goes with it.

The Soviet Union, always rather old-fashioned in matters of taste, took longer than the west to adopt the near-nude look. In the meanwhile, Soviet designers, anxious to get away from the stylization of formal tutus and to achieve a more natural and lyrical look, developed long flimsy dresses, fairly closely fitting and reaching down to the calves, which became the 'uniform' of Soviet ballerinas in works ranging from *Romeo and Juliet* to short *divertissements*. These dresses were often popularly described in the West as 'nightdresses' and are now used also in some Western works.

Coupled with the trend towards less and less clothing in classic and abstract ballets, there has also been a trend towards more realistic costumes in character ballets. Traditionally character costumes are stylized. In Birgit Cullberg's *Miss Julie*, for instance, Sven Erixon dressed the heroine in a riding hat and blouse-jacket, and gave her a riding whip to brandish, but she wore a short classical tutu and her legs were in tights. In Ashton's *Enigma Variations*, on the other hand, Julia Trevelyan Oman dressed the dancers as much as possible like the characters they were playing, and Ashton showed that it was possible to choreograph dancing in formal Edwardian clothes. Much more attention than before is now paid to authentic period fashions and national styles in clothes. Critics and the public are quick to point out mistakes which previously would have been ignored, or simply accepted as one of the artificial conventions of ballet.

One of the most distressing twentieth-century innovations is the noisy, hard blocked point-shoe now worn regularly by most ballerinas and female corps de ballet. Originally the point shoe was absolutely soft, padded with cotton wool and darned by the dancers to get a better grip on the stage. The dancers still darn their shoes, but the points of the shoes are now often 'blocked', glued so solidly that sometimes they make a noise like tap-dancing. This ruins the effect of romantic, ethereal ballets like *Giselle* or *Les Sylphides*, but does help dancers to remain on *pointes* much longer than they otherwise might.

10
The critics

The critics are the most maligned members of the
ballet community. They speak with many voices,
and are useful in providing a wide range of opinions
about ballets and performers

Critics are the most abused members of the ballet community. Managements of ballet companies and the dancers themselves often resent them for writing unfavourable reviews and despise them for not understanding all the finer points and all the problems in a production. Ordinary readers get irritated when they disagree with the critics, often alleging that the critics are incompetent or even that they do not actually attend the performances they review! Many people think that critics serve no useful purpose, but are simply parasites, living off ballet without contributing anything to it. Critics sometimes secretly feel that way themselves.

In fact, critics serve several useful functions. Their first duty is to their employers, and to their readers. The nature of this duty will vary, according to what sort of publication employs them.

The criticism which usually appears in daily newspapers, or on the radio or television immediately after a performance, is a snap judgement. Very often it is scarcely more than a boo or hurray, with very little supporting argument. Aimed at a general readership, much of which will not be interested in ballet, it is often written in a newsy or even sensationalist way, to arouse readers' interest and even perhaps to lure them to a form of entertainment they might not otherwise try. Many critics feel a missionary zeal for their art, even that this is their main function.

There is no doubt that a critic can widen the ballet audience by writing in such an interesting or exciting way that readers find their appetite aroused. Some critics are very conscious of the need to do this; others think it unnecessary, or are incapable of doing it, and think it sufficient to preach to the converted. Even the 'converted', the regular ballet-goer, can be given new insights about ballets and dancers by a perceptive critic, and encouraged to think about ballets in new ways.

The more serious the newspaper or magazine, the more thoughtful the reviews it will aim to publish. The most detailed studies of ballets and performances are likely to appear in weekly magazines or in specialized ballet journals. Critics writing these reviews not only have more space to develop their arguments, but they also have more time to think.

Wherever they write, critics need to be enthusiasts. Far from being the crabbed, ballet-hating people of popular image, anxious to sneer and destroy, they are in fact passionate ballet fans. Nobody would take up ballet criticism for the financial rewards, which are meagre. Most ballet critics have to do some other work to earn an adequate living. Professional critics have to attend far more performances than most of them really want; they have to do so even when they are not 'in the mood' and

when they can be fairly certain the performances will not be enjoyable. The same is true, of course, of every other kind of critic, whether it be of plays, films, concerts or art.

There used to be a tradition of ballet being covered by music critics. It makes more sense for it to be covered by a theatre critic, as ballet is a total theatrical experience. The British critic Clive Barnes was for many years theatre *and* dance critic of the *New York Times*, and now does both duties for the *New York Post*. Sometimes an art critic also makes a good dance critic; Nigel Gosling, half of the husband-and-wife ballet critic known as 'Alexander Bland' is also *The Observer*'s distinguished art critic, under his own name. Sometimes music critics develop into important ballet critics, as Andrew Porter and Noël Goodwin did in London.

Many people assume that ballet critics must be dancers or ex-dancers, or that they must at least have studied dancing. This is not the case. There have been critics in this category, and they have not been notably better or worse than any others. Dancers often make bad critics, being too concerned with technical details to notice the impact of a performance in the theatre. On the other hand, once they give up dancing and become members of the audience, they may develop sufficient of an outsider's point of view. They have the advantage of knowing technical terms and spotting technical errors, though few of these mean much to most readers.

Most critics acquire their knowledge and understanding of ballet simply by watching it and reading about it. They meet dancers and choreographers, and learn something about their techniques and their problems. They may also watch occasional ballet classes. They increasingly acquire knowledge and standards of comparison.

There is no guarantee, however, that anyone writing about ballet necessarily knows much about it. Newspapers and magazines quite frequently publish articles by people who write well and who express an interest in ballet, but who have not actually seen very much. The editors, not being interested in ballet themselves and not knowing anything about it, are mainly concerned with the quality and liveliness of the writing, rather than with the accuracy of the facts or the value of the opinions expressed. There have been at least three cases in recent years of British national newspapers launching new ballet critics who knew little or nothing about their subject when they started writing.

There is equally no guarantee that someone who has seen a great deal of ballet, and knows a lot about it, will make a good critic. The first requirement for a critic is journalistic skill, rather than knowledge of ballet. The critic has to form his opinions and express them on paper very quickly, and ensure that his review is factually accurate, interesting, and not libellous! None of this is as easy as it may sound.

When writing at great speed, for next day's newspaper, it is very easy to leave out vital details—even the name of the ballet or the choreographer. It is equally easy to write something in the heat of the moment which is regretted later, or to sit on the fence, not making any real judgement of the ballet.

Readers gradually discover for themselves which critics are worth reading. Inevitably every critic has personal tastes and prejudices which will appeal to some readers, and infuriate others. There is no such thing as objective criticism. One critic may be particularly susceptible to a particular sort of ballet, or a physical type of dancer. Another may mainly judge ballets in terms of their musicality, or their dramatic effect, or the extent to which they successfully blend all the ingredients.

A new type of criticism has recently been developed in the United States, more detailed, more technical and supposedly more 'objective' than conventional writing. Writers of this new criticism try to describe and analyse exactly what happens on the stage, often finding elaborate significances in the slightest movements and going into considerable detail about the appearance and individual styles of the dancers. At the same time, these writers—like most American ballet-goers—generally have very dogmatic opinions about what ballet should be, and how it should be danced.

Theoretically, this kind of writing should be most valuable. In practice, many people find it boring and sometimes unintelligible. The British critic Noël Goodwin described it as being written 'as if the grammar of dance is more important than the result'.

Many American writers are anxious to stress the importance of dance as a serious art. Perhaps the British are more willing to treat it simply as entertainment. In any case, British writers are rarely given the amount of space which their American colleagues are regularly expected to fill. British ballet writing benefits, in conciseness and readability, from the limited space available.

Not all American critics are guilty of excessive length and over-seriousness. There are several distinguished practitioners of the older, more readable school of criticism, led by the veteran Walter Terry.

There is not only a difference between modern American and British styles of criticism, but also a difference in the judgements expressed, resulting from what can best be described as a trans-Atlantic taste gap. Many Americans now reserve their highest praise for neo-classical abstract ballets by Balanchine, or in his style. They like ballet as mobile sculpture or architecture, rather than as an emotional or dramatic experience. British audiences and critics tend to prefer their ballets with a little more heart, a suggestion of romance if not actually a story. They generally think more highly of Ashton than of Balanchine.

It seems a pity that critical enthusiasm should be limited to any one type of ballet, or that a whole genre should be condemned on theoretical grounds.

This is one of the dangers of taking ballet *too* seriously. Another danger is that writers have no time to keep up with developments in the related arts of theatre, music and cinema. Some of the exaggerated critical enthusiasm for certain forms of *avant-garde* dance has come from critics who were unaware that the dancers were only doing feeble imitations of work that had already been better done in experimental theatre.

Critics inevitably see too much ballet. Their appetites become a little jaded and their tastes become ultra-sophisticated. As a result, they tend to over-praise the new and the different, and to under-value conventional ballets and performances. This explains why critical taste often diverges quite markedly from public taste. Critics also feel a duty to encourage new styles, dancers and choreographers. If sufficient critics praise a dancer, that dancer is likely to be given more opportunities. Even a single critic singling out a young dancer for special mention may help that dancer's career. Critical demand for a new production of a familiar classic may accelerate the process of getting a new production mounted. It is of course extremely satisfying to a critic's ego when critical suggestions or complaints are acted upon. The critic then feels like a real contributor to the art of ballet. But it is not the critic's main job to guide choreographers and dancers; ballet companies have directors and ballet-masters for that.

The fact that critics inevitably get to know some dancers and choreographers personally may inhibit their criticism, or tempt them into unjustified flattery. It used to be argued that critics should never meet the artists they write about, so as to preserve their independence and freedom of judgement. In the modern world, that separation is impractical. Critics are often asked to interview artists for television, radio or for publications. They travel to out-of-town premieres in small places and to summer festivals, where dancers, artists, critics and the general public all mingle in the same hotels, restaurants and bars. Moreover the critic actually gains in knowledge and understanding from conversations with the artists. Obviously the critic will still try to maintain his independence, and will probably be extra careful not to over-praise an artist he knows personally. In recent years, two British critics (James Monahan and Nicholas Dromgoole) married ballerinas of the Royal Ballet (Merle Park and Lesley Collier respectively) and promptly stopped reviewing them. This meant that each ballerina actually suffered from not being reviewed by an important critic and an unqualified admirer, and it may also have meant that other ballerinas suffered from the conscious or unconscious comparisons the critic must make between one ballerina and another.

Sometimes critics are afraid of criticizing too harshly, because they want to remain on good terms with managements. Being human, they are flattered at being asked for advice. Some managements invite critics to accompany their companies on foreign tours. Naturally most critics enjoy free trips of that kind, and do not want to bite the hand that provides them.

There may also be 'political' reasons for not writing freely. A critic may feel that a company needs encouragement and support, particularly when it is new, and that the bitter truth about its achievements should be sweetened to ensure its survival. He may believe that a sensitive choreographer will improve with encouragement, or be destroyed by truthful but brutal criticism. Yet if a critic is not truthful and honest about his own judgement, he soon loses credibility.

A critic should also be honest about his personal tastes and prejudices. Some professional critics deny that they have any prejudices; they may also deny that they are influenced by their mood, their health, or the weather. Those are the dangerous ones. Critics are only human and must be affected by all these things. Nobody can enjoy a performance as much when developing 'flu, or after getting soaked on the way to the theatre, or when a close relative has just died. Similarly a critic may enjoy a performance more than usual when it is sunny, he has just got engaged to be married, or is in the theatre in the company of a loved one.

Nevertheless a professional critic does develop a certain skill in discounting these things, and in analysing the reasons for his pleasure or discomfort at a performance. Most critics are fairly consistent about their likes and dislikes. They may occasionally change their minds about a ballet or a dancer, and when they do so they must have the honesty to say so. The author's first impression of a new ballet usually remains fairly constant at later performances, though it may be qualified in various ways. The most dangerous time for him to judge is after the second performance, when a new work usually seems not quite as good or not quite as bad as it did

at first. But different critics think and feel in different ways, and what is a good method of reaching a conclusion for one may not be so good for another.

Readers may be shocked to find that criticism is so personal and so subjective. Some critics have indeed tried to follow certain rules, such as judging ballets by the Fokine principle that music, décor, story and dance must be of equal importance and perfectly suited to each other. But the mere decision to adopt such a rule is subjective, and means dismissing many popular and successful ballets. The interpretation of the rule must also be highly personal and subjective.

There is in fact no absolute answer, right or wrong, to the question whether a ballet or a dancer is good. At best, there is only a general consensus of opinion. Even the greatest dancers and choreographers have had, and still have, their detractors, more conscious of their faults than of their virtues. The ballet regarded as a masterpiece today can easily seem tasteless or boring tomorrow, or be totally forgotten, because of changing standards of taste.

Critics vary as much in their techniques as they do in their tastes and opinions. Some write notes conscientiously during performances, inevitably missing some of the stage action while they do so. They may try to remain as detached as possible from the performance, always remembering they are critics, posing criticial questions to themselves even while the performance is in progress, and refraining from anything so 'committed' as applause at the end. There used to be an unwritten rule that critics never applaud, but this seems to have largely disappeared, except with a few of the older generation. One reason for the rule was said to be that a critic should not reveal his reaction to a performance to anyone before it became available to his readers!

Other critics find it chilling or even impossible to be self-consciously a critic while a performance is in progress. They try to enjoy it as much as an ordinary member of the audience, waiting till afterwards to do the necessary analysis of why they did or did not enjoy it. In practice, most critics have to use a little of both methods. The most austere and disciplined critic must sometimes get carried away with enthusiasm or disgust; the most openly responsive sometimes needs to start planning his review while the performance is still in progress, to save time, and may need to note down some details—a sequence of dances, the colour of a dress, the nature of the scenery—before they are forgotten.

Some critics prefer to write immediately after a performance, while it is fresh in their minds; others prefer time for reflection.

Whatever their different methods and tastes, critics also have a great deal in common. There is such a thing as a critical mentality—the ability to judge, to make comparisons, and to give reasons for the judgements. Many critics apply these techniques to everything they do—the meals they eat in restaurants, the journeys and holidays they take—as well as to the art they are paid to review.

All critics share some of the same professional temptations. The principal one is to exaggerate. A review saying that a new dancer is the best since Pavlova or Fonteyn, or so bad that she should never have been allowed on the stage, is more fun to write, and more fun to read, than an article saying the new dancer is neither particularly good nor particularly bad, and in fact indistinguishable from dozens of others. Yet the latter is far more likely to be a truthful judgement. Critics go to considerable lengths to find something extreme and exciting to say, to make sure their papers print their notices and to keep their readers interested and entertained. A critic who is always moderate, and sound, may also be very often a bore.

Some critics consistently look for something to sneer at, which makes for lively, controversial writing. The result may be an ego-trip for the critic and a flashy piece of journalism, but not a very fair appraisal of the performance. It may also be cruelly wounding to the artists concerned. However dancers and other artists usually prefer even the most damaging review to no review at all, to being ignored. There is a great deal of truth in the saying that 'all publicity is good publicity'. If the public reads about a dancer or choreographer often enough, that artist bcomes well-known, even famous. Most people remember the names they have read more easily than they remember *what* they have read about them.

Britain still has the benefit of a fairly large number of more or less equally influential newspapers, so that there are a large number of published critical voices. No single opinion can dominate. In the United States the *New York Times* seemed for a long time the only critical voice that mattered, which gave its critics an embarrassing and dangerous amount of power. Since Clive Barnes moved to the *Post*, there have at least been two rival voices, and the *Times* no longer seems to have quite the critical power of former years.

It is sometimes alleged that it does not matter how many critics there are, as they all 'gang up' together and take a united line. This is quite untrue. Although there are certain types of performances which are likely to appeal to any experienced critic, it's amazing what a diversity of tastes and views are represented by ballet critics. Perhaps because they are people of strong individual tastes and prejudices, many of them have low opinions of each other, and in some cases there is considerable personal hostility between critics. They do not meet to agree on a line, though obviously critics who are friendly and generally see eye to eye do sometimes compare notes after a performance. Critics do not sit together in a solid critical phalanx in the theatre, but are generally split up among the audience. This is partly for their own good, as most critics prefer not to be in close proximity with each other, but to get an 'ordinary' audience reaction. It is also for the audience's good, as critics sitting next to each other at a performance usually succumb to the temptation of exchanging clever remarks and gossip during the performance, which can be infuriating to their neighbours. A critic should of course be at least as well behaved as he expects the rest of the audience to be. In fact, ideally the critic should be an example to the rest of the audience on how to attend and appreciate the ballet.

11
The audience

The audience does not need any specialised
knowledge to enjoy ballet. But it does help to do a
certain amount of preparation, and to know how—
and how not—to relax and get the most out of a
performance

Much more telling a story rather than breakdance

Those going to the ballet for the first time often ask what they need to know in advance, how they must approach the performance. There really are very few rules, and the most helpful tips are of a fairly negative character—not so much 'dos' as 'don'ts'. Of course it does help to know something about the programme in advance. People who have no idea what they are about to see till the curtain goes up are less likely to enjoy the performance than those who have done a little preparation. If it is a story-ballet, it helps to read the story in advance, either in the programme at the theatre or in a reference book at home. Whatever the ballet, it may help to read some reviews of it, so as to know what other people think about it, what special points may be worth noting, and what performances to watch out for. After that, the best thing is just to relax, clear one's mind as far as possible of other thoughts and worries, and abandon any preconceived notions of what a ballet should be. To achieve that relaxation, arrive at the theatre at least fifteen minutes before the performance, settle in, read the programme, absorb the atmosphere of the theatre, and avoid last-minute worries. People who read a book or a newspaper till the last minute do not seem to me to be clearing their minds for the ballet, but maybe what works for one person does not work for another.

One of the advantages of studying the programme before the ballet begins is that it should not then be necessary to glance at it during the performance. Looking at the programme during the performance inevitably means missing some of the action. What is worse, it also means interrupting one's mood and concentration on the ballet, and distracting neighbours in the audience. Even someone gazing around the auditorium, instead of looking at the stage, is distracting to others sitting near. There really is no point in looking at a programme to identify a dancer during a performance; that can perfectly well be done after the curtain falls.

When a great star is appearing in a ballet, there is a temptation to watch out for the star and ignore everyone else on the stage. Sometimes a considerable portion of a ballet is missed by those waiting for the star to appear, and anxiously wondering if each new entrant on the stage is in fact the star or not. In many ways it is easier for a newcomer to appreciate a ballet as a whole when it is not a 'star vehicle'. In that case, the best thing is to 'make one's own stars', looking up the names of any dancers who were particularly impressive immediately after the performance, and noting their names for the future. Even when an established star is appearing, there may also be new talents on the stage, waiting to be discovered by the critics and by the general public.

Not everyone realizes that the performance of a ballet begins as soon as the music starts, which in some cases may be well before the curtain goes up. The audience should be as quiet during the overture and during orchestral interludes between scenes as during the actual dancing. If the composer had wanted the sound of human voices, he would have written it into the score!

It is difficult to formulate general rules about the right time to applaud. The usual practice in Britain is not to applaud till the music ends. When an exciting dance, full of virtuosity, comes to an end, the audience has a spontaneous need to explode into applause, and indeed the dancers expect it. Most dancers give better performances when they are applauded, and rapidly go 'off form' if the audience seems unresponsive. This was one of the problems faced by the first Western ballet companies to visit China, where the audiences did not applaud until they had been told that the dancers must be treated 'like athletes'.

On the other hand there are certain places where applause shatters the atmosphere, even when the music has temporarily stopped. It is obviously correct to applaud the various bits of the 'Black Swan' or 'Blue Bird' *pas de deux*. It is not so obviously correct to applaud separate numbers in the lakeside scenes of *Swan Lake*, though that is probably a lost battle—nothing will prevent audiences applauding a particularly well-danced *pas de deux* by Odette and her Prince, or the lively high-stepping number for the four cygnets. Fokine hated applause after each dance in his *Les Sylphides*, interrupting the flow and shattering the atmosphere, but nearly all audiences today are determined to do just that. Usually, in the ballets of this kind, the dancers do their best to maintain the mood by ignoring the applause, remaining still till it has died down, or acknowledging it in character. Giselles, for example, often flit daintily from one side of the stage to the other during their applause, instead of stopping to make a formal curtsey.

In some countries, notably the United States and Denmark, it has become customary to applaud an exciting bit of dancing even while it is happening, and while the music is still playing. Most people would agree that this is an obnoxious practice, though many dancers actually like it. When New York City Ballet was in London in 1979, Balanchine said that one of the things he preferred about British audiences was that they did not destroy the music by drowning it in applause.

Ballet companies could do more to guide audiences, by putting notes in the programmes suggesting when applause is and is not appropriate. This *is* sometimes done at song-recitals and operas.

The best time of all for applause is at the end of the performance, when both audience and dancers

many rules of etiquette in ballet.
also many rules in how it is danced—critics

can relax, and enjoy their mutual admiration. Some artists make their curtain-calls as interesting and dramatic as their actual performances. It would have been worth going to a Fonteyn-Nureyev performance for the curtain-calls alone, even if one missed the preceding performance! Sometimes there is an unexpected or amusing moment during the curtain calls, when one dancer pays tribute to another, or when the audience throws flowers, or when a dancer is overcome with emotion. Newcomers to the ballet are well advised to stay till the end of the curtain-calls if they possibly can, and not rush away the second the curtain falls.

All this may sound pompous and didactic, as if one was not supposed to relax and enjoy oneself at the ballet. But unthinking behaviour can all too easily spoil other people's enjoyment. Everything said here about distracting behaviour also applies, naturally, to audiences at concerts, plays, films or any other cultural event. But there is something about the nature of ballet which makes care in these matters particularly important. The bond between the spectator and the performers on the stage is fragile, not reinforced by the spoken word as in a play. The spectator is frequently transported, forgetting where he is and receiving a direct aesthetic and emotional communication from the dancers. This mood, and the empathy which is established to produce it, is very easily shattered.

Quite apart from all these questions of how to behave, there are even more important questions of how to watch. Those questions are difficult to answer. First there is the technical question —should one try to watch the whole stage at once, or focus on a particular dancer or group of dancers? And if one does focus, should one use artificial aids like opera glasses or even more powerful binoculars?

With experience, people find out for themselves what is the best way for them. Those who have seen a ballet many times begin to develop a pattern of watching, always looking out for certain things, focussing on certain dances at certain times, and perhaps ignoring others. When only one or two dancers are on the stage, it is fairly easy to decide which to watch. When there is a lot of activity all over the stage, it is far more difficult. That is one reason why it is often necessary to see a big complicated production several times before one can 'take it all in'.

Methods of watching depend a lot on personal taste. Some are more interested in studying groupings, looking at the décor, noting lighting effects; others prefer to focus nearly all the time on the principal dancers. Whatever one does, one is bound to miss something. People who use opera-glasses gain considerable detail, and lose the general picture;

they may easily miss something that happens out of range. Those who never use binoculars miss a great deal of facial expression and detailed movement, unless they have exceptionally good eyesight or always sit very close to the stage.

Again, sitting close to the stage means missing general patterns and groupings, while sitting far away means missing detail. Floor patterns and ensembles are generally better seen from above, from one of the tiers; jumps look more impressive from stage-level. In some theatres, the music will sound much better in one part of the house than in another. So will the dancers! At Covent Garden, for example, the brass and percussion often sound unpleasantly loud at the rear left of the stalls while the dancers may seem gloriously light on their feet. Move upstairs, to one of the top tiers, and the orchestra will sound much better balanced, but the dancers may appear to be doing a tap-dance in their toe-shoes.

Ideally, regular ballet-goers should experiment, sitting in different parts of the theatre and watching in different ways at different performances. Critics are normally kept in their 'regular' seats, to which they become possessively accustomed, but it is good for them too to be moved around; it is amazing how different the same ballet can look from different distances and angles. Similarly, some ballets look better in big theatres while others, created for a more intimate setting, get 'lost' when transferred to a big opera-house.

Then there is the hardest and most important question of all—what to watch for and how to judge? Just as the critics vary in their tastes and approaches to ballet, so of course do the rest of the audience. Some are interested mainly in dance virtuosity, others in style and musicality, the creation of a mood, or the telling of a story. Some people would rather see great dancers in a conventional display of virtuosity than see unknown dancers doing interesting and original new choreography. Others would far prefer the opposite. Some are mainly concerned about the appearance of the dancers, and may really watch only one sex, and only the better-looking members of that sex at that. Some scarcely hear the music, while others are so sensitive to it that their enjoyment is ruined if it is badly played, or if they think it unsuitable for the dancing. Or they may enjoy quite an ordinary ballet more, because they like the music. Some cannot appreciate a ballet unless it has pretty décor and costumes; others prefer body-fitting tights, wanting to see as much as possible of the dancers' bodies.

So there can be no dogma. Even experienced and knowledgeable ballet-goers approach performances with quite different expectations and demands. Their expectations and standards of

67

judgement also change over the years. What I want from a ballet today is not necessarily what I wanted twenty years ago. One of the joys of ballet is that there are so many ways of enjoying it.

12
British ballet: the background

Dame Ninette de Valois, who founded the Vic-Wells
Ballet and guided its fortunes till it became the
Royal Ballet. Without her faith and determination,
British ballet would not have achieved such rapid
success, at home and abroad

Ballet as we know it in Britain today owes its existence largely to two women: Dame Marie Rambert and Dame Ninette de Valois. Indirectly it also owes its existence to Diaghilev, with whom both women worked and who re-kindled the taste for ballet in Britain, which had been dead for some time.

What Diaghilev brought to Britain was of course Russian ballet, and for a long time after his death many people continued to think that ballet must be Russian, that only Russians could dance. British dancers had to adopt Russian names. Rambert and de Valois had a hard struggle overcoming that prejudice. Eventually they succeeded in establishing British ballet to such an extent that British teachers, dancers and choreographers—at least as much as Russian—became in demand all over the world.

Rambert was born Cyvia Rambam in Poland in 1888. She studied music and movement with Jaques-Dalcroze and was engaged by Diaghilev to help Nijinsky choreograph the complicated rhythms of Stravinsky's *Le Sacre du Printemps (The Rite of Spring)*. She danced in Diaghilev's company, studied with Cecchetti, fell in love with Nijinsky, and married Ashley Dukes, a British playwright. She opened a ballet school in London in 1920, which started giving performances in 1926. From 1930 she organized regular performances by a group called the Ballet Club, which in 1935 became Ballet Rambert. She 'discovered' and encouraged Frederick Ashton and Antony Tudor, who did their first choreography for her, and she

Marie Rambert dancing Massine's The Snow Maiden *in London, in the early thirties*

Dame Marie Rambert, the founder of Britain's oldest ballet company and the discoverer of Frederick Ashton and Antony Tudor. Her production of Giselle *set a standard in its time*

also trained a number of the most distinguished dancers in the early days of British ballet. She was made a Dame of the British Empire in 1962.

Ballet Rambert was based at the tiny Mercury Theatre in London, where Rambert had her school. It specialized in miniature, 'chamber' ballets suitable for the Mercury's very small stage. Other choreographers who worked for Rambert included Andrée Howard, Frank Staff and Walter Gore.

During the Second World War, Ballet Rambert made extensive provincial tours under the sponsorship of CEMA (The Council for the Encouragement of Music and the Arts), which later became the Arts Council. It was one of the companies which brought ballet to wide new audiences during the war, and helped to create the nation-wide public for ballet which has existed ever since.

After the war, Ballet Rambert toured overseas, developed new choreographers, most notably Norman Morrice, and staged dramatically coherent and intelligent productions of classics like *Giselle* and *La Sylphide*. For a long time, the Rambert production of *Giselle* was regarded in Britain as the standard by which others should be judged. It caused other companies to pay more attention than before to dramatic consistency and credibility.

Because of its small scale, Ballet Rambert could never afford to pay its artists rates comparable with what they could get elsewhere, and after the war there was a steady drain of talent to other, younger companies.

In 1966, Rambert and Morrice decided that it was no longer practicable or desirable to compete with the Royal and Festival ballet companies. They reduced the group to an even smaller size, making it essentially a 'modern dance' ensemble, the first of

Left: top, *Ninette de Valois in 1933 and* below, *de Valois with the Vic-Wells Ballet in 1931, when she founded it*

Lillian Baylis, the founder of the Old Vic, who encouraged de Valois to start a ballet company

its kind in Britain. The full-length classics were totally abandoned; some of Tudor's works were retained for a time. However the attempt to mix 'classical' and 'modern' did not work, and the group became entirely devoted to 'modern' techniques and styles.

Morrice introduced the American choreographer Glen Tetley to Britain, and for a time Ballet Rambert relied heavily on him for its new productions.

Morrice retired from Ballet Rambert in 1974, leaving it to his assistants, John Chesworth and Christopher Bruce. Increasingly the choreography was done by members of the company, which acquired a new audience, interested in the experimental and the *avant-garde*. Morrice returned to his first love, classical ballet, becoming director of the Royal Ballet in 1978.

Like Rambert, De Valois, born Edris Stannus in Ireland in 1898, danced in Diaghilev's company. She married an English doctor and started a ballet school in London in 1926. Lilian Baylis, the founder of the Old Vic Theatre, asked her to teach movement to the actors and to supply dancers for some of the productions. She staged a ballet of her own at the Old Vic in 1928, as a curtain-raiser to an opera. Other ballets followed, and in 1931, Baylis asked de Valois to transfer her ballet school to the newly-opened Sadler's Wells Theatre, The Vic-Wells Ballet was born, giving its first performance at Sadler's Wells on 15 May, 1931; performances were soon being given regularly, every two weeks. Two British dancers who had been with Diaghilev—Alicia Markova and Anton Dolin (real names Alicia Marks and Patrick Healey-Kay)—appeared regularly with the company, Markova as prima ballerina and Dolin, her partner, as a guest artist. Robert Helpmann joined as a dancer in 1933, performing Dolin's role as Satan in de Valois' *Job*. The very young Margot Fonteyn joined the Sadler's Wells School in 1934 and danced with the company in the same year. In 1935, the Vic-Wells Ballet gave its first West-End season and also made its first provincial tour. Also, Ashton joined it as choreographer. In 1937 it went to Paris.

From the beginning, the full-length classics were included in the repertoire, in authentic versions based on the notation brought from Russia by Nicolai Sergeyev. *Swan Lake* Act 2 was given in 1932, *Coppélia*, with the Russian ballerina Lydia Lopoukhova as guest, in 1933. *Giselle, The Nutcracker* and the complete *Swan Lake* followed, and *The Sleeping Beauty* was mounted in 1939, shortly before the outbreak of war. It was given one gala performance at Covent Garden that year, for President Lebrun of France.

With the outbreak of war, Sadler's Wells Theatre was closed, and the company—now called the Sadler's Wells Ballet—toured. It was in the Netherlands in 1940 when the Germans invaded, and escaped, losing some of its scenery. During the war, it did extensive provincial tours, like Ballet Rambert, and had West-End seasons at the Princes and New Theatres. With Ashton away on war service, Helpmann joined de Valois as the company's choreographers.

After the war, the Sadler's Wells Ballet moved into the Royal Opera House, Covent Garden, as the resident company, giving extensive seasons, alternately with opera performances, for most of the year. They made their début at Covent Garden with *The Sleeping Beauty*, in a new production—the first big spectacular production to be seen in the London theatre after the war. It established the Sadler's Wells Ballet as a major company, and Margot Fonteyn as a leading ballerina.

Guest choreographers and guest dancers soon came to work with the Sadler's Wells Ballet at Covent Garden. The choreographers included Massine, Balanchine and Petit, the dancers, Danilova, Massine, Markova and Dolin. Ashton, back from the war, rejoined the company as principal choreographer. A second company was formed at Sadler's Wells Theatre to cater for local audiences and others who could not afford Covent Garden prices, and to give opportunities to new young dancers and choreographers. It was this company, known for several years as the Sadler's Wells Theatre Ballet, which developed the choreographic talents of John Cranko and Kenneth MacMillan, and such dancers as Nadia Nerina, Svetlana Beriosova, Elaine Fifield, Maryon Lane, Patricia Miller, David Blair, Stanley Holden, Donald MacLeary, David Poole and Pirmin Trecu.

In 1949, the main Sadler's Wells Ballet made its first visit to New York, opening at the Metropolitan Opera House with *The Sleeping Beauty*. The visit was a revelation to American critics and audiences, who immediately hailed the company as one of the finest in the world, and recognized Fonteyn as an outstanding ballerina. Other stars of the company at that time were Beryl Grey, Violetta Elvin (a Soviet-trained dancer from the Bolshoi who had married an Englishman), and Moira Shearer, a red-haired beauty who achieved film-star fame in *The Red Shoes*. The male roster, apart from Helpmann, who 'doubled' the roles of the Prince and Carabosse in *The Sleeping Beauty*, included Michael Somes, Alexis Rassine, Brian Shaw, John Hart and John Field.

Regular visits to New York followed after that, helping to establish the Sadler's Wells Ballet as one of the world's leading companies. Americans came to think of it as 'their' company, and it was often

De Valois returns to the stage for a special gala at Sadler's Wells, 15 May 1950, as Webster, the maid, in Ashton's A Wedding Bouquet, *a role she created in 1937*

Margot Fonteyn as Princess Aurora with Robert Helpmann in the 1939 production of Sleeping Beauty

said that the company danced even better in New York than it did in London.

On 31 October 1956, the Queen granted a charter naming the whole Sadler's Wells organization—both ballet companies and the school—as The Royal Ballet. Considerable confusion was caused for a time by both the Covent Garden and Sadler's Wells companies appearing under the new name, confusion which was worse when both companies made their frequent foreign tours. Different titles were subsequently tried to distinguish the two companies, the most recent of which was to call the Covent Garden company simply 'The Royal Ballet', while the smaller group became known as 'The Sadler's Wells Royal Ballet'. There are of course other 'Royal' ballets in the world, in Sweden and Denmark, so there is still scope for confusion abroad.

In 1962, Rudolf Nureyev, who had escaped from the Kirov Ballet in Paris the previous year, began to dance regularly with the Royal Ballet. His partnership with Fonteyn, who had been on the brink of retiring, became legendary, in the classics, in Ashton's *Marguerite and Armand* which was created specially for them, and in Nureyev's own stagings of previously neglected Petipa works like *La Bayadère* and *Le Corsaire*. Nureyev's example encouraged a remarkable rise in the standard of British male dancing, inspiring Christopher Gable, Anthony Dowell and David Wall, among others. He also immensely broadened the classical repertoire, stimulated considerable re-thinking of standard works like *The Nutcracker*, and started the practice of inserting extra solos for the principal male dancers in Petipa's works.

In 1963, de Valois officially retired as director of the Royal Ballet, though she continued to supervise the School and to exercise great influence over the company's policies. Her successor was Sir Frederick Ashton, who continued choreography and brought Bronislava Nijinska to the Royal Ballet for the first time with her productions of *Les Biches* and *Les Noces*. In 1970, Ashton was succeeded by John Field and Kenneth MacMillan, in a joint directorate which did not work. Field soon resigned, and Peter Wright became MacMillan's assistant.

MacMillan's period as director of the Royal Ballet was extremely controversial. Fewer Ashton works were performed, being replaced by Mac-Millan's own ballets, including his full-length *Anastasia* and *Manon*. (He had already made *Romeo and Juliet*, a huge box-office and artistic success, during Ashton's period in charge.) MacMillan seemed remote and inaccessible to some of the dancers, morale in the company fell, and many dancers left. He resigned in 1978, remaining as principal choreographer and being succeeded as director by Norman Morrice, a surprise choice as he had never been a member of the Royal Ballet, though he had choreographed for it. On becoming director, he announced that he would not be doing choreography for the company. One of his first policy decisions was to stop all guest artists, including Makarova, Nureyev and Baryshnikov, who had recently appeared regularly with the company, in an attempt to give more opportunities to the company's own dancers and to develop new stars.

From 1964 till 1979, the Royal Ballet also ran Ballet For All, a small touring group which gave lecture demonstrations, sometimes amounting to miniature performances, in college halls and small theatres around the country. This group was

The Royal Ballet production of Anastasia *with (from right to left) Lynn Seymour, Vergie Derman, Jennifer Penney, and Lesley Collier*

transferred from the Royal Ballet to the Royal Academy of Dancing in 1979, mainly for financial reasons, and soon disbanded.

From 1967, the Royal Ballet Choreographic Group gave occasional workshop performances of new ballets by would-be choreographers, drawn both from the Royal Ballet and from outside. This group, devised and directed by Leslie Edwards, one

Maina Gielgud as the Siren in Balanchine's The Prodigal Son, *with the Sadler's Wells Royal Ballet*

of the Royal Ballet's veteran character dancers and mimes, was intended to provide opportunities for dancers to try their hands at choreography without all the expense and critical exposure of a full-scale production by a company. Most major ballet companies now have similar workshops, though the amount of choreographic talent that emerges remains meagre.

De Valois always stressed the importance of the School as a key element in providing the Royal Ballet with dancers and giving them a specific style. In 1947 the School expanded from Sadler's Wells Theatre to Baron's Court, and started giving academic education as well as ballet training. In 1955 the junior section moved to the beautiful White Lodge, in the middle of Richmond Park, where it remains. The Royal Ballet's own classes are conducted at the senior school, in Baron's Court, as there are no studios at the Royal Opera House, but three studios have been built at Sadler's Wells Theatre for use by the Sadler's Wells Royal Ballet when it is in residence there.

A number of other comparatively short-lived companies, now almost forgotten, also played an important part in the development of British ballet. In 1938, Antony Tudor formed his own company, The London Ballet, for which he choreographed

Antoinette Sibley and Anthony Dowell, one of Britain's most famous ballet partnerships, in Kenneth MacMillan's three-act Manon

two of his most enduring works, *Judgement of Paris* and *Jardin aux Lilas*. This company only lasted a year as Tudor went to the United States in 1939.

Two companies which toured Britain during the Second World War and the years immediately after, introducing many new audiences to ballet, were the Anglo-Polish Ballet and International Ballet. The Anglo-Polish, founded in 1940 by the Polish *émigré* dancers Alicia Halama and Czeslaw Konarski, had a mixed repertoire of short classics, *divertissements* and folk-lore works, of which the

most popular was *Cracow Wedding*. International Ballet was founded in 1941 by Mona Inglesby, a wealthy lady who was also the company's ballerina. It performed a number of specially created short works including a masque of *Everyman* in which the Shakespearian actor Leslie French had a speaking role. Later it also mounted the Russian classics, in stagings by Nicolai Sergeyev. At various times the company's roster included such distinguished dancers as Nina Tarakanova, Harold Turner, Algeranoff (who had been in Pavlova's company),

Moira Shearer and Sonia Arova. After the war, the American dancers Nana Gollner and Paul Petroff appeared with International as guest artists.

In the 1950s and early 1960s, Walter Gore briefly ran various companies, putting on his own ballets, and starring Paula Hinton, the dramatic ballerina, who was his wife. In 1964, Norman McDowell, a designer, founded London Dance Theatre, a company which only lasted a year but became famous for its high standards of design, including décors by McDowell himself and by other young British designers, including Peter Farmer. This was the first time a British company had concentrated on décor, in the French tradition. The principal choreographer was Jack Carter, and there were also works by Andrée Howard, Terry Gilbert and Janine Charrat.

In 1972, André Prokovsky left Festival Ballet (see p.78) to form his own group, the New London Ballet, with his wife, the Soviet-trained ballerina Galina Samsova. This company gave Prokovsky his first opportunities to do choreography and also commissioned works by other choreographers. It achieved remarkably high standards, touring at home and abroad, but financial problems brought it to an end in the late '70s. By this time, Prokovsky was in international demand as a choreographer and Samsova was dancing with the Royal Ballet.

A small company which had considerable influence and which was later reincarnated in a larger form was Western Theatre Ballet, founded in Bristol in 1957 by Elizabeth West and Peter Darrell. It was the first 'regional' company in Britain, and its title, apart from being a pun on the name of one of its founders, made it clear that it wanted to be thought of as regional. It also wanted to concentrate on dramatic or 'theatre' works. Elizabeth West was killed in a climbing accident in Switzerland in 1962 and the company continued under Peter Darrell till 1969. It danced with Béjart's company in Brussels, and later became resident company at Sadler's Wells Theatre, dancing in the operas as well as giving its own performances. In 1969, the company was invited to move to Glasgow, where it became Scottish Theatre Ballet. It gradually evolved into a larger and much more classical company, changing its name, in 1974, to become The Scottish Ballet.

Although based in Glasgow, The Scottish Ballet has toured throughout Britain, while concentrating on Scotland and the north. Peter Darrell did his own production of *Giselle* and made his own original version of *Swan Lake*, as well as making some new full-length ballets. The company became the first British group to mount Bournonville's *Napoli*, and was also for a long time the only British company performing his *La Sylphide*. Very few of

Mona Inglesby and Algeranoff as Swanilda and Dr Coppélius in the International Ballet production of Coppélia. *Inglesby's company toured Britain during the second world war, introducing ballet to new audiences*

the principal dancers were Scottish, and some principals were engaged from Europe and the United States. The company made some foreign tours, and is now established as an important ensemble, similar in many ways to Festival Ballet.

A smaller regional company, Northern Dance Theatre, was formed in Manchester in 1969 by Laverne Meyer, a Canadian dancer who had been a member of Western Theatre Ballet. Meyer's idea was to provide the Midlands with something similar to the company Elizabeth West had formed in Bristol, but it did not attract big audiences. Meyer was forced to resign in 1975 and, after a short interim period, Robert de Warren, who had run classical and folk-lore companies in Iran, was appointed director. The company changed its name to Northern Ballet Theatre and shifted its emphasis from short modern ballets to longer classical-style ones.

Both The Scottish Ballet and Northern Ballet Theatre found it easier to attract audiences with classics or full-length works in classical style than with mixed programmes of modern ballets. The London-based companies had the same experience when on tour, and even in London the full-length works tended to be the most popular.

In the late 1970s Maina Gielgud produced occasional performances by a small group called Airs and Graces. This was a new form of lecture-demonstration, which included dancers being rehearsed and coached in public by well-known directors like Ninette de Valois, Anton Dolin and Robert Helpmann. It was extremely popular, with critics and the public, and could well become a permanent way of introducing ballet to new audiences and helping existing audiences to understand it better.

The most important new company to emerge

Dr Julian Braunsweg (right), the founder and administrator of London Festival Ballet, talking with Alexandre Benois, the famous designer

in Britain since the Second World War was Festival Ballet. Named in honour of the Festival of Britain in 1951, its title eventually acquired a second meaning, as the company gave regular Christmas and summer seasons at the Royal Festival Hall in London. It grew from a small group formed to support Markova and Dolin on a British provincial tour in 1949, managed by Dr Julian Braunsweg, a Polish-born impresario who exercised considerable financial skill and ingenuity in keeping it going as a private venture. He survived various crises until 1965, when a spectacular production of *Swan Lake* drove him bankrupt, much as an earlier London production of *The Sleeping Beauty* had nearly ruined Diaghilev.

A public trust was formed to run Festival Ballet, with considerable financial support from the Greater London Council, and Sir Donald Albery, a well-known West-End theatre impresario who had managed the Sadler's Wells Ballet during the war, agreed to serve as director. In 1968, Beryl Grey

The Western Theatre Ballet's production of Sun into Darkness *first staged at Sadler's Wells Theatre in 1966. The ballet was choreographed by Peter Darrell and the score, which was specially commissioned, written by Malcolm Williamson*

Beryl Grey, who danced the full-length Swan Lake *with the Sadler's Wells Ballet on her 15th birthday*

took over as artistic director, and remained till a revolt by the dancers led to her resignation in 1979. She was succeeded by John Field, her former dancing partner with the Royal Ballet, who had in the meanwhile run the Royal Ballet's touring company, the company at La Scala, Milan, and the Royal Academy of Dancing.

Festival's official name changed slightly from time to time, as it survived and re-emerged from various financial crises and came under new boards of management. Since 1968 it has officially been known by the rather cumbrous and faintly ungrammatical title of London Festival Ballet. It now has its own offices and rehearsal studios, but it never had a theatre or school of its own. Its first London season, in 1950, was at the old Stoll, and since then it has been seen mainly at the New Victoria cinema and the London Coliseum, as well as the Festival Hall.

From the beginning, the company always had well-known international stars and an eclectic repertoire, including the nineteenth-century and Fokine classics. In its early days the stars, apart from Markova and Dolin, were Belinda Wright and John Gilpin. Danilova, Arova, Kovach and Rabovsky, Toumanova, Chauviré and Slavenska are just a few of the star names who appeared with the company. Natalie Krassovska was resident ballerina for a long period, as was Toni Lander. Flemming Flindt got much of his early experience with Festival Ballet, before becoming a star of the ballet at the Paris Opéra and then director of the Royal Danish Ballet. André Prokovsky joined Festival Ballet at the beginning of his career, and returned to the company after a spell with New York City Ballet. Galina Samsova also joined Festival as ballerina. She and Prokovsky, whom she married, followed Markova and Dolin, Belinda Wright and John Gilpin, to

become the third great Festival partnership. In recent years, regular guests with Festival included Patrice Bart of the Paris Opéra, Peter Breuer from Dusseldorf, and Peter Schaufuss, a Danish dancer who appeared regularly with several of the world's major companies. Eva Evdokimova, the most cosmopolitan of all ballerinas, divided the greater part of her time between Festival and Berlin.

Festival gave British audiences a chance to see a number of well-known twentieth-century ballets which were not in the Royal's repertory. These included numerous works by Fokine (*Le Spectre de la Rose, Carnaval, Prince Igor, Schéhérazade,* and *Petrouchka*), Harald Lander's *Etudes*, a popular display of technique for the company's stars and *corps de ballet*, David Lichine's *Graduation Ball* and Massine's *Gaieté Parisienne* and *Le Beau Danube*, all operetta-style romps. Numerous new ballets were also created for Festival by choreographers including Jack Carter, Michael Charnley, Ronald Hynd and Barry Moreland. Few of these remained long in the repertoire but Carter's *Witch Boy*, a dramatic work based on the play *The Dark of the Moon*, was for years a successful vehicle for Gilpin, and Moreland's *The Prodigal Son (in Ragtime)* was equally successful for Paul Clarke.

Since Beryl Grey took over the company in 1968 it became rather more like a second edition of the Royal Ballet, and acquired a number of Royal Ballet dancers. Emphasis shifted to the nineteenth-century classics and—when Nureyev no longer worked with the Royal Ballet—to his productions of *The Sleeping Beauty* and *Romeo and Juliet*. Nureyev joined Festival for a gala season in London every summer for several years, and they also appeared together in the United States.

John Field seems likely to continue broadly the same policies, collaborating closely with the Royal Ballet School and the Royal Academy of Dancing for the recruitment of dancers. In his first year there were new ballets by Geoffrey Cauley and Michael Pink, both graduates of the Royal Ballet. Cauley had made ballets for the Royal Ballet some years earlier while Pink had early choreographic experience while at the Royal Ballet School. In 1981, Field was forced by financial difficulties to abandon new ballets, and to concentrate on established classics.

Festival remains, and presumably will remain, a more international company than the Royal Ballet, with a lingering vestige of Ballets Russes style and repertoire. What it lacked in style and coherence, it nearly always made up for in showmanship and gusto. It was never afraid of commercialism or of virtuoso guest artists. There is room in ballet for this sort of company, as well as for the more 'respectable' Royal Ballet image. Britain has been lucky, in recent years, to have had both.

13
Britain today
and tomorrow

The future of ballet depends above all on the
schools. Children from the Arts Educational Schools
appear in Festival Ballet's annual Christmas
Nutcracker, and sometimes go on to join the
company

In 1980, Britain had one world-famous ballet company (The Royal Ballet), three highly professional touring groups (The Sadler's Wells Royal Ballet, London Festival Ballet and The Scottish Ballet), and one regional company (Northern Ballet Theatre) which could not compete with the others in full-scale classical productions or in dancing strength but which performed a useful service in staging smaller-scale ballets in the Midlands. In addition there were two well-established modern dance groups (Ballet Rambert and London Contemporary Dance Theatre), and various smaller ones of no great quality or importance.

It is impossible to predict which of these companies will survive and prosper or what new ones may arise. In the 1970s the Royal Ballet no longer held quite the high place in world opinion—or even in British opinion—which it had won earlier. It had found no real successor to Ashton as a supreme choreographer or to Fonteyn as a ballerina assoluta. Its new ballets were often perfectly adequate but not universally accepted as masterpieces and its leading dancers, though good, were not international stars. The repertoire relied too much on repetition of certain over-familiar works; regular ballet-goers—and some of the dancers—grew bored. Nevertheless it remained an important company—certainly the best in Britain—with great potential resources of talent and repertory. All companies have their ups and downs; some never recover from their downs, while others—like the Paris Opéra—suddenly shine again after a long period of decline.

The Royal Ballet is essentially the resident company of the Royal Opera House. There are very few theatres in Britain large enough to take its bigger productions on the scale they are presented at Covent Garden. For several years, the Royal Ballet gave up touring in Britain, as it felt it could not do itself justice in touring conditions. A few regional theatres have now been modernized, and their orchestra pits enlarged, to enable touring to be resumed, at least on a limited scale.

The other companies all tour regularly, and indeed that is insisted on by the Arts Council, on which they are all financially dependent. This is just one way in which public subsidy for the arts, now generally accepted as inevitable and desirable, can actually affect the nature of the art provided.

Before the Second World War, British ballet companies—like all other theatrical ventures—had to raise their own money to survive. Lilian Baylis regularly appealed for funds from the stage of the Old Vic. Ballet Rambert lost dancers to bigger companies which could afford to pay them more. It was difficult enough for two small London ballet companies to survive; there was no question of companies existing in the regions.

On the continent of Europe, of course, the big opera and ballet companies were always supported by the state, and appeared mainly in state-owned opera-houses. Diaghilev showed that a ballet company could be run privately, but he had exceptional skills as a fund-raiser, as well as as an artistic director. Even Diaghilev could only survive so long as he satisfied the public, or his rich patrons, that he was providing something they wanted to support.

Public subsidy of the arts in Britain started during the Second World War, when the Council for the Encouragement of Music and the Arts organized and financed 'culture for the people'. This role was continued after the war by the Arts Council, which obtains its money from the Government but distributes it free of political pressure. (Ironically, indeed, many of the theatrical groups financed by the Arts Council were strongly anti-establishment, regularly biting the hand that fed them.)

Since the establishment of the Arts Council, the idea has gained ground that any cultural or artistic enterprise has only to announce its existence to qualify automatically for a public subsidy. Occasionally the Arts Council itself has even appeared to share that view. It is inevitably faced with very difficult decisions in distributing its limited funds—for example to what extent its first duty is to the preservation of existing excellence, mostly in London, as opposed to the support of smaller and less established groups which want to take dance to more far-flung parts of the country. Political and philosophical attitudes must obviously influence these decisions.

The 'left-wing' argument is that as the Arts Council is financed by taxpayers from all over the country, it is wrong for the greater part of the money to be spent on the minority who live or work in London, and who have a wide choice of entertainments and the arts in any case. It is also argued that it is the Arts Council's duty to act as a missionary, introducing the arts to people who have not had much opportunity to see them and who may not yet appreciate them when they do.

One result of this philosophy is that some experimental and not very talented dance groups have sometimes obtained Arts Council grants. Once the Arts Council gives a grant, it is very difficult to withdraw it, as it is then accused of 'killing' a company. Yet there must obviously be some limit to the number of dance companies Britain needs and to the number the Arts Council can be expected to support. The Council must also maintain its right to discontinue a grant to a company which has failed to live up to its expectations or whose standards have seriously deteriorated. The public can just as easily be 'turned off' dance by pretentious or boring performances as it can be 'hooked' by good ones.

The Arts Council is no longer the only source of public subsidies for the arts. There are now regional arts associations, set up to further the policy of disseminating culture as widely as possible throughout the country and to encourage local talent. Local authorities are also empowered to support the arts, though few of them do so on any worthwhile scale. One exception is the Greater London Council, which has generously supported London Festival Ballet for many years; others are the Greater Manchester Council, which supports Northern Ballet Theatre, and Glasgow Corporation, which supports the Scottish Ballet.

A dance company was supported in Wales by the Welsh Arts Council, and the East Midlands Arts Association backed the EMMA dance company, but neither of these groups achieved much success. Private industry and business also give substantial grants to the performing arts, sometimes sponsoring specific productions, especially 'prestige' opera and ballet productions in London.

Ballet could not survive in Britain today (or anywhere else in the world) without public subsidy. The future of British ballet is thus inextricably bound up with the level of subsidy permitted by various Governments, and therefore with the whole state of the national economy. It will also be affected by the policies adopted in distributing such funds as are available. Too much concentration on 'taking art to the people' all over the country could mean a serious threat to the best art, which tends to be concentrated in London, as it is in most capital cities. People who are particularly interested in the arts, or who regard them as essential to their lives, make a point of gravitating to capital cities. They put up with the expense, violence, noise and transportation problems precisely because they want the superior artistic amenities which capital cities provide. That may result in 'élitism'; it is also inevitable.

There could be something to be said for a more widespread adoption of the American system of 'matching grants', to check that public money is not wasted on art or supposed art which nobody wants. Grants given by the National Endowment for the Arts (the American equivalent of the Arts Council) are virtually always 'matching grants'—the grant is only given to the extent that an equivalent amount is raised from private sources. On the other hand this can put a premium on popular or commercial enterprises. It would be much less practical in Britain, where high taxation prevents much private sponsorship of the arts.

Another American practice which could revolutionize the situation in Britain would be the adoption of tax exemption for grants to the arts. Even private individuals buying tickets for fund-raising performances in the United States can claim tax deductions for the amount of their contribution. Unfortunately it seems unlikely that the British Treasury would risk such a reduction in its revenues.

The problems about subsidizing ballet are not specific to ballet, or to Britain. They affect all the arts, and all organizations which try to support them. The problems facing the Arts Council, and the criticisms it receives, are remarkably similar to those which face the National Endowment for the Arts in Washington. 'Art' has come to cover such a wide variety of activities in recent years that it is almost impossible for anyone to be sure what is experimental art and what is a confidence trick. The Tate Gallery in London incurred much ridicule for spending public funds on an exhibition of a pile of bricks; public television in the United States outraged opinion with an 'art' film showing a dog being shot in the head, repeated over and over again for thirty minutes! Much *avant-garde* dance is in that same highly controversial area, on the boundary between creative experiment and fraud. Public benefactors of the arts face the dilemma of supporting junk or risking failure to encourage important innovative work.

All art has always been to some extent 'élitist' and will probably remain so. Art only appeals to a minority of the population and is only judged with experience and discrimination by an even smaller minority. Moreover, with present-day mobility and ease of transport, it is often easier for people to come to the art than for the art to go to them. This is certainly true of people living in the London suburbs and in the Home Counties, who often prefer to get to a West-End theatre and see a performance in something like ideal conditions rather than have it brought to them in less satisfactory ones.

The demand for ballet in central London is enormous, and there would probably be room for at least one full-time ballet theatre. At present Covent Garden is shared between the Royal Opera and the Royal Ballet, which means there are not enough ballet performances to satisfy the audience or to give dancers and choreographers the opportunities they need. Festival Ballet has to find itself a home each time it wants a London season. The Sadler's Wells Royal Ballet can only appear at Sadler's Wells for limited periods, because the theatre is also run as a London home for visiting companies from the regions and abroad. The number of ballet performances given in London does not compare favourably with the number given in New York.

The audience for ballet in what used to be called the provinces but are now referred to as 'the regions' is naturally not as great or as discriminating. It tends to support only well-known works, especially the full-length classics. Ballets with unfamiliar titles and even premieres of new works have often played to empty houses outside London. It is difficult to resist the conclusion that talent has often been squandered on places where it is neither wanted nor appreciated, while London has been comparatively deprived.

It can be argued, on the other hand, that the only way to develop a ballet audience is by giving ballet performances. There is considerable truth in this.

Northern Ballet has gradually built up something of an audience for itself in Manchester; a bigger and more obviously talented company would probably have built a bigger one, more quickly. But at a time of financial stringency, the question needs to be asked whether it is more important to be building new audiences where they do not exist, or preserving and developing talented companies and audiences which do exist but which could easily dwindle or die.

For years the Royal Ballet has not been able to afford the number of older character dancers, orchestral musicians or new productions which ideally it should. Unsatisfactory or fading productions of the classics have been retained longer than they should. Talented dancers have become bored with the small repertoire or with the inadequate number of performances they were able to give. All this and the lack of a much more comprehensive pension and welfare scheme for injured and retired dancers have played a part in the decline of the Royal Ballet's prestige and morale. One of our great national treasures has been jeopardized.

For the Royal Ballet is essentially a national company. It has always restricted itself to British and Commonwealth dancers—apart from occasional guests. Indeed the departure of South Africa from the Commonwealth in 1961 deprived the company of one of its best sources of overseas talent, a source that had produced the ballerina Nadia Nerina and many other leading dancers. New laws connected with Britain's becoming a member of the European Common Market gave all European citizens of the Market freedom of employment in Britain, and made it more difficult to employ Commonwealth citizens. It seems likely that, as a result, the Royal Ballet may be able to use European talent, including perhaps the excellent male dancers produced by the French and Danish schools. This might be some compensation for the loss of Commonwealth talent.

The future of the Royal Ballet, and of all ballet, obviously depends on maintaining high standards, so as to retain, renew and expand its audience. This means, among other things, producing new generations of talented dancers and choreographers. As we have seen, choreographers can only be guided and encouraged; they are really born, not made, and

cannot be trained as such. Dancers *must* be trained and the Royal Ballet School has a good record of doing that. It now produces far more first-class dancers, year after year, than can possibly find work in the Royal Ballet and the other British companies, which do not have their own schools. Many of these dancers seek and obtain work abroad. The School has generally achieved higher standards with girls than with boys, and British-trained girls are more in demand internationally than the boys. There are various reasons for this: the difficulty of persuading suitably strong and athletic boys to take up ballet training and a shortage of good male teachers are among them. The standards of male dancing in Britain have risen enormously in the past twenty years, partly due to the stimulating example of Rudolf Nureyev. Anthony Dowell, a product of the Royal Ballet School, became an international star, leaving the Royal Ballet to become a much-acclaimed star of American Ballet Theatre. Stephen Jefferies starred for a time with the National Ballet of Canada; he and Mark Silver, with their combination of stylish technique and dramatic ability, are among the brighter hopes of recent British male dancing. Nevertheless the standards of British male dancing in general are still lower than in the Soviet Union, the United States, Denmark and France, where the schools have also progressed in recent years. This is one of the most pressing problems for British ballet training.

It used to be thought that a major company could not exist and prosper without its own school. However when John Field took over the direction of Festival Ballet, he expressed himself content to rely on other schools, rather than to continue the campaign for sufficient funds for the company to have its own. A year later, when Baryshnikov took over the direction of American Ballet Theatre, he too seemed content to rely on other schools, rather than continue the company's own, which had not recently produced many dancers suitable for the company. Both Field and Baryshnikov felt able to rely on the abundance of talent produced by their rival companies' schools—the Royal Ballet School and the School of American Ballet (attached to New York City Ballet).

There are also several good private ballet schools. In Britain, the Arts Educational Schools, which train children for all the performing arts, regularly provide dancers for London Festival Ballet, including the corps of children who appear in the annual Christmas production of *The Nutcracker*. John Gilpin, for many years the virtuoso male star of Festival Ballet and one of the greatest British male dancers of all time, was trained at an Arts Educational School. The Elmhurst School (which trained the Royal Ballet's ballerina Merle

situated at the company's headquarters, known simply as The Place.

Ballet training in British private schools, and indeed in many parts of the world, is supervised by the Royal Academy of Dancing. This was founded in 1920, becoming 'Royal' in 1936. The Danish ballerina Adeline Genée was President till 1954, when she was succeeded by Margot Fonteyn. The RAD conducts examinations, awards scholarships, and holds various conferences, lectures, and residential courses. It now holds special training courses for teachers. It awards diplomas for dancers and teachers who pass its examinations, and also special prizes to young dancers and to outstanding personalities in British ballet. By setting the syllabus for examinations it is extremely influential in determining the type of teaching given in private schools. Its inspectors travel constantly at home and abroad. It is one of Britain's greatest contributions to world ballet.

Dame Adeline Genée, the Danish ballerina who settled in London and became first President of the Royal Academy of Dancing

Park) and the Bush Davies School also regularly produce highly trained girls who get jobs in the major ballet companies.

Ballet Rambert has always had its own school though in recent years this became quite separate from the company. A new Rambert school was then formed specifically to train dancers in the company's present modern style. The principal 'modern' school in Britain is associated with the London Contemporary Dance Theatre and is

Dame Margot Fonteyn, who succeeded Genée at the Royal Academy in 1954

14
The United States

New York City Ballet in Balanchine's *Square Dance*, abstract classical dancing set to chamber music by Vivaldi and Corelli. The ballet originally (1957) had a square dance caller, but he has now been eliminated and the work only retains slight suggestions of square dance. This is typical of the way Balanchine has gradually revised several of his ballets, to make them even more abstract

The United States now has the biggest ballet and dance boom in the world. There are more companies—classical and modern—than anywhere else, and there is a greater variety of dance styles, from the nineteenth-century classics to the most experimental *avant-garde*. Dance is now taught in almost every American university; there is even a subject called the 'philosophy of dance'! There are annual conferences of dance critics, and a devoted dance audience, especially in New York. All this is a very recent phenomenon. The growth of a native American classical ballet tradition began even later than in Britain.

As in Britain, the taste for classical ballet in the United States in this century was first aroused by touring Russian companies. Pavlova toured the States a great deal, as well as having New York seasons. Nijinsky danced in the States with the Diaghilev company but at the time he was quarrelling with Diaghilev. The various Ballets Russes companies which succeeded Diaghilev spent a great deal of time in the States: Colonel de Basil and René Blum brought their Monte Carlo company to New York in 1933, with the teenage ballerinas Baronova, Riabouchinska and Toumanova, and with Massine and his ballets. Balanchine, who had worked briefly with this company, was invited to New York by Lincoln Kirstein about the same time, and started the School of American Ballet, from which New York City Ballet eventually grew. During the Second World War Sergei Denham's Ballet Russe de Monte Carlo was resident in the States, where it continued for some years after the War.

Adolph Bolm, a star character dancer who had worked with Pavlova, left the Diaghilev company in the States and worked there till his death in 1951. He produced and choreographed ballets at the Metropolitan Opera, New York, and at the Chicago Opera, where one of his young dancers, Ruth Page, was later to direct and choreograph ballets for many years. In 1933, Bolm was the first choreographer of the San Francisco Ballet, which he helped to found and which remained, under a succession of directors, one of the most important regional companies in the States.

Mikhail Mordkin, one of Pavlova's regular partners, settled in New York where he formed a company in the 1930s. His manager, Richard Pleasant, and one of his dancers, Lucia Chase, became co-founders of American Ballet Theatre in 1940. The link between Russian and American ballet is clear and close. Sol Hurok once advertised American Ballet Theatre as 'the finest in Russian ballet'!

The protégé of Diaghilev's who ultimately came to have the widest and most long-lasting influence in the States was George Balanchine. A

Lincoln Kirstein (left) and George Balanchine the founders of New York City Ballet. Kirstein is the company's General Director, and Balanchine its principal choreographer

company attached to his school and called the American Ballet gave its first performance in 1934 in Hartford, Connecticut, and then danced at the Metropolitan Opera till 1938. In 1936, Balanchine's business associate and impresario Lincoln Kirstein also formed a touring company, Ballet Caravan, and the two groups joined forces in 1941. New York City Ballet (NYCB) as such was not born till 1948, when the company acquired a home at the New York City Center. It came to London in 1950, achieving international recognition at Covent Garden in much the way that the Sadler's Wells Ballet had achieved recognition in New York the previous year. In 1964, NYCB transferred to the newly built and specially designed New York

Adolph Bolm, who danced with Pavlova and in the Diaghilev company, later settled in the United States. He choreographed the first version of Stravinsky's Apollo

The Dance Theatre of Harlem: **left,** *the* Don Quixote pas de deux, *performed by Elena Carter and Joseph Wyatt,* **above,** *Judy Tyrus in* Le Corsaire *and,* **below** *from left to right, Peter Hunter, Gregory Stewart and Darrell Davis in* Forces of Rhythm *the music for which is a mixture of Tchaikovsky and popular rock*

making revivals as authentic as possible, recreating the original decors and dissuading choreographers from modernizing or 'improving' their works. At the same time, he was also interested in trying out new choreographers and even experimenting with the *avant-garde*. The Joffrey Ballet was the first in New York to mount works by Oscar Araiz, an Argentinian choreographer who had worked in Canada and in Europe, and whose full-length *Romeo and Juliet* was extremely controversial but struck many critics as a valid and interesting new way of treating the old story. The Joffrey was also the first American company to acquire a work by Jiri Kylián, *Return To the Strange Land*, in 1980.

Even more experimentally, the Joffrey was the first classical ballet company to commission a work from Twyla Tharp, who made the successful pop ballet *Deuce Coupe* in 1973. In 1980, Joffrey engaged an even more *avant-garde* choreographer, Laura Dean, who made *Night*, a controversial work with deliberately repetitive and monotonous choreography and music.

One of the reasons for the remarkably high standard of the Joffrey dancers is that they are mostly trained in the company's own school. This was founded in 1952 as the American Ballet Center and is now known as The Joffrey School (American Ballet Center).

Eliot Feld, who previously danced with both NYCB and ABT, formed a company called the American Ballet Company to display his own choreography in 1969. It was disbanded, for financial reasons, in 1971, but re-formed in 1974 as the Eliot Feld Ballet. Feld set up his New Ballet School in 1978. The company consists of about 20 dancers and only performs Feld's own works. He is a musical and sometimes witty choreographer, as well as a stylish and ebullient performer, but the comparatively limited nature of the repertoire and the company restricts its appeal to regular dance-lovers and critics rather than the general public. It is almost 'chamber ballet'.

The Dance Theatre of Harlem and its associated school, were established by Arthur Mitchell who felt that black dancers were not given equal opportunities in the predominantly white companies. His repertory mixed classical and 'ethnic' works; in 1980 they mounted a one-act version of *Swan Lake*, dressing the 'swans' in pale blue to avoid too great a contrast between the costumes and their skin colours. The company also performs classical *pas de deux*, like *Le Corsaire*, and one of its virtuoso dancers, Paul Russell, joined the Scottish Ballet as a principal and later moved to the San Francisco Ballet. Another, Ronald Perry, was engaged by Baryshnikov for ABT, becoming the company's first black soloist. DTH's vitality and

virtuosity make it very popular in London, where it has given several visiting seasons at Sadler's Wells Theatre. In 1981 it became the first black company to appear at the Royal Opera House, Covent Garden.

Most New York companies have to make do without any regular theatre of their own. NYCB has the New York State Theatre, and ABT is officially 'resident' at the Kennedy Center in Washington, which in fact means giving regular seasons there. ABT has performed at various New York theatres, most recently giving regular seasons once or twice a year at the Metropolitan Opera. The Joffrey Ballet is attached to the City Center, where Dance Theatre of Harlem also gives regular seasons. The Eliot Field Ballet had no home for many years, and indeed was unable to appear in New York City in 1979 or 1980. However, it plans to have its own theatre, the Elgin, a renovated cinema which is to be shared with other dance companies.

All these companies tour, though NYCB, ABT and The Joffrey Ballet can only visit the larger theatres. Both ABT and Joffrey have formed second 'junior' companies to tour smaller places, and to give opportunities to young dancers and choreographers. Dancers straight from school often go first into these companies, gaining experience in leading roles, before 'starting again' in the corps of the principal companies. In New York, both companies have given occasional seasons at Brooklyn College. ABT's second company, called Ballet Repertory Company, was formed in 1972, under the direction of Richard Englund, who supervised the repertoire and contributed some choreography, including his own version of the full-length *Romeo and Juliet*, specially adapted for a small cast and for small stages. Joffrey's junior company, simply called Joffrey II, was started in 1970. Both companies played a valuable role in training dancers and in taking ballet to new audiences.

San Francisco, Chicago, Washington, Philadelphia and Boston have had classical ballet companies of their own for many years. In recent years, practically every other American city has also acquired its own company, usually associated with a prominent local school or with a university dance department. Since 1977 Boston has even had two companies, the smaller Boston Repertory Ballet aiming for a more 'modern' image than the Boston Ballet. From 1963 to 1974, Washington also had two companies, the fully professional National Ballet directed by Frederic Franklin and the semi-professional Washington Ballet, associated with the school run by Mary Day. The National Ballet collapsed financially, but the Washington Ballet gained strength in the late 1970s from its new resident choreographer, Choo San Goh, regarded by some American critics as one of the most promising young talents.

Ruth Page, who danced with Pavlova and studied with Bolm, ran ballet companies in Chicago from the 1930s to the 1970s, engaging prominent foreign dancers and choreographers as well as developing local talent and creating her own ballets. She was finally forced to give up in the late 1970s, for financial reasons. There was some uncertainty about the future of ballet in Chicago, though various schemes for a new company were being mooted.

In 1980 the most successful and highly praised companies outside New York were the San Francisco Ballet, Ballet West in Salt Lake City, and the Pennsylvania Ballet in Philadelphia. The San Francisco Ballet was directed from 1938 by Willam (*sic*—not William) Christensen and then by his brother Lew, who between them choreographed most of the repertoire. Lew Christensen, the first American to perform the title-role in Balanchine's *Apollo*, had a speciality of injecting incongruous jokes in seemingly abstract ballets, like *Con Amore* (1953) and *Scarlatti Portfolio* (1979). Several of his ballets are also in the repertory of other American companies. Willam's comic, Massine-like *Nothin' Doin' Bar* (1950), set in a speakeasy to Milhaud's *Le Boeuf sur le Toit*, was revived in 1980 with great success. Under the direction of the Christensens, the San Francisco Ballet was always mainly classical, and staged the first American productions of the full-length *Coppélia* (1939), *Swan Lake* (1940) and *The Nutcracker* (1944).

In 1973, Michael Smuin, who had been a soloist with ABT, returned to San Francisco as a choreographer and an artistic director of the company. His ballets ranged from abstract neo-classical works, to dramatic slices of Americana like *A Song for Dead Warriors* (1978), about the oppression of the American Indians. His setting of Mozart's *C Minor Mass* (1978) was an exciting and vivacious non-literal vision of the religious music, which had a big success. He also made full-length versions of *Romeo and Juliet* (1976) and *The Tempest* (1980).

The San Francisco Ballet also performs Ashton's *La Fille mal Gardée*, being the only company in the United States to have it in the repertoire. The company does the ballet full justice. One of the company's leading men, David McNaughton, scored a particular success as Colas. He was hailed as an exciting new dance talent during the company's 1980 New York season. The company visits New York regularly and is highly praised by New York critics.

The Pennsylvania Ballet, which visits New York once or twice a year, is also very highly

Ruth Page, who started her dancing career with Pavlova and Adolph Bolm, and later founded and directed ballet companies and a ballet school in Chicago. Miss Page is also a well-known choreographer

regarded. It developed from Barbara Weisberger's school in Philadelphia in 1963, and she directed the company. Its repertoire originally consisted largely of works by Balanchine. Benjamin Harkarvy became artistic director of the company in 1972 and choreographed for it regularly since then. The company has a reputation for always having good dancers, American and foreign, and has been praised for performing Balanchine's abstract works with more warmth than NYCB! In 1980 its ballerina Magali Messac transferred to ABT as a principal.

Willam Christensen moved from San Francisco to Salt Lake City to teach dance at the University of Utah and to found Ballet West there in 1963. Under his direction, and mainly with his choreography, the company made some successful European tours. Bruce Marks, formerly a principal dancer of ABT, joined Christensen in 1976, becoming artistic director of the company in 1978, when Christensen retired. Bruce Marks undertook his own choreography for the company, while his wife—the former Danish ballerina Toni Lander—became the principal teacher. In 1978, Ballet West moved into its own new theatre in Salt Lake City. The repertoire has broadened to include Balanchine and the Petipa classics. By 1980 the company had become the fifth largest in the United States and made its first visit to New York. It was well received by the critics, some of whom found its dancers had a distinctive 'Western' vitality.

The Boston Ballet, founded in 1964 by E. Virginia Williams, and directed by her since then, also has a mixed repertoire ranging from Petipa and Bournonville to Balanchine and Robbins. The company inaugurated an annual international choreographic contest in 1979 and makes a special effort to find and employ new choreographers. In 1980 the Boston Ballet became the first American company to tour China. In the same year the former French ballerina Violette Verdy joined the company as associate artistic director and it was hoped to raise standards of dancing to match those of the other principal American companies.

These standards are astonishingly high. There are so many good, highly-trained dancers in the United States that it is impossible for them all to find adequate employment, despite the large number of ballet companies. At Christmas, virtually every company, big and small, fully professional or semi-amateur, stages a version of *The Nutcracker*, often based on Balanchine's NYCB production. It is estimated that there are over 200 *Nutcrackers* in the United States each Christmas!

It is impossible to keep track of all these numerous companies and it is often difficult to define their status. In Britain, a 'regional' company is any company based outside London; in the United States, 'regional' has a specialized meaning, usually referring to semi-professional or amateur companies consisting largely or mainly of school pupils. Large, well-established fully professional companies like the San Francisco Ballet, Ballet West and the Pennsylvania Ballet do not like to be described as 'regional'.

Many companies, like the Washington Ballet, use a combination of professional dancers and school students. Some apparently well-established companies disappear. The National Ballet of Washington, for example, directed by Frederic

Kathleen Crofton, the British dancer who started her career with Pavlova and later became a famous teacher. She founded regional American ballet companies in Buffalo, New York, and Baltimore, Maryland

Franklin, an English dancer who had been with the Ballets Russes, was founded in 1963, and was joined by Ben Stevenson, another English dancer, from Festival Ballet, as assistant director in 1971. It seemed to thrive, and numbered Fonteyn among its guest artists. It collapsed financially in 1974, leaving Washington without a major ballet company of its own, though ABT plays regular seasons there at the Kennedy Center.

During the 1980–81 season, a large number of these companies visited New York, possibly setting a precedent for future seasons. In addition to the San Francisco and Pennsylvania companies, the Ohio Ballet, the Cleveland Ballet, the Los Angeles Ballet and the Houston Ballet came to the elegant and spacious Brooklyn Academy. Dennis Nahat and Ian Horvath, both former dancers of ABT, became joint artistic directors of the Cleveland Ballet in 1974. The Los Angeles company was formed in 1973 by John Clifford, a virtuoso dancer and young choreographer from New York City Ballet. The Houston Ballet, directed by Ben Stevenson, made a particularly good impression on New York audiences and critics. It seemed destined to become much better known. Smaller companies—Cincinnati, Atlanta, Oakland, the Garden State and Washington—came to Brooklyn College's Center for the Performing Arts.

Other American companies at this time included the Maryland Ballet, which had been run successively by Kathleen Crofton, a British dancer who had been with Pavlova, and Petrus Bosman, formerly of the Royal Ballet. (Miss Crofton had earlier run a company in Buffalo, New York, which had even undertaken a European tour with Nureyev.) Bosman was replaced in 1980 by Alfonso Cata, a Cuban ballet master and choreographer.

The renowned Russian dancer André Eglevsky formed a small company in Long Island, attached to his school, which he directed till his death in 1977. Edward Villella, formerly a virtuoso dancer with NYCB, took over as artistic adviser.

Many of these companies have already achieved high standards of performance and production; their weakness is usually in the new choreography created specially for them. Their brief visits to New York have helped the New York public and critics to become increasingly aware of balletic activity outside the city. Favourable reviews in New York of course help regional companies to get further support and prestige in their home cities.

There are several theatres in New York City which have become semi-permanent homes for dance. On Lincoln Center, both the Metropolitan Opera House and the New York State Theatre have regular ballet seasons—the Met in the spring and

New York State Theatre, Lincoln Center, the home of New York City Ballet — the first theatre designed and built specifically for dance, though it is also the home of New York City Opera. (Inset), exterior of New York City Center, where New York City Ballet started, which now provides a home for visiting dance companies. It was originally a masonic temple

summer, when the opera is not performing, the State Theatre for most of the year, alternating with seasons by the opera. The City Center on 55th Street, like Sadler's Wells in London, houses regular seasons by itinerant companies, from New York, the regions and abroad, and is devoted to dance virtually all the year round. There are also numerous smaller venues which provide regular homes for modern dance. In Brooklyn, both Brooklyn Academy and Brooklyn College have regular dance seasons, especially by regional companies.

There are also frequent ballet seasons on Broadway. American Ballet Theatre used to appear at the modern Uris Theatre, where Nureyev has

also had several seasons, and where Roland Petit's and Makarova's companies appeared in 1980. Even Eliot Feld's smaller company had a Broadway season in 1978, aided by the presence of Baryshnikov as a guest, while Nureyev has enabled several companies to dance on Broadway by appearing with them.

Ballet and modern dance have also had a tremendous influence on the Broadway musical. Ever since Agnes de Mille choreographed what was virtually a complete ballet, the 'dream' sequence, for *Oklahoma*, most big musicals have contained a dance scene, connected with the story. *West Side Story* was almost as much danced as sung, and was choreographed as well as directed by Jerome Robbins. The popularity of dance became so great that Bob Fosse, a successful choreographer of films and musical shows, was able to stage a Broadway show consisting almost entirely of show-biz dancing, not linked by any story line and with scarcely any songs. It was called simply *Dancin'* and ran for several years from 1978. Michael Bennett's *A Chorus Line* and David Merrick's *42nd Street* both owed their Broadway successes largely to their dance ensembles, though these were of the traditional tapping and high-kicking chorus variety rather than ballet or 'modern'. Michael Bennett also attempted to repeat the success of *A Chorus Line* with a musical called *Ballroom*, dedicated to ballroom dancing, but this was not a success. Nevertheless there is no doubt that dancing has become a major ingredient, and sometimes virtually the only ingredient, in the success of Broadway shows.

Despite the new importance of dance in New York, a contrary trend is also now emerging. Important foreign ballet companies visiting the United States are starting to omit New York from their itineraries. This would have been unthinkable a few years ago.

In 1979, the British Royal Ballet toured the United States and Canada, omitting New York for the first time. In 1980, the Royal Danish Ballet went to Chicago for a special week of Bournonville performances, organized by Mrs Geraldine Freund who has sponsored a summer ballet festival in Chicago for some years. In both cases, economic factors made a New York season impossible. Companies of this size and importance expect to play at one of the few large theatres of the highest prestige—the Metropolitan Opera and the New York State Theatre. These are not always available, and in recent years New York managements have preferred visiting companies to guarantee the box-office by having a famous guest star. Nureyev appeared with London Festival Ballet, the National Ballet of Canada, the Australian Ballet, and the Berlin Ballet in their New York seasons, and it was his participation which guaranteed full houses and made these seasons possible. A projected visit by the Paris Opéra in 1980, on the other hand, was cancelled when the dancers of the company objected to Nureyev and Peter Schaufuss appearing as guests.

This situation highlights two recent trends in international ballet. One is for star dancers, like famous opera singers, to form a kind of 'jet set', rushing hither and thither around the world to appear with various companies. Nureyev is the most conspicuous example of this; he has also organized regular summer seasons in which one or more companies, or simply an *ad hoc* group of dancers, acted as supporting groups while he appeared nightly in a series of leading roles in classical and modern works. Sometimes these seasons, in London, Paris and New York, were simply billed as 'Nureyev and Friends'. In 1980 Makarova launched a similar venture for herself in New York, with star male dancers—Anthony Dowell, Fernando Bujones and Peter Schaufuss—joining her for a special Broadway season.

The other trend is for ballet to become more 'regionalized' and decentralized. Economics now make touring by large companies more and more difficult. It is easier to run regional companies and to invite famous guest artists. Places like Chicago and Los Angeles, which are trying to establish and develop new ballet companies of their own, may increasingly play host to visiting artists instead of to complete companies from abroad.

Ballet throughout the United States is now publicly subsidized, as well as receiving generous support from private donors. Public subsidy for the arts is even more recent in the United States than in Britain, a European tradition which has been slow to take root across the Atlantic. The National Endowment for the Arts—the American equivalent of the Arts Council in Britain—was only set up in 1965. It is a federal agency, with its headquarters in Washington. Within ten years, it was supporting 167 dance companies! Each State also has its own Council on the Arts, which often subsidizes local dance companies. (Major companies obtain financing from both National and State Councils.) Charitable foundations set up by private industry—most notably the Ford Foundation—have also supported dance companies. It was the Ford Foundation, in 1963, which saved the lives of several regional companies threatened with bankruptcy and extinction. It was criticized by some people at the time for mainly supporting those companies which leaned heavily towards Balanchine's style and repertory, notably the companies in San Francisco, Boston, Philadelphia and Salt Lake City.

The National Endowment for the Arts, just like the Arts Council in Britain, has also been criticized for supporting minor and sometimes mediocre companies at the expense of those which have already achieved high artistic standards. Certainly the very existence of the National Endowment encouraged the formation of new dance companies. The number of companies eligible for grants rose from a mere 37 when the Endowment was set up to 200 in 1978. (A similar growth took place in theatre and opera companies, and in symphony orchestras.) To some extent the growth simply represents the boom in the arts which has been taking place in the United States. But during the late 1960s, the Endowment was so generous with its funds for touring companies that many companies were formed to undertake unnecessary and unpopular tours simply as a means of collecting the money.

As in Britain too, it is very painful and difficult to cut off a grant to a company, once it has been given. Ending a grant may well amount to killing a company, especially as it will be more difficult to raise money from private sources once the company has been publicly condemned as unworthy of a grant. Private patronage, both from corporations and from individuals, is still important and comparatively plentiful in the United States.

Many of the companies supported with public funds are small and experimental 'modern' groups. The value of these is particularly difficult to assess; well-meaning public bodies are reluctant to seem blind to the latest developments in art and are sensitive to charges of élitism if they support only established successes. As a result, much public money is wasted on amateurism, pretentiousness, and valueless experiments.

15
Ballet
around the worlc

Ballet has flourished in Copenhagen since the
sixteenth century. The pantomime theatre is the
oldest building in the Tivoli gardens and the
commedia dell'arte tradition is regularly maintained
with daily performances throughout the summer

The Royal Ballet, American Ballet Theatre and New York City Ballet are generally numbered among the six great companies of the world. The others are the two major Soviet companies, the Bolshoi and the Kirov, and the Royal Danish Ballet. Companies with historical claims to importance are the Royal Swedish Ballet and the ballet troupe of the Paris Opéra. In recent years, German companies in Stuttgart, Hamburg, and Berlin, and the national ballets of Australia, Canada and the Netherlands have laid claims to equal fame, while promising new groups from Cuba, Venezuela and Japan have become internationally known. Here is a brief survey of companies around the world today.

The Soviet Union

The Bolshoi Ballet

The company was started in 1776, and the present Bolshoi Theatre in Moscow opened in 1825. It had some importance in the nineteenth century, giving the first performance of Petipa's *Don Quixote* (1869) and the first, unsuccessful, version of *Swan Lake* (1877). However it was not considered the principal ballet company in Russia until after 1917, when Moscow became the capital city instead of St Petersburg. Before the revolution, sophisticated Russian ballet-goers, who were mainly in St Petersburg, regarded everything about Moscow, including its ballet, as rather provincial. To some extent, this reputation still attaches to the Bolshoi, despite every effort to make it the showcase of Russian ballet. Performances in Moscow are mainly given for visiting diplomats, and workers' delegations from all over the Soviet Union and the Soviet satellites, so that the audience is not an expert one. Acrobatic effects and elaborate spectacle have always been stressed in an effort to appeal to this general audience, and to fill the Bolshoi Theatre (whose name means 'large') and the even bigger hall in the Kremlin Palace where the company now also performs.

The Bolshoi Ballet first acquired real artistic importance at the beginning of this century, when Alexander Gorsky was its ballet-master. Trained in St Petersburg, as most of the Bolshoi's best artists have been, he went to Moscow in 1898 to stage *The Sleeping Beauty*. He became principal dancer and producer there in 1900, and proceeded to revise many of the Petipa classics, including *Don Quixote* and *Swan Lake*. He is now thought to have been a pioneer in making those ballets more dramatic and realistic, and is credited with considerable influence over later Soviet productions. Balanchine too admits to being influenced by him.

In the 1930s, the Bolshoi had two great ballerinas, Marina Semyonova and Olga Lepeshinskaya. Semyonova, trained in Leningrad, was scarcely known outside Russia, as Soviet artists rarely appeared abroad at that time. She did, however, dance Giselle at the Paris Opéra in 1935. She excelled in the classic and romantic roles. Lepeshinskaya, one of the few Bolshoi ballerinas who was actually trained in the Bolshoi school, was famous for her very strong technique and lively personality. She specialized in soubrette roles; a brief glimpse of her in the *Don Quixote pas de deux*, when the Bolshoi Ballet visited Brussels in the 1950s, was sufficient to reveal her greatness. Even in the twilight of her career, she gave a performance which ranked with the most brilliant and most charismatic ever seen. Unfortunately, neither Semyonova nor Lepeshinskaya was ever seen in Britain or the United States.

A new chapter in the history of the Bolshoi Ballet began in 1945, when the company returned home to Moscow after its wartime evacuation to Kuibyshev. Galina Ulanova, who had been the leading ballerina in Leningrad for some years, transferred to Moscow. She was said to be Stalin's favourite ballerina. Lepeshinskaya danced the first performance of Prokofiev's *Cinderella*, which had its world première at the Bolshoi in 1945. Another Prokofiev ballet, *The Stone Flower*, had its première there in 1954.

In 1956, the Bolshoi made its first appearance in the West, at the Royal Opera House, Covent Garden. Ulanova scored enormous personal successes as Juliet and Giselle. Raissa Struchkova, who alternated with her, was also much admired. London was also stunned by the virtuosity of the male soloists in roles like the Blue Bird and the *Swan Lake pas de trois*. But the leading men—the Romeos and Princes—seemed old, heavy, and out-of-date in their costumes and performing style. *Giselle* was highly praised as the most realistic and convincing production yet seen in London, and *Romeo and Juliet*, in the Lavrovsky version, was a revelation of the new Soviet choreographic style—dancing integrated with drama and a ballerina role which used exciting high lifts, ecstatic runs across the stage, and ardent *pas de deux* to express Juliet's youthful passion. *Swan Lake* and *The Stone Flower* were less successful.

Since then, the Bolshoi Ballet has paid regular visits to London, Paris and New York. The company is so large that it can split into several groups, performing at home and in two foreign tours simultaneously. In recent years, for example, the star dancers Ekaterina Maximova and Vladimir Vasiliev, who are husband-and-wife, led their own section of the Bolshoi on several international tours, and rarely appeared in Moscow itself.

Above: *General view of the* Prologue *to* The Sleeping Beauty *at the Bolshoi Theatre, Moscow and,* **below,** *Galina Ulanova, the great Soviet ballerina, tying the ribbons on her shoes in preparation for a performance at the Bolshoi*

Maya Plisetskaya and Nicolai Fadeyechev as Odette and the Prince being menaced by Rotbart in the Bolshoi Ballet's version of Swan Lake

Similarly Maya Plisetskaya, who succeeded Ulanova as the Bolshoi's principal ballerina, spent a lot of her time abroad. She was particularly popular in Paris, where Roland Petit created a ballet for her. Other western choreographers who created roles for her were Béjart and the Cuban, Alberto Alonso. She was not so popular in London, where her style struck many people as too exaggerated for the classic roles. Her interpretation of Odette in *Swan Lake* was famous for the serpentine rippling of her arms. She brought great humour and personality to *Don Quixote, The Stone Flower* and *The Little Humpbacked Horse.* Her melodramatic acting style was well suited to Aegina in *Spartacus.* Both her performance and Alberto Alonso's version of *Carmen* were disliked in London as vulgar and brash.

Since 1964, the Bolshoi Ballet had a talented but controversial director in Yuri Grigorovitch. He came from Leningrad, where he had already been very successful as a producer and choreographer.

His biggest success in Moscow was his new version of *Spartacus* (1968), which is generally regarded as the standard version of that ballet. He also revised many of the other full-length productions, and eventually incurred considerable unpopularity with senior members of the company by staging his own version of *Romeo and Juliet* despite the fact that the Lavrovsky version had come to be accepted as a classic.

Grigorovitch modernized the repertoire by changing production and dancing styles. His versions of the full-length ballets eliminated a lot of mime, aiming to tell the stories almost entirely through dance. He encouraged young dancers to take over leading roles, discarding the Bolshoi tradition of allowing veterans to continue well past their prime. The dancing became less acrobatic and closer in style to what had always been the tradition in St Petersburg-Leningrad, and what is regarded in London and New York as a purer classical tradition. Grigorovitch narrowed the gap between the Bolshoi

Crassus on his chariot in the spectacular Bolshoi production of Spartacus, to music by Khatchaturyan

and the Kirov, to such an extent that there was no longer a marked disparity in styles between the two companies.

The leading Bolshoi dancers in the 1960s and early 1970s were Maximova and Vassiliev. She had a youthful, girlish manner, which was particularly well suited to *The Nutcracker.* Her touching, vulnerable femininity also made her most moving as Phrygia in *Spartacus.* Vassiliev's heroic features, blond good looks, and strong technique made him an ideal exponent of the title-role in *Spartacus.* Together they gave a dazzling technical display in *Don Quixote.*

The new generation of Bolshoi dancers, coming into prominence in the late 1970s, was headed by the young ballerinas Ludmilla Semenyaka and Nadezhda Pavlova. Semenyaka, who was trained in Leningrad, is probably the purer and more remarkable classical dancer. Her Odette-Odile in *Swan Lake* with the Bolshoi in New York in 1979 was an outstanding performance, without the mannerisms which Plisetskaya brought the role. Her performance recalled both Fonteyn and Makarova. Pavlova (no relation to Anna Pavlova) was trained in Perm, where the Kirov Ballet had been evacuated during the Second World War and where the ballet school is closely based on the Kirov tradition. She achieved fame while still in her teens and is popular both in the Soviet Union and abroad in a variety of roles. She is married to Vyacheslav Gordeyev, one of the two leading male dancers of the Bolshoi's new generation, and they normally dance together, following the husband-and-wife tradition of Maximova and Vassiliev. The other leading Bolshoi male dancer of this generation, Alexander Godunov, was less brilliant and refined technically but had a more dramatic stage presence, allied with remarkable good-looks. He had an enormous popular following in New York, and scored a big success in the heroic dramatic role of Spartacus, before he left the Bolshoi to stay in the west in 1979. He was the first Bolshoi dancer to 'defect'.

The Bolshoi has always contained an extra-ordinary mixture of dancers of varying ages and talents, ranging from the young and sensational to the old and mediocre. Its repertoire has embraced masterpieces like *Giselle* and *Romeo and Juliet,* controversial but popular modern works like *Spartacus,* banal folk-tales like *Legend of Love* and political works like *Flames of Paris* which have not been shown, except in brief extracts, in the west. The Bolshoi's future, more than that of most ballet companies, is unpredictable. In addition to all the usual problems and uncertainties affecting every ballet company, and the internal dissensions between Grigorovitch and dancers like Plisetskaya, Maximova and Vassiliev, the company is subject—like

Ekaterina Maximova and Vladimir Vasiliev in the Bolshoi's production of The Nutcracker

all Soviet institutions—to political winds of change from the Kremlin. The defection of Godunov, closely followed by those of Leonid and Valentina Kozlov, probably undermined Grigorovitch's authority and made it more difficult for the Bolshoi to undertake foreign tours. Political censorship in the Soviet Union always makes new productions a risk, and experiments difficult. Periods of extra repression and conservatism in Soviet policy must inevitably have a numbing and depressing effect on Soviet choreography and lower the morale of the dancers. Periods when choreographers are allowed to try new ideas, and when choreographers and dancers can keep in close touch with their colleagues abroad, are obviously healthier and more stimulating. It is impossible to say which way the Soviet Union—and Soviet ballet—is going to move.

The Kirov Ballet

The Kirov is the present name of the historic and lovely theatre which is the home of the Leningrad ballet and opera. It opened in 1860, as the Maryinsky Theatre, and ballet performances have been given there since 1880. After the Bolshevik revolution of 1917, the theatre's name was changed to State Academic Theatre for Opera and Ballet, and in 1935 it was renamed the Kirov, after the Communist leader who had been assassinated the previous year, probably on Stalin's orders.

The Maryinsky Theatre was the birthplace of most of the Petipa-Ivanov classics. During the end of the nineteenth century and the early years of the twentieth, it was the home of what was undoubtedly the world's greatest ballet company. The most famous ballerinas of that period—Kschessinska, Preobrajenska, Trefilova, Karsavina and the legendary Pavlova—all started their careers there. So did male stars like Gerdt, Legat, Bolm—and Nijinsky.

Many of the most important Soviet ballets also had their premières at the Kirov, and the majority of leading Soviet dancers were trained there. The school attached to the Kirov, now named after Vaganova, the famous Soviet ballet teacher, is the most famous ballet school in the world.

The Kirov Ballet made its first western tour—to Paris, London and New York—in 1961. It was immediately hailed as one of the world's great companies. Many critics preferred its purity of style and technique to the more flamboyant and acrobatic style of the Bolshoi. Kirov dancers have been par-

Below, *The grand staircase at the Kirov Theatre, Leningrad, formerly the Maryinsky Theatre, St Petersburg and* **right,** *the interior of the Kirov*

ticularly admired for their performances of the fairy variations in the first act of *The Sleeping Beauty* and for their dancing in *Chopiniana*, an early version of Fokine's *Les Sylphides*.

The prima ballerina of the Kirov in the late 1940s and in the 1950s was Natalia Dudinskaya, whose husband Konstantin Sergeyev was artistic director of the company for many years. His authority was undermined by the 'defection' to the west of many of the Kirov's leading dancers. Until Godunov left the Bolshoi, all the Soviet dancers who transferred to the West were Kirov stars—Nureyev, Makarova, Baryshnikov and the Panovs.

Left, *Irina Kolpakova and Vladilen Semyonov in the Kirov's* Sleeping Beauty *and* **below,** *Natalia Dudinskaya and Konstantin Sergeyev in the same company's* Giselle

Dudinskaya's successors were the strong but hard ballerina Irina Kolpakova and the slight and girlish Alla Sizova, who was a particular favourite with London audiences. The Kirov also had another sensational male virtuoso, Yuri Soloviev, who did not move to the west; instead, he committed suicide in Russia. The reason for his suicide has never been made public, but it is believed to have been a combination of loneliness, following the departure of his colleagues to the west, and dissatisfaction at a sterile artistic career.

The barren repertoire and the political pressures on the company, which made experiment and new work difficult, were the main reasons given by the Kirov artists who fled to the west, though some also complained of the lack of personal freedom in the Soviet Union. In recent years, and especially since Grigorovitch moved to Moscow, the Kirov seems to have taken a definite second place to the Bolshoi.

Other Soviet companies

There are second ballet companies in Moscow, the Stanislavsky Ballet, and in Leningrad, the Maly Theatre of Opera and Ballet, formerly the Mikhailovsky. Both these companies have done important experimental work. Vladimir Bourmeister was the director of ballet at the Stanislavsky from 1930 till his death in 1971, making numerous dramatic revisions of the classics, including his internationally acclaimed version of *Swan Lake*. Fyodor Lopoukhov, the brother of the ballerina Lydia Lopoukhova, was the first director of the Maly ballet (1931–36) and acquired a considerable reputation as an *avant-garde* choreographer. In the decade from 1963, the Maly again became famous for experiment, under the direction of the choreographer Igor Belsky. He also did new versions of the classics, mostly eliminating the mime and story-telling and concentrating on dancing. He became artistic director of the Kirov Ballet in 1972, and was succeeded at the Maly by Oleg Vinogradov.

Other major Soviet ballet companies are based in Kiev, which produced the popular western ballerina Galina Samsova, Perm, which produced the Bolshoi's star Nadezhda Pavlova, and Novosibirsk, where Vinogradov got his first choreographic experience, doing a controversial 'abstract' version of *Romeo and Juliet*, among other works. All these companies now have their own schools and produce good dancers. The Perm and Novosibirsk companies have toured abroad, and were well received in Italy and France.

Left, *Mikhail Baryshnikov and Alla Sizova in the Kirov's production of* The Stone Flower, *music by Prokofiev*

Hungary

Since 1945, ballet has been officially sponsored and encouraged in the Soviet bloc countries of eastern and central Europe. The best-known and most successful of these companies is the one in Budapest, where there was already a flourishing ballet tradition. The company has ballets by several Soviet choreographers and its dancers get Soviet training. In the 1940s and 1950s, Hungary had its own outstanding ballet teacher, Ferenc Nadasi, who trained a large number of excellent dancers, several of whom became well-known abroad. These included Nora Kovach and Istvan Rabovsky, the first dancers from a Communist country to escape to the west—in 1953. A number of other Hungarian dancers appeared as guests with London Festival Ballet—Gabriella Lakatos, Zsuzsa Kun, Viktor Fülöp, and Ferenc Havas—while another, Viktor Rona, partnered Fonteyn on some of her international tours.

The company from Budapest has also toured abroad, including the Edinburgh Festival. Its own choreographer, Laszlo Seregi, has been highly

Zsuzsa Kun and Ferenc Havas of the Budapest State Opera Ballet, regular guests with London Festival Ballet in the early 1960s

praised by foreign critics for his versions of *Spartacus, The Miraculous Mandarin*, and *Sylvia*. He has worked in Germany, Austria and Switzerland, and his *Spartacus* was taken into the repertoire of the Australian Ballet.

Denmark

There has been ballet in Copenhagen since the sixteenth century. The old *commedia dell'arte* tradition still survives there, at the open-air pantomime theatre in Tivoli Gardens. Danish ballet first achieved distinction in the last quarter of the eighteenth century, when the Italian ballet-master Vincenzo Galeotti was in charge. One of his works, *The Whims of Cupid and the Ballet Master* (1786), is the oldest ballet to survive anywhere today.

Right, *Anna Laerkesen as the Sylph, entering through the window to seduce Henning Kronstam as James in the Royal Danish Ballet's production of* La Sylphide. **Below,** *Toni Lander, the Danish ballerina who danced for many years with London Festival Ballet and then with American Ballet Theatre*

The French dancer and choreographer Antoine Bournonville went to Copenhagen in 1792. It was his son August who created the repertoire which has remained the basis of the Royal Danish Ballet's fame and popularity. After August's death in 1879, there was a decline in the prestige and talent of the Royal Danish Ballet—in the first part of the twentieth century many of Bournonville's ballets were actually abandoned and forgotten. Fokine and Balanchine worked in Copenhagen in the 1920s and 1930s but did not do any of their major creative work there.

The company's next successful period began in 1930, when Harald Lander became balletmaster, as the Danes call the artistic director of their company. He encouraged and supervised revivals of the major works by Bournonville, and made new ballets of his own. One of these, *Etudes* (1948), a brilliant display of romantic and bravura dancing styles for soloists and *corps de ballet*, has taken its place in the international repertoire; it has been particularly associated with London Festival Ballet.

In 1950, Lander persuaded the Danish Government to sponsor an annual ballet festival, which was held in May for several years. Foreign critics were invited and the Royal Danish Ballet, until then virtually unknown outside Denmark, was 'discovered'. Bournonville's ballets were hailed as a revelation, and the dancing style of the company, especially the men, was much admired. The company paid its first, highly successful, visit to Covent Garden in 1953.

Lander also engaged the Russian teacher Vera Volkova to teach at the Danish Ballet's historic school. She stayed in Copenhagen from 1952 till her death in 1975. There was some criticism that, in acquiring a more Russian technique, the Danes were forgetting how to do Bournonville. In recent years it has become apparent that they have simply become more versatile. Bournonville revivals are still as stylish and well received as ever.

Lander left Copenhagen for Paris in 1951, and was succeeded by the veteran dancer and mime Niels Bjørn Larsen. The years between 1951 and 1965 were indecisive ones for the Royal Danish Ballet, with a retreat from the Bournonville repertoire and with the acquisition of a motley bag of modern ballets from all over the world. The company was in danger of losing its specific character. In 1966, however, the young Danish dancer Flemming Flindt, who had been pursuing a successful international career in London and Paris, was appointed director. He again revived the Bournonville repertoire, and contributed several distinctive modern works of his own. He was succeeded in 1977 by another distinguished Danish male dancer, Henning Kronstam.

Danish ballet is now more famous for its male dancers than for its ballerinas. Erik Bruhn became an international star and was widely regarded as the most stylish classical male dancer of the 1950s. Another Dane with a pure classical line and elegant style, Peter Martins, has become one of the top favourites in New York City Ballet. Balanchine was so impressed by Danish male dancing that he engaged three other Danes—Peter Schaufuss, Adam Luders and Ib Andersen—for his company. (Peter Schaufuss went on to become an international freelance star. Egon Madsen, another Dane, was for years a star of the Stuttgart Ballet, but he was not a product of the Royal Danish school.) Henning Kronstam, who pursued most of his career in Copenhagen, was another equally elegant stylist, while Fredbjørn Bjørnsson and Niels Kehlet were character dancers of outstanding virtuosity and dramatic and humorous ability.

In recent years, the Danes have not had a ballerina of world class. They have always produced a number of excellent female soloists, who tend to specialize in particular roles. In recent years, Kirsten Simone, Anna Laerkesen and Sorella Englund were all tipped as future ballerinas but never quite fulfilled their full promise. Lis Jeppesen was, in 1980, the latest hope for this position.

The last Danish ballerina to achieve international fame was Toni Lander, Harald Lander's second wife. She danced for several years (1954–59) with London Festival Ballet and then for a further decade with American Ballet Theatre.

The last important ballerina to remain faithful to the Royal Danish Ballet was Margrethe Schanne, who danced the leading roles in the 1950s and early 1960s, specializing particularly in Giselle and La Sylphide. Harald Lander's first wife, Margot Lander, was 'prima ballerina' of the Danish Ballet from 1942 till 1950. She was the only Danish dancer to be given that title officially. She was enormously admired by all who saw her, especially in soubrette roles like Swanhilda, and in the folksy Bournonville repertoire. Unfortunately she was not known abroad.

Earlier Danish ballerinas who did achieve international fame were Lucile Grahn, the nineteenth-century ballerina who left Copenhagen to escape from Bournonville and became a star in France, Russia, Germany and England, and Adeline Genée, who starred at various London music-halls from 1897 till 1917, gave enormous help to British ballet in its early days, becoming the first president of the Royal Academy of Dancing, and was made a Dame of the British Empire in 1950.

Danish dancers have always been famous for their lively personalities, natural acting style, and light, bouncy dancing. This tradition is maintained

The Royal Danish Ballet in Harald Lander's Etudes, *a showpiece which was also for many years in the repertoire of London Festival Ballet*

today. The Royal Danish Ballet radiates warmth and enthusiasm, so that even when it has no big stars, it is always one of the most enjoyable companies to watch. If it had a top-ranking ballerina or a major present-day choreographer of its own, it would not need to fear comparison with any other company.

France

The Paris Opéra

The company which first produced some of the great nineteenth-century ballets is now more distinguished for its dancers than for its new works. In the early years of this century, the Paris Opéra was often the home of the Diaghilev company. From 1930 almost continuously till 1959, its ballet was under the direction of Serge Lifar, one of Diaghilev's last protégés. Lifar choreographed a substantial part of the repertoire; his ballets were popular with French audiences and critics, but had less success abroad and have not survived in the Opéra repertoire since Lifar's retirement.

After Lifar, the company had a series of directors, none of whom stayed long. Guest choreographers were engaged from all over the world, including Balanchine, Grigorovitch, Nureyev, Petit and Robbins—Petit was even director of the company for a short time in 1970. American 'modern' choreographers included Merce Cunningham, Glen Tetley and Carolyn Carlson, who was a resident dancer and choreographer for some time. Pierre Lacotte restaged *La Sylphide* and *Coppélia* in something like their original forms. But no ballets created at the Opéra in recent years have won international acceptance.

The most recent directors of the company were the French ballerina Violette Verdy (from 1977 to 1980) and the American ballerina Rosella Hightower (from 1980), who promptly commissioned further works from American 'modern' choreographers—Alwin Nikolais, Douglas Dunn and Lucinda Childs.

Throughout all these régimes, the school attached to the Opéra continued to produce a succession of first-class dancers, many of whom won international fame.

Yvette Chauviré, who was a ballerina at the Opéra from 1941 till 1972, was acclaimed as one of the world's great Giselles. Lycette Darsonval was another distinguished ballerina at that time. Liane Daydé, who became a ballerina at the Opéra in 1951, left in 1959 and danced with various French and international companies.

More recently, the Opéra's Ghislaine Thesmar became a regular guest with New York City Ballet

Top, *The* corps de ballet *of the Paris Opéra in* Etudes.
Centre, *Galina Samsova and Viktor Rona in the Cuevas Ballet's production of* Cinderella, *Paris 1963, designed by Raimundo de Larrain with choreography by Orlikowsky*
Bottom, *Yvette Chauviré and Alexis Rassine in* The Sleeping Beauty *at Covent Garden, 1958, when Chauviré appeared as a guest*

and danced with Nureyev in Lacotte's *La Sylphide* (with the Boston Ballet) in New York. Dominique Khalfouni left the Opera in 1980 to join Roland Petit's Marseilles company, and also to make guest appearances with American Ballet Theatre.

The Paris Opéra has always produced exciting virtuoso male dancers. Stars during the 1940s and 1950s included Michel Renault, Alexandre Kalioujny, and Serge Golovine, who joined the Cuevas Ballet (see p.114) in 1950 and became one of the world's leading exponents of virtuoso roles like the Blue Bird and Spectre de la Rose.

More recently, male stars of the Opéra who have appeared as guests with foreign companies included Patrice Bart, seen regularly with London Festival Ballet, and Michael Denard, who appeared with American Ballet Theatre. The very young Patrick Dupond appeared with Ballet Theatre in 1980 and seemed destined for a brilliant career.

Other French companies

In addition to the Opéra school and company, France has for years had a number of distinguished private teachers and interesting small ballet companies. Emigré ballerinas from Russia, notably Kshessinskaya and Preobrajenska, set up their own studios in Paris and were responsible for training some of the outstanding dancers of our time. Vladimir Skouratoff, who starred with many French companies in the 1940s and 1950s, studied partly with Preobrajenska, and did not dance at the Opéra. Jean Babilée, the greatest French male star of the 1940s and 1950s, who was famous for virtuoso roles like the Blue Bird and also for dramatic ones like the hero in Petit's *Le Jeune Homme et la Mort*, trained at the Opéra but spent most of his career with Roland Petit's companies and as a guest abroad.

The most notable French companies since the Second World War have been those run by Petit, and the French-based but very cosmopolitan one run by the Marquis de Cuevas. Roland Petit, who started his career at the Opéra, left in 1944 at the age of 20. His first company was Les Ballets des Champs-Elysées, formed in 1945, which had a big success on its visits to London and a considerable influence on choreography and design. Later Petit

Previous pages, left, *Mary Skeaping, the British expert on reviving forgotten historic ballets, adjusting a dancer's dress on stage at the Drottningholm Court Theatre, near Stockholm.* **Right,** *Members of the Vienna State Opera Ballet posing in their Opera House in* Les Sylphides *costumes*

von Aroldingen, trained in Hamburg, became a leading ballerina of New York City Ballet, one of the few foreign dancers to do so. The Hamburg ballet week, an annual event designed to show off the company's dancers and repertoire, attracted as many foreign critics and ballet-goers as the Stuttgart week had done in Cranko's day.

The other important ballet company in Western Germany is in Berlin. Like other German opera houses, Berlin had lost its ballet tradition between the late nineteenth century and the middle of the twentieth. In between, dance was mainly 'modern'. Tatjana Gsovsky began the classical revival in the late 1940s; Kenneth MacMillan took it further, staging the nineteenth century Russian classics, when he was director of the company from 1966 to 1969. He did not, however, succeed in giving the company a prestige or repertoire equal to Cranko's in Stuttgart. Gert Reinholm, a former dancer with the company, was director of the company for five years before MacMillan, and took over again on MacMillan's departure. He achieved greater international recognition of the company by engaging the Panovs, giving Valery Panov his first opportunities to do major choreography. Panov's version of *Cinderella* was highly praised by German critics, and both this and *The Idiot* were taken to New York by the company. The repertoire also included Nureyev's production of *The Nutcracker,* and Nureyev also appeared in the role of Myshkin in *The Idiot.* The international ballerina Eva Evdokimova danced regularly with the Berlin Ballet from 1969 and was officially appointed its prima ballerina in 1973. The company also boasted another ex-Soviet dancer, Vladimir Gelvan, who scored a big personal success as Myshkin, a role he created. When the company visited New York in 1980, many American critics were impressed by the strength of the German soloists and corps.

There is also a big ballet company in Munich, which at one time shared the Cranko repertoire with Stuttgart. It has had a series of directors, including the Royal Ballet ballerina Lynn Seymour, but has not achieved the international recognition given to Stuttgart, Hamburg and Berlin. A much smaller company in Frankfurt has also had some success, especially when it was run by Neumeier, before he went to Hamburg. It too has toured abroad, including a visit to Britain.

Austria

Fanny Elssler, the great nineteenth-century ballerina, was Viennese, and Bournonville worked with the Vienna State Opera ballet in 1855. All the greatest stars of the ballet appeared there regularly in the nineteenth century, but then the ballet was neglected until the 1950s. There have been numerous directors of the ballet since then, Nureyev staged productions and danced there regularly, and John Neumeier made a highly praised version of *Legend of Joseph* for the company. The Viennese dancer Karl Musil appeared as a regular guest with various foreign companies, including London Festival Ballet, in the 1960s and he partnered Fonteyn on some of her international tours. The company has toured, but has never achieved real distinction, always remaining subservient to the renowned Vienna opera company. The Austrian ballet critic Gerhard Brunner was appointed director of the ballet in 1976 and succeeded in engaging more eminent guest choreographers and dancers than before.

Italy

There are long-established ballet companies at the major Italian opera-houses, though they have never achieved the fame, importance and popularity of the opera. John Field, formerly of the British Royal Ballet, was director of the ballet at La Scala, Milan, from 1971 to 1974; Nureyev has danced and produced there regularly. Aurel Milloss was director of the ballet at La Scala and at the Rome Opera at various times since 1938; he choreographed numerous ballets for both theatres. Other directors of the Rome ballet, in recent years, included Vaslav Orlikowsky, Anton Dolin and André Prokovsky. None succeeded in establishing the company's importance and none stayed long.

Italy does still keep up the tradition of Taglioni, however, by producing some good dancers, especially romantic ballerinas. Carla Fracci, trained in Milan, and Elisabetta Terabust, trained in Rome, both had successful international careers, appearing as guests with British and American companies. A more athletic, technically strong dancer, Luciana Savignano, has become a star in Italy, specializing mainly in Béjart and other modern works.

Two Italian male dancers have also achieved international recognition in recent years. Paolo Bortoluzzi made his début in a company organized by Massine at Nervi, and later danced with Béjart's company in Brussels and with American Ballet Theatre. Luigi Bonino joined Roland Petit's Marseilles company and scored a big success when he took over Petit's character roles during the New York season of 1980.

Fracci and her husband, Beppe Menegatti, have also run various touring groups in Italy, appearing at various festivals. The principal Italian ballet festival is at Nervi, Genoa, where Italian and foreign companies perform in a charming open-air theatre nearly every summer. Ballet is also featured at the Spoleto Festival.

Carla Fracci and John Gilpin in a revival of Fokine's Le Spectre de la Rose *by Festival Ballet*

Liliana Cosi, formerly of La Scala, Milan, and a frequent guest artist with London Festival Ballet

The Netherlands

The main classical company in Holland is the Dutch National Ballet, formed in 1961 when two smaller companies merged. During most of its first years, the artistic director was Sonia Gaskell, a Russian dancer who had worked with Diaghilev. She tried to create a company similar to the British Royal Ballet, but without the benefit of a classical choreographer like Ashton. The company and repertoire lacked a coherent style, though creditable performances of classic ballets were given. Audiences were disappointingly small. Based in Amsterdam, the company toured all the cities of The Netherlands, rarely giving more than three performances in any one place. That continues to be the pattern for all Dutch ballet companies.

Rudi van Dantzig, originally a pupil of Gaskell's but later much influenced by Martha Graham, started choreographing for the company in the early 1960s. He became assistant to Gaskell and succeeded her as director in 1968. His ballets, often dealing with homosexuality and other complex emotions, are modern in style though using classical technique. He made the company's image much more modern, though it still performs the classics. He also enhanced its international reputation with his own works, in which Nureyev has appeared on several occasions. In 1973 Hans van Manen joined him in running the National Ballet, and choreographed for it regularly. The third member of the directorial team was Toer van Schayk, a dancer, designer and very modern choreographer.

The company has not achieved the distinction Gaskell intended but is well regarded and has interesting ballets and dancers.

The other important Dutch company, Netherlands Dance Theatre, was founded in 1959 by a group of dancers who wanted to do more modern work than was being performed by either of the Dutch ballet companies at that time. It is based in The Hague, but tours extensively in Holland and abroad. It became internationally known as a modern dance company, and had several very successful seasons at Sadler's Wells in London. Its principal Dutch choreographer was Hans van Manen, though Rudi van Dantzig and Jaap Flier also worked with it. It had numerous American choreographers. The company also achieved a certain notoriety by staging the first ballet with a totally nude scene—*Mutations*, choreographed by Tetley and van Manen to music by Stockhausen, produced in 1970. This caused considerable controversy and was a huge box-office success everywhere, including Sadler's Wells.

The young Czechoslovak dancer and

Left, *Sylvester Campbell and Marianna Hilarides in the Dutch National Ballet's production of* Le Corsaire pas de deux.

Below, *Netherlands Dance Theatre in* Mutations, *by Glen Tetley and Hans van Manen, a ballet which achieved notoriety in 1970 by including nude dancers*

choreographer Jiri Kylián became joint artistic director of the company (with the Swiss dancer Hans Knill) in 1975, and took over its sole direction in 1976. Originally trained at the Royal Ballet School and with John Cranko in Stuttgart, Kylián's choreography is more classical than that of most of his predecessors with Netherlands Dance Theatre.

He brought the company to New York in 1979 with a repertory consisting almost entirely of his own ballets. He was acclaimed by many American critics as the most important new choreographer to have emerged from Europe for many years. His company too was extremely favourably received.

The third Dutch ballet company is Scapino.

Founded in 1945, it is the oldest of them, and is the only classical ballet company in the world specifically designed to give performances for schoolchildren. It has a remarkably high standard of production and performance, and has perfected various techniques of explaining and introducing ballet to very young audiences.

Switzerland

There are ballet companies attached to the various Swiss opera houses. A succession of international choreographers and directors have run the companies in Basle, Geneva and Zurich in recent years. Nicholas Beriosoff took the Zurich company to the Nervi Festival in Italy in 1908, and Patricia Neary, a former member of New York City Ballet, took the company to London in 1979 as a support group for Nureyev. The Argentinian choreographer Oscar Araiz became director of the ballet in Geneva in 1980. The Swiss companies contain some good dancers, and several Balanchine ballets have been staged by the companies run there by Miss Neary. But none of the Swiss companies has yet achieved international distinction.

Australia

The Australian Ballet was founded in Melbourne in 1962, with a number of dancers from the defunct Borovansky Ballet. There was already a tradition of ballet in Australia: Pavlova toured there extensively, and so did the Ballets Russes companies of the 1930s. Eduard Borovansky was one of several Ballets Russes dancers who settled in Australia and started schools there; his company performed there throughout the late 1940s and the 1950s.

Dame Peggy van Praagh, a former Sadler's Wells ballerina who founded and directed the Australian Ballet, with members of her company

The first director of the Australian Ballet was Peggy van Praagh, an English dancer who had created roles in several of Antony Tudor's ballets and had been a famous Swanhilda with the Sadler's Wells Ballet. In the late 1940s and early 1950s she ran the Sadler's Wells Theatre Ballet. She took over the Borovansky Ballet in 1962, converting it into the Australian Ballet. She based the company firmly on the Royal Ballet, importing several of its dancers and John Lanchbery, its musical director. She developed a mixed classical repertoire, including Ashton's *La Fille mal Gardée* and *Cinderella*, and Nureyev's *Don Quixote*, which the company also made into an extremely successful film. Robert Helpmann choreographed several new works for the company and became associate director with van Praagh, before taking sole command of the company for a year in 1974. He was succeeded by Anna Wolliams, who had been Cranko's ballet mistress in Stuttgart and director of the ballet school there. She in her turn was speedily succeeded, after a disagreement with the administration, by the ballerina Marilyn Jones.

Australia has for many years produced first-class dancers. In recent years the company's ballerinas have included several Australians —Elaine Fifield (who was previously a ballerina of the Royal Ballet), Kathleen Gorham, Marilyn Jones and Marilyn Rowe. Other ballerinas of the Australian Ballet included Lucette Aldous, who was born in New Zealand. Prominent male dancers included Kelvin Coe, who appeared as a guest with London Festival Ballet, and John Meehan, who partnered Fonteyn on a world tour and then joined American Ballet Theatre.

Recent successful productions by the Australian Ballet included Ronald Hynd's *The Merry Widow* and André Prokovsky's *Anna Karenina*. The company is always full of vitality and talent. It scored successes in London and New York, and toured extensively with Nureyev. It suffered in recent years from frequent changes of direction and conflicts over artistic policy. Its problem, like that of most companies today, is of finding choreography which is both artistically and commercially successful.

There are also various regional ballet companies in Australia, and some modern groups.

Canada

There are three major ballet companies in Canada. The largest, which is similar to the Australian Ballet and also closely modelled on the Royal Ballet, is the National Ballet of Canada. It was founded in Toronto in 1951, and directed till 1974 by Celia

Lucette Aldous, trained in New Zealand and at the Royal Ballet School, who danced with Ballet Rambert, Festival Ballet and the Royal Ballet, ending her career as ballerina with the Australian Ballet

Franca, who had danced with the principal British companies and choreographed for the Sadler's Wells Theatre Ballet. The repertoire includes the major classics and modern works by many of the world's leading choreographers. Erik Bruhn was a producer and artistic advisor to the company for many years; Nureyev produced for them and danced with them regularly. Other choreographers included Roland Petit, Flemming Flindt and John Neumeier.

Franca was succeeded in 1976 by Alexander Grant, the distinguished Royal Ballet character dancer. In general, he continued Franca's policies, acquiring more ballets by Ashton. Peter Schaufuss, who danced with the company for several years, produced Bournonville's full-length *Napoli* for it in

1981. Karen Kain, the company's ballerina, also appeared as a regular guest with other companies, including Roland Petit's Ballet de Marseille and in Makarova's Broadway season of 1980. Nureyev danced with her regularly when he was a guest with the company. The company's Canadian *premier danseur*, Frank Augustyn, left to join the Berlin ballet in 1980.

The National Ballet of Canada has made several visits to London and New York. It is sometimes criticized for lacking a specific style or repertoire of its own.

The other two Canadian companies are smaller, less classical, but more distinctive. The oldest of them all is the Royal Winnipeg Ballet, the successor of various Winnipeg companies which

Elaine Fifield, the Australian ballerina who spent several years leading the Sadler's Wells Theatre Ballet and dancing at Covent Garden before returning to her native country. She created the title-role in Cranko's Pineapple Poll

Yoko Morishita and Tetsutaro Shimizu, Japanese dancers who often appear as guest artists in New York and London, in the Don Quixote pas de deux

Zhandra Rodriguez and Zane Wilson of the International Ballet of Caracas in Vicente Nebrada's Lento, A Tempo e Appassionata, *to music by Scriabin*

16
Modern dance

The Alwin Nikolais company in *Imago* (1963). This
was Nikolais' first full-length work, using many of
the multi-media effects which he developed and
which have become typical of much modern dance

'Modern' and 'contemporary' are terms used interchangeably to describe a form of theatrical dancing which does not use the techniques of classical ballet. They are generally admitted to being unsatisfactory terms: they are imprecise and cover a wide variety of dance styles. Some 'modern' dance dates from the beginning of the twentieth century and scarcely remains modern; some of the most 'contemporary' dancing is to be found in discos, and not in theatres at all. That is not the kind of dancing meant by 'contemporary' when it is used to describe an artform which takes itself extremely seriously.

'Modern' dance as we know it today originated in the United States and Germany in the first three decades of this century, when there was not yet any classical ballet tradition in those countries. Today its most distinguished exponents are all American. The recent rise of modern dance in Britain owes its existence entirely to American example and guidance. Ironically, modern dance has almost died out in Germany, where it has been replaced by the enormous new popularity of classical ballet.

The great names of German modern dance were Mary Wigman, Harald Kreutzberg, and Kurt Jooss, all of whom had international fame and success. Jooss and his company took refuge in Britain

Above, *Isadora Duncan, a high priestess of modern dance*

Below, *Scene from Kurt Jooss' satirical anti-war dance drama,* The Green Table *(1932)*

during the second world war, and acquired a considerable following, but his style of dance-drama did not take root in Britain after his return to Germany. *The Green Table*, created by Jooss in 1932, had a new lease of life, however, in recent years, and is now performed by several classical ballet companies in Britain and the United States. Hanya Holm, who studied with Wigman, settled in the United States and became an influential teacher there.

The great names of early American modern dance included Loie Fuller, Ruth St Denis and Ted Shawn, Isadora Duncan, Charles Weidman, Doris Humphrey, José Limon, Erick Hawkins and Martha Graham. Of these, only Graham and Hawkins were still alive and working by the end of the 1970s. The great names of present-day modern dance are all American: Alvin Ailey, Merce Cunningham, Louis Falco, Pearl Lang, Murray Louis, Lar Lubovitch, Meredith Monk, Alwin Nikolais, Paul Taylor and Twyla Tharp are the best-known. They have very different talents, their works ranging from inaccessible and highbrow (Cunningham and Monk) to dances which could easily be part of a Broadway show (Tharp) or are performed by classical ballet companies (Ailey, Limon, Louis, Taylor and Tharp).

Martha Graham, another of the great 'high priestesses' of modern dance in her Phaedra *(1962)*

'Modern' dance started as a reaction against the formality and alleged artificiality of ballet. The watchword was freedom; the dancers wanted to express their moods and emotions, and sometimes to comment on life. They wanted to be up-to-date and 'relevant'. Isadora Duncan espoused the cause of the Russian Revolution, and Kurt Jooss's most famous work, *The Green Table*, was a dance-drama satirising the League of Nations and showing war as capitalist exploitation. Some of these dancers, like Kreutzberg and Fuller, had very little technique of any kind. Fuller was essentially a revue-artiste, using transparent dresses and elaborate lighting effects, Kreutzberg studied briefly with Wigman but mainly relied on the force of his personality as a performer. On the other hand Wigman developed a technique and a school, originally based on Dalcroze eurythmics, a system of music and movement, part dance and part gymnastics, developed by the Swiss teacher, Emile Jaques-Dalcroze. The system was popular all over the world in the 1920s and 1930s and is still used to help young dancers fit their movements to music. St Denis and Shawn, who were married, ran schools known as 'Denishawn' which taught quite an elaborate technique.

Martha Graham, herself a pupil of Denishawn, started her own school in New York in 1927. Her company started performances two years later, and has appeared, with some breaks, ever since. She created an enormous repertoire of works, some consisting simply of abstract dancing but many, which she preferred to call 'plays', telling stories based on Greek tragedy, the Bible, and American folk-lore.

Her productions were notable not only for her original and dramatic choreography but for the use of contemporary music, often specially composed by distinguished composers, and of décor and costumes by leading designers. For many years Miss Graham favoured abstract sets by the Japanese sculptor Isamu Noguchi. She herself devised an ingenious dress, usually worn by her female dancers, which had a tight bodice and seemed close-fitting down to the ankles but in fact swirled out, being made of stretch material and allowing maximum freedom of movement. In recent years Halston, the well-known American fashion designer, designed a variety of colourful briefs for her male dancers, who usually appeared almost nude. The dance technique which Graham developed is now taught in many parts of the world, including Israel, Canada, and the London School of Contemporary Dance. It can be seen clearly demonstrated and explained in her fascinating documentary film, *A Dancer's World*. Her company has become completely accepted by the dance 'establishment'. Balanchine played a crucial role in making Graham 'respectable' in ballet circles, by inviting her to collaborate with him and New York City Ballet in a ballet called *Episodes*, in 1959. In the end, this was not really a collaboration, being a ballet in two separate parts, one an abstract work by Balanchine and the other a dramatic one about Mary Queen of Scots by Graham. Both used music by Webern. Paul Taylor, then a member of the Graham company, danced in the Balanchine section. Later the two sections were performed separately, both under the name *Episodes*, by New York City Ballet and the Graham Company.

More recently, Nureyev has danced with the Graham company on several occasions, enabling it to have seasons on Broadway and at the Metropolitan Opera, and Graham created some roles specially for him. Liza Minelli, a guest from a very different sphere of show business, has also appeared with the Graham company, narrating a pop version of *The Owl and the Pussycat* both at the Metropolitan Opera and at Covent Garden.

It is fairly easy for a ballet dancer to master the basic elements of Graham technique though Graham aficionados tend to find something too lightweight and stylistically wrong when this happens. It goes without saying that 'modern' dancers cannot acquire ballet technique.

What all the 'modern' techniques have in common is negative—a rejection of the formal *five positions* of classical ballet, and of pointwork for the women. Modern dance is usually performed barefoot, which is often claimed to give greater contact with the earth, to be more flexible and in some ways more natural. Whereas ballet dancers train from an early age to develop turn-out and skill in aerial steps and jumping, modern dancers deliberately turn their feet *in*, and concentrate on much looser movements, especially those performed while sitting or lying on the stage. They devote particular attention to various ways of balancing at an angle, falling to the ground and getting up again. The Graham technique includes special breathing exercises, allied with 'contractions' and 'releases' of the body which are meant also to express emotional contraction and release.

These techniques are easier to learn than classical ballet techniques, and it is not necessary to start training in early childhood. One of the reasons for the popularity of modern dance is that adolescents or even young adults who suddenly decide to become dancers can learn it. Modern dance is so free and so varied that almost any reasonably fit person can attempt it, regardless of physique. As there are no rules, modern dance is difficult to criticize; its exponents can always counter criticism by saying they are expressing themselves, or the music, in a way which the public or the critic has not yet learned to understand.

Some of them profess not to care whether they are understood or not.

At its best, modern dance can be exciting, moving, amusing and expressive. A lot of it depends for its success on the personality and commitment of the performer. There is controversy about how much technique Isadora Duncan actually had; there is no controversy about the enormous effect her interpretations of great musical classics had on her audiences. Attempts to revive her dances, performed by other people, have never achieved any great popularity or success, though they have intrigued critics and specialists. Sir Frederick Ashton created a very successful suite of dances in the style of Duncan for the ballerina Lynn Seymour, but these were very brief and were more an evocation of Duncan by other great artists than a recreation of her work. Duncan was as famous as Pavlova, partly because of her revolutionary dancing, but also because of her 'shock' tactics — baring her breasts in public, having open love affairs, and touring the United States with the drunken revolutionary Soviet poet Essenin.

Graham's psychological and mythical plays are still performed regularly but lose something without the participation of their creators. Miss Graham herself had a dominating stage personality and a compelling belief in her own work which have never been equalled by any of her successors while her dancers seem to have lost dramatic strength while becoming more adept technically.

Alwin Nikolais became famous mainly as an originator and experimenter with what are now known as multi-media techniques. He composed his own sound scores and designed the lighting, décor and costumes for his works. Frequently his dancers are totally depersonalized, appearing enclosed in stretch material on which various lights are projected. The visual effects are often striking and unusual, like watching mobile sculpture set to strange and eerie sound effects.

Merce Cunningham enjoys an enormously high reputation in modern dance circles, being highly regarded by certain critics, by young dancers and by art students. He worked closely with John Cage, the *avant-garde* composer, and with Robert Rauschenberg, the painter; together they developed aleatory art in which a great deal of the dance, music and décor was left to chance. Dancers improvised, or appeared to do so; random objects were picked up around the theatre to be used as décor, trays were dropped and piano lids banged. All this had very little appeal to the general public, and did not fill large theatres, but it did impress a coterie and was influential on other modern choreographers and dancers.

More recently Cunningham has specialized in

Previous pages, left, *Liza Minelli and Charles Brown in Martha Graham's staging of* The Owl and the Pussycat *and,* **right,** *Paul Taylor (with Bettie de Jong) in his* Public Domain *(1968) to a collage of music arranged by John Herbert McDowell.* **Below,** *Merce Cunningham, a contemporary 'high priest' of modern dance, regarded by many dancers and critics as the most important recent innovator*

presenting 'events' rather than complete dance works—more like studio works in progress. He has also created for television, and has experimented with trying to speed up live dancing to make it look as if the viewer was switching quickly from one television channel to another. The movements he uses often seem like ordinary walking or running, rather than specific dance steps, and he has stressed that he regards all physical movement as part of dance. He choreographs in silence, even though music or sound-effects are usually added later. Although he has no specific technique, Cunningham has for many years run a successful school in New York, where would-be 'modern' dancers and choreographers are stimulated and try out their ideas.

Although Robert Wilson does not call his works 'dances' but 'operas', they are in a way danced and mimed plays, and have influenced modern choreographers. Wilson has specialized in extremely slow motion and minimal movement, deliberately testing the patience of his audiences. His marathon works have lasted up to twelve hours! Naturally they are extremely controversial,

arousing reactions ranging from irritation and boredom to ecstatic admiration for an original experimental artist.

Meredith Monk also specializes in welding dance with other theatrical forms, including speech. Although there is often very little dance, she regards herself primarily as a choreographer. Her works are often presented in non-theatrical settings, notably museums and art galleries, highlighting the very close links between avant-garde dance and modern art. Both Wilson's and Monk's work often looks more like an animated picture or sculpture than a ballet. It is not surprising that art sudents are often among the most enthusiastic supporters of dance events of this kind, and of Merce Cunningham's experiments.

Other experiments which achieved a certain popularity and critical favour in the United States include Stephanie Evanitsky's Multigravitational Aerodance Group, which performed on trapezes, and Pilobolus, a company whose work was based on gymnastics. It had a novelty appeal, and appeared on Broadway and at the Edinburgh Festival.

José Limón's works are much more conventional; his *The Moor's Pavane*, a danced quartet for the four principal characters in Shakespeare's *Othello*, has been taken into the repertoire of several ballet companies and has been danced by leading ballet stars, including Nureyev and Bruhn.

The most accessible and popular of all the present-day 'modern' choreographers are Paul Taylor and Twyla Tharp. Taylor's works are always musical and often witty; his abstract *Aureole*, full of fast and lyrical movements to music by Handel, has been performed by various ballet companies, including the Royal Danish Ballet and the Paris Opéra. His *Airs* entered the repertory of American Ballet Theatre in Baryshnikov's first season as director. Taylor himself had a highly individual and attractive humorous personality as a dancer, but his presence was not essential to his works, which are now performed without him by the admirable, highly-trained company which he founded in 1954. Nureyev has frequently appeared with it as a guest artist. He has also appeared with the Murray Louis company as a guest, enabling it too to have a Broadway season, and Louis has choreographed specially for Nureyev. Like Paul Taylor, Louis ranges in style from happy, bouncy accessible musical works to elusive ones, with more intellectual content. He has choreographed for the Royal Danish, the Scottish and the Berlin Ballets.

In 1980, Twyla Tharp and her company ventured on a Broadway season, without any superstars as guests. Tharp had become very popular and well-known, partly as a result of her *Push Comes To Shove*, a vehicle for Baryshnikov mixing classical and jazz dancing, which had received critical and public acclaim when produced by Ballet Theatre and had also been televised. In addition Tharp choreographed the dances for the film of *Hair*, while many of her recent stage works had been in popular, near-disco style, using blues and jazz music. There was nothing inaccessible or avant-garde about them.

However Tharp did start her career as a 'modern' dancer, in Paul Taylor's company, and her early choreography was extremely avant-garde; she used to walk behind the audience, or drop eggs on the floor, to test audience reactions. She still retains something of the reputation of a 'serious' and 'experimental' choreographer, while doing much more conventional work.

For her Broadway season, she attempted an ambitious version of A.A. Milne's *When We Were Very Young*, with a narrated script by the playwright Thomas Babe, who provided an adult and slightly depressing version of the children's tale, and with a mixture of dancing styles. It did not find much critical or public favour.

Alvin Ailey is another special case who does not fit easily into any category. He studied both 'modern' dance and classical ballet, and incorporates both, as well as folk-dance elements from negro culture, in his work. He formed his own company in 1958, with a mixed repertoire of his own works and others by contemporary 'modern' and 'ethnic' choreographers. The music used ranges from negro spirituals and jazz to classical symphonic music. Ailey himself used music from Vaughan Williams to Duke Ellington. The company is mainly, but not exclusively, black.

Ailey's most famous and most popular work, *Revelations* (1960), performed in almost every Ailey programme, is set to negro spirituals. His *Memoria* (1979), a tribute to the choreographer and dancer Joyce Trisler, starts like a lament but builds up to a joyous, fast-moving finale, akin to a Broadway show. Among Ailey's works for classical ballet companies were *Feast of Ashes* to music by Carlos Surinach for the Joffrey Ballet (1962) and *The River* to Duke Ellington for Ballet Theatre (1970). He also choreographed for Baryshnikov when he appeared as a guest with Ailey's company.

It is evident from the way classical ballet dancers now appear in modern dance and modern choreographers work with classical companies that the traditional hostility and rigid divisions between the two types of dance have broken down. Many classical ballets now incorporate 'modern' movements and some 'modern' works may even use point-work!

An American choreographer who has been particularly successful in bridging the gap is Glen

Above, *Members of Alvin Ailey's company in the famous 'Wadin' in the Water' sequence from his* Revelations *and,* **below,** *Ailey's company in his* Blues Suite *(1958), to music by Duke Ellington*

Tetley. He started his creative work entirely in the modern idiom, and moved into the classical while retaining some distinctive aspects of his original style. He had his own company for a short time in 1969 but has mainly worked as an international freelance choreographer. He was a director of Netherlands Dance Theatre in the 1960s, making several successful 'modern' works for the British Ballet Rambert around the same time. By the time he became director of the Stuttgart Ballet in 1974, he had developed a much more classical style, which he continued after leaving Stuttgart in 1976. His best-known and most popular work, *Voluntaries* (1973) was created for the Stuttgart Ballet but later adopted by the Royal Ballet and by American Ballet Theatre. It is a mainly abstract interpretation, with some religious undertones, of Poulenc's concerto for organ, percussion and orchestra. Tetley also made other works for the Royal Ballet and ABT, as well as working regularly in Germany and the Netherlands. His critical reputation has always been higher in Europe than in the United States.

There are many modern dance groups, especially in the States but now in Britain too, which make no effort to bridge the gap with ballet or with intelligibility. There are 'dances' which contain walking, running, lying on the ground, talking, singing, simulated sex—indeed anything but actual dancing. There are 'musical' scores which consist of recorded noises, snatches of conversation, speeches in foreign languages, and bits of poetry. The movements performed by the 'dancers' often have no recognizable connection with the sounds or the words being spoken, and are frequently less interesting. In 1980, at the New York Dance Festival in Central Park, supported with public money, a group of dancers skipped about while a recorded voice spoke of steamers on the Hudson, thickly carpeted rooms, and a Buddhist monastery! A female soloist stood stock-still and then did very slow ballet exercises while a recording was played of a Johann Strauss waltz. These items were quite typical of the sort of thing regularly staged recently as 'modern dance', frequently supported by public funds, and taken seriously by many critics.

These more experimental and supposedly 'revolutionary' dances, and their followers, are often openly hostile to classical ballet, even though the mainstreams of modern dance and of ballet now merge and mix happily together. Any suggestion that all dancers should have some technical standards is met by these people with accusations of cultural snobbery and élitism, and of being blind to new trends. Ballet itself is sometimes attacked also for being 'sexist', because the men and women play different and contrasted roles, and wear different styles of costume, and because the old classical

ballets are display pieces for ballerinas. It is also frequently claimed that modern ballet is easier to understand and more popular than ballet, which is alleged to be both old-fashioned and obscure.

In fact, despite this sort of propaganda to the contrary, it is classical ballet—not 'modern dance'—which has won a huge audience today. In London, ballet companies can fill large theatres like Covent Garden and the Coliseum for long seasons, and can often fill two or three such theatres simultaneously. Modern dance companies generally play in much smaller theatres, and by no means always fill those. The London Contemporary Dance Theatre and Ballet Rambert have won themselves audiences which fill Sadler's Wells for short seasons, but outside London modern dance companies often play to tiny audiences. Even in London, the Dance Umbrella (a modern dance festival with a number of visiting American companies) could not fill the small halls it used for its performances in 1981.

The same is true, incidentally, in New York, the home of modern dance. Most of the companies appear in very small studios and halls; when they appear in larger theatres, they usually need a well-known guest star, or have to be content with half-full houses and with selling seats at discount rates.

It is true that many young people, especially art and music students, get 'hooked' on modern dance. They are often people who have not had the chance to see and appreciate the more subtle skills of classical ballet. It is also true that modern dance is sometimes only too easy to follow and understand, so literal in its mime and movement that one may question its artistic purpose. Many forms of modern dance are certainly easy to learn and perform, cheap to stage, and difficult to criticize. Almost anybody who feels a compulsion to express his feelings in movement can proclaim himself to be a modern dancer, and then demand public and critical attention, to say nothing of financial support. Some of these 'dancers' have no visible technical skill or creative imagination, and some have bodies which are so ungainly that they are, by most normal standards, quite unsuited to public display.

Fortunately, not too much of this kind of thing has spread across the Atlantic from the United States to Britain and the European continent. Mainstream modern dance is now established in Britain, but it was slow to take root. When Martha Graham first came to London with her company, in 1954, a small group of critics and dance-lovers were impressed, but audiences were small. Miss Graham did not come back to Britain till 1963, when she had a big success at the Edinburgh Festival and in London. This emboldened Robin Howard, a hotelier and businessman who had come under

Two scenes from productions by the Ballet Théâtre Contemporain in the early 1970s. **Above,** Hopop *with pop music of the time, choreographed by Dirk Sanders. In* Violostries, **below,** *choreography was by Michel Descombey to music by Bernard Parmegiani and Devy Erlih*

Graham's spell, to set up the London School of Contemporary Dance in 1966 and the London Contemporary Dance Theatre emerged in 1967. Originally financed largely by Howard himself, the school eventually succeeded in giving Britain a generation of dancers trained in Graham technique. Under the direction of Robert Cohan, a former Graham dancer, the London Contemporary Dance Theatre performed works by a number of established choreographers, not just Graham, and gradually encouraged its dancers to attempt choreography. Cohan himself provided the repertoire with several of its more popular and spectacular works. Good designers, notably Peter Farmer, were used from the beginning.

At least two of the choreographers developed by LCDT went on to successes elsewhere. Robert North, like Cohan an American but largely educated and trained in Britain, made *Troy Games*, a dance for male athletes, which was subsequently performed in even more virile style by the Dance Theatre of Harlem and then, rather surprisingly, by the Royal Ballet. Another of London Contemporary Dance Theatre's choreographers, Richard Alston, left to form Strider, a company of his own, and later, in 1980, became resident choreographer of Ballet Rambert. In 1981, Robert North followed Alston to Rambert, becoming the company's artistic director.

Ballet Rambert, converted into a 'modern' company by Norman Morrice in 1966, was the first British company to stage works by Glen Tetley, who was at that time working mainly with the 'modern' Netherlands Dance Theatre. Tetley became for several years Rambert's principal choreographer, in practice though not in name, while Morrice and several of the company's dancers, notably Christopher Bruce, John Chesworth and Jonathan Taylor, also made works for it.

London Contemporary Dance Theatre and Ballet Rambert have for several years been friendly rivals, the two leading exponents of various styles of modern dance in Britain. They attract a mainly young audience, and their mixed repertoires are very similar. This similarity might seem likely to become even more marked since Robert North's appointment as Rambert's director though he has expressed a desire to revive some of Rambert's more classical tradition. Various smaller modern groups have come and gone, without achieving any great distinction. The 'EMMA' dance company, sponsored by the East Midlands Arts Association, was considered for some time to be above average,

though critics expressed some doubt even about its value.

Modern dance, even more than classical ballet, depends for its future on outstanding choreographers. Because of its very determination to be up-to-date and 'relevant', modern dance goes out-of-date more quickly than ballet. It also loses more when its original creators disappear, taking their special personal talents and inspiration with them. None of the modern choreographers who have emerged in Britain seem to have the stature of a Martha Graham, a Paul Taylor or even a Glen Tetley. There have not yet been any British 'modern' equivalents of balletic giants like Ashton, Tudor and Cranko. Only time can tell whether they will arise or whether the present vogue for modern dance in Britain will turn out to be a sterile and passing fad.

Modern dance is also developing, following American inspiration, in many other countries, including Australia, Canada, Israel, France and Germany. The European country where it has been most successful recently is The Netherlands, where a whole group of choreographers have blended classical and modern techniques. This sort of experiment started with Netherlands Dance Theatre, which was founded in 1959. Apart from Tetley, other Americans like John Butler, Anna Sokolow and Benjamin Harkarvy, who founded the company, worked with it regularly.

'Modern' groups in France recently included Ballet Théâtre Contemporain, which started in Amiens in 1968 and moved to Angers in 1972, toured internationally, and blended classical and modern styles. It was later succeeded in Angers by Alwin Nikolais, the American choreographer and multi-media designer, who received a big French subsidy to run a school there. Joseph Russillo, another American choreographer, founded his own modern dance company in Paris in 1971, which has also done extensive international tours, and in 1973 Jacques Garnier and Brigitte Lefèvre formed yet another Paris-based group, the Théâtre du Silence. In 1980 there were plans for Garnier to do 'modern' work at the Opéra, where another American, Carolyn Carlson, had held sway in the 'modern' field in the 1970s.

Modern dance, which flourished in Germany in the 1920s and 1930s, is less popular there now and the Tanz-Forum of Cologne has toured abroad, including Britain, Pina Bausch, a pupil of Jooss, who has directed the Wuppertal Dance Theatre since 1973 winning great critical acclaim.

17
Some great dancers

Merle Park in *Coppélia*. Starting her career with the Royal Ballet as a soubrette, Park went on to become a leading classical ballerina. She danced regularly with Nureyev, and in 1981 she created the title role in MacMillan's *Isadora,* a part requiring strong dramatic gifts

Auguste Vestris (1760–1842)

Vestris was the first legendary male ballet star. Born in Paris, he was a principal dancer at the Opéra there from the 1770s until 1816! He danced in London for several years immediately after the French Revolution. He was famous for his elevation, his pirouettes and his nimble footwork. He ended his days as a teacher in Paris; his famous pupils included Perrot, Bournonville and Taglioni.

Marie Taglioni (1804–1884)

Taglioni came from a famous Italian dancing family and became one of the most famous ballerinas of all time. She was notable for her lightness and romantic ethereal style; she created the title-role in *La Sylphide* at the Paris Opéra, which was choreographed for her by her father in 1832. After starring in Paris for many years, she also appeared triumphantly in other European capitals, including London and St Petersburg. Her farewell performance was in London in 1847, and she taught there in her old age. She choreographed one ballet, *Le Papillon*, to music by Offenbach, at the Paris Opéra in 1860.

Marie Taglioni, the great 19th-century romantic ballerina who was the first interpreter of La Sylphide. *She triumphed in all the capitals of Europe, choreographed* Le Papillon *at the Paris Opéra, and eventually taught ballroom dancing in London!*

Fanny Elssler (1810–1884)

An Austrian dancer, Elssler became Taglioni's greatest rival. Instead of romantic ethereality, she specialized in a more dramatic and sensual style, including various gypsy and Spanish roles. A solo in *La Fille Mal Gardée* is still named after her, and her lively cachucha solo was recently revived in Britain by Ballet for All. She had triumphs in all the capitals of Europe, and on an American tour in 1840. She was particularly successful in St Petersburg and Moscow. Her farewell performances were in Vienna, where she spent the last years of her life.

Jules Perrot (1810–1892)

Perrot was Taglioni's regular partner at the Paris Opéra and was considered the greatest male dancer of his time. He appeared regularly in London from 1833 to 1836; he met Grisi in Naples and became her partner, lover and choreographer. He was ballet master in St Petersburg in the 1850s and married a Russian ballerina, with whom he retired to France.

Fanny Cerrito (1817–1909)

Like Taglioni, Cerrito was an Italian ballerina who conquered the whole of Europe, including London and St Petersburg. Like Elssler, she was an exciting and erotic personality.

Carlotta Grisi (1819–1899)

Yet another great Italian ballerina of the romantic period, Grisi became a star of the Paris Opéra and was the first Giselle. Jules Perrot, one of the choreographers of *Giselle*, was her lover, and Théophile Gautier, who married her sister, wrote the scenario specially for her. During the 1840s she created the leading roles in a number of other full-length ballets at the Paris Opéra; she also appeared regularly in London, Vienna, Milan and St Petersburg. Gautier placed her style as a dancer between Elssler and Taglioni.

Lucile Grahn (1819–1907)

Grahn is the only Danish ballerina to achieve major international fame. She studied with Bournonville, created the lead in his version of *La Sylphide*, and left Copenhagen for Paris in 1838 to escape his attentions. She danced regularly at the Paris Opéra, alternating with Elssler in *La Sylphide*. She also danced in London and St Petersburg. She spent her final years in Germany, working as a ballet mistress and choreographer in Munich, where a street is named after her.

Taglioni, Cerrito, Grisi and Grahn appeared together in the romantic *Pas de Quatre* created by Perrot at Her Majesty's Theatre, London in 1845. This quartet has been reconstructed at various times in recent years, notably by Keith Lester and by Anton Dolin, and is an excellent gala display-piece for four great ballerinas, with a humorous hint of the rivalry between them.

Russian Ballet Yesterday

Mathilde Kschessinska (1872–1971)

The reigning ballerina of St Petersburg in the last decade of the nineteenth century and the first decade of the twentieth century, Kschessinska was also famous as the mistress of the Tsar's heir, Nicolas, who became Nicholas II, the last Tsar of Russia. She was the only Russian ballerina to be given the official title *prima ballerina assoluta*, and was also the first Russian to perform the famous 32 *fouettés* in *Swan Lake*. She was celebrated for her vivacity, glamour, and wealth. She specialized in sparkling gypsy-style roles like Kitry in *Don Quix-ote* and the title role in *La Esmeralda*. She appeared in London with the Diaghilev ballet in 1911, wear-ing a great deal of jewellery in the Aurora *pas de deux* from *The Sleeping Beauty*. She also danced in *Carnaval* and a two-act version of *Swan Lake*. She was highly praised though some critics found she lacked Pavlova's inspiration. Kschessinska left Russia in 1920, and lived in France till her death. Her farewell performance was at a charity gala in London in 1936. She ran a very successful ballet school in Paris from 1929, and published her very entertaining memoirs in 1970. Her name was originally Kschessinskaya, but she shortened it slightly for the West.

Anna Pavlova (1881–1931)

Pavlova is still the most famous ballerina of all time. Her name is a household word: every little girl who wants to dance dreams of 'being another Pavlova'. She started her career in Russia, becoming a leading ballerina in St Petersburg at a very early age. In 1907, Fokine made his famous *Dying Swan* solo for her. She started European tours in 1908, and ap-peared with the Diaghilev company during its first seasons. She did not like Stravinsky's 'modern' music, nor did she wish to share star billing with Nijinsky, or to be subservient to Diaghilev. She cut her ties with Diaghilev in 1911 and with Russia in 1913, touring the world with her own company un-til her sudden death from pneumonia in The Hague. She lived with Victor Dandré, a Russian business

man who managed her company, at Ivy House in Golders Green, London. Her principal dancing part-ners were Mikhail Mordkin, Laurent Novikoff and Pierre Vladimirov.

Pavlova toured every part of the globe, in-cluding North and South America, India, Japan and Australia. She was famous for her lightness and spirituality, displayed in various short solos and also in the full-length *Giselle*. She also excelled in humorous and soubrette roles, which made her unusually versatile. Driven by some inner compul-sion, she danced an average of two items at every performance, including matinées, and thought nothing of one-night stands or even travelling from one town to another between the matinée and the evening performance!

All who saw her remembered her forever, and used her as a standard by which to judge subsequent ballerinas. She inspired Sir Frederick Ashton and Sir Robert Helpmann to take up ballet as a career, and her dancers settled and became teachers all over the world.

Tamara Karsavina (1885–1978)

A ballerina in St Petersburg from 1909 till 1918, Karsavina was also the leading ballerina of the Diaghilev ballet, creating the principal roles in most of Fokine's ballets. She was much admired for her classical technique and her versatility, which enabled her to range from the nineteenth-century classics to modern works by Nijinsky and Massine. She married Henry Bruce, a British diplomat in Russia, and they settled in London from 1918. Kar-savina danced as a guest with Ballet Rambert in its first seasons, and played an influential role in the development of British ballet. She was Vice-President of the Royal Academy of Dancing till 1955, taught mime till an advanced age, and personally coached Fonteyn in *The Firebird* and *Spectre de la Rose*. *Theatre Street*, her autobi-ography first published in 1930, is a classic of ballet literature.

Vaslav Nijinsky (1888 or 1889–1950)

Pavlova's contemporary and early partner, Nijinsky is the most famous male dancer of all time. He was a leading dancer in St Petersburg from 1907 till 1911, when he left because of a row about the allegedly over-revealing costume he wore in *Giselle*. He became Diaghilev's lover and star dancer, creating leading roles in a series of famous ballets by Fokine. His jumps out of the window in *Spectre de la Rose* became legendary, but he was also famous for his romantic poeticism in *Les Sylphides*, his

141

Vaslav Nijinsky, as Albrecht in Giselle. *He created leading roles in numerous ballets by Fokine, his leap in* Le Spectre de la Rose *becoming legendary*

dramatic Albrecht in *Giselle*, and his moving *Petrouchka*. He gave remarkable performances in his own dramatic ballets, which are discussed in Chapter 18.

The tale of Nijinsky's marriage to Romola de Pulszky, a rich Hungarian admirer, in 1913, and his consequent breach with Diaghilev, has become notorious. His marriage hastened the end of his very brief dancing career and possibly the onset of his insanity. He gave his last public performance in 1916. He spent his final years in various asylums, ultimately in London, where he died. Herbert Ross's film about him, released in 1980, mixed fact with fantasy. There is an authoritative and detailed biography by Richard Buckle, as well as a famous, though biased, memoir by his widow.

Lydia Lopoukhova (1891 – 1981)

Lopoukhova joined the ballet company in St Petersburg in 1909 and the Diaghilev company the following year. She was famous for her creation of light, soubrette roles, notably in Massine's *La Boutique Fantasque* and *Le Beau Danube*. She was one of the Auroras in Diaghilev's London production of *The Sleeping Beauty* in 1921. She married the British economist John Maynard Keynes, later

Lord Keynes, in 1925. Together they founded the Arts Theatre in Cambridge; later Lord Keynes became first chairman of the British Arts Council. Lopoukhova's final appearances were with young British ballet companies: she created the tango and the milkmaid in Ashton's *Facade* in 1931 and danced Swanilda in *Coppélia* with the newly-formed Vic-Wells Ballet in 1933.

Olga Spessivtseva (b.1895)

Spessivtseva, whose name was shortened in the West to Spessiva, was a leading ballerina in St Petersburg from 1918 till 1923. She appeared with the Diaghilev company in the United States and in London (in the ill-fated *Sleeping Beauty* of 1921). When she left Russia, she became a star of the Paris Opéra, dancing there till 1932. She danced again in London with the Camargo Society in the early 1930s; her farewell performance was in Buenos Aires in 1939. Her most famous role was Giselle, in which some people preferred her to Pavlova.

After her retirement from the stage, Spessivtseva settled in the United States. She advised on the formation of Ballet Theatre, but had a mental breakdown in 1943, and has lived in hospitals and institutions since then.

Alexandra Danilova (b.1904)

Trained in St Petersburg before and after the Revolution, Danilova left the Soviet Union on a tour with other dancers (including Balanchine) in 1924, and was engaged by Diaghilev. Later she danced with various Ballet Russes companies in Western Europe and the United States. She gave her farewell performance in New York in 1957 and has taught and staged ballets there since then. Danilova was particularly famous for her sexy, soubrette roles, especially in Massine's ballets. She appeared at Covent Garden as guest artist with the Royal Ballet, partnered by Frederic Franklin, in 1949, and also as a guest artist with Festival Ballet in 1952 and 1955.

Léonide Massine (1895–1979)

Massine joined the Bolshoi Ballet in Moscow in 1912, and was 'discovered' by Diaghilev in 1914. He created roles in a large number of ballets, starting with the title-role in Fokine's *Legend of Joseph*. He was most famous for his comedy and pathos as Petrouchka and in his own ballets, which are discussed in Chapter 18. He continued dancing into his sixties, appearing with the Royal Ballet in London regularly in the late 1940s. In later years he specialized in mounting revivals of his own ballets. He published *My Life in Ballet*, his autobiography, in 1960.

Serge Lifar (b.1905)

Lifar, who studied with Nijinska in Kiev, joined the Diaghilev company in 1923. Noted for his sensational good looks, he created roles in various ballets by Massine, Nijinska and Balanchine—the latter including *Apollo* and *Prodigal Son*. He became director and principal dancer of the Paris Opéra in 1929, staying there till 1945. During that time he danced leading roles in most of the repertoire, as well as choreographing a very large number of ballets. After the war, he was accused of collaboration with the Nazis, and formed his own company—the Nouveau Ballet de Monte Carlo—which came to the Cambridge Theatre in London in 1946. Lifar returned to the Paris Opéra in 1947, remaining there for a further decade. He continued dancing till a late age, appearing in his own *Icare* at Covent Garden with the Paris Opéra Ballet in 1954. Lifar was the chief force in French ballet for many years. He was known for his strong personal opinions, expressed in a large number of books.

Irina Baronova (b.1919), Tatiana Riabouchinska (b.1917) and Tamara Toumanova (b.1919)

These were the 'baby ballerinas' of de Basil's Ballets Russes in the 1930s. All three of them were trained by émigré Russian ballerinas in Paris (Baronova and Toumanova by Preobrajenska, Riabouchinska by Volinine and Kshessinskaya). They all had strong techniques and personalities, and were very attractive. Baronova retired to England, where she played an advisory role in the Royal Academy of Dancing. Riabouchinska continued dancing into the 1940s, and then retired with her husband, David Lichine, to run a school in Los Angeles. Toumanova, who had the strongest technique and personality, continued doing flashy virtuoso *pas de deux* into the 1950s.

Russians in the West

Rudolf Nureyev (b.1938)

It is impossible to over-estimate the impact of Nureyev on Western ballet. As a dancer, he raised the status of all male dancers, gave audiences new and more demanding expectations, and stimulated Western male dancers into new feats of virtuosity and artistry. As a partner, he gave Margot Fonteyn, who was on the verge of retirement, a new and sensationally successful lease of life as a roving international star. Later, he provided support, encouragement, and fame for a host of younger ballerinas and for comparatively unknown companies. As a producer, he showed how the principal male roles in the nineteenth-century classics could be made more interesting, dramatically and in terms of their dance content. He introduced us to various 'forgotten' Russian classics and aroused a taste for the lesser-known works of Petipa. On television and on the cinema screen, he introduced ballet to vast new audiences. And as a flamboyant and exciting personality, he put himself, male dancers and ballet in general 'on the map'.

Nureyev was born in Siberia (on a train) and started dancing as an amateur with local folk groups. His professional training began late—he did not get to the Leningrad school till 1955. On graduating, in 1958, he persuaded the authorities to admit him to the Kirov, by going to Moscow and threatening to join the Bolshoi! He had various conflicts with the authorities in the Soviet Union, and further endangered his status when appearing with the company in Paris in 1961 by staying out at night, 'fraternizing' with French friends. On reaching the airport to fly to London with the company, he was told that he must return to the Soviet Union instead. Taking an instant decision, he fled across the airport, demanding political asylum from the French police and becoming the first Soviet dancer to 'defect' to the West.

Nureyev had a big success during that Kirov season in Paris, and was already a major star at the age of 23 when he came to the West. He was immediately invited to join the Cuevas company, which was dancing *The Sleeping Beauty* in Paris. Margot Fonteyn then invited him, unseen, to appear in a charity gala she was organizing in London, for which Ashton created a spectacular solo to Scriabin's *Poème de l'Extase*. This was Nureyev's London debut. His electrifying, romantic personality and strong virtuoso technique immediately made an enormous impact on London audiences and critics.

Following this, Nureyev's regular partnership with Fonteyn, first with the Royal Ballet and then on various international tours, became world famous. They danced the full-length classics, Nureyev's own stagings of extracts from forgotten classics like *La Bayadère* and *Corsaire*, and various modern ballets. Nureyev also learned more and more modern roles in the Royal Ballet's repertoire.

In the 1970s, Nureyev danced all over the world with various ballet companies, big and small, and partnered a large number of ballerinas, ranging

Famous dancers from the Soviet Union: **above, left,** *Alexandra Danilova as Odette in* Swan Lake. **Above, right,** *Rudolf Nureyev in the role of Romeo, taking a curtain call.* **Below, left,** *Valery Panov, formerly of the Kirov Ballet, came to the West in 1974 after a long struggle to escape the Soviet Union with his wife, Galina Rogozhina.* **Below, right,** *Mikhail Baryshnikov in* Rhapsody, *created for him by Sir Frederick Ashton*

from famous stars to young beginners. He developed an amazing versatility, appearing not only in classical-style works, but in more modern choreography by Rudi van Dantzig and Glen Tetley. Most leading classical choreographers, including Ashton and Balanchine, created works for him. He also pioneered the idea of ballet dancers appearing as guests with modern dance companies, appearing with the Martha Graham, Paul Taylor and Murray Louis groups, and having new roles created for him by those choreographers.

Another pioneering venture by Nureyev was the group of dancers, usually known as 'Nureyev and Friends', in which other stars and a small ensemble joined him in a mixed repertory for a short season on Broadway and in commercial theatres in Paris and London. Nureyev, an indefatigable and seemingly inexhaustible worker, normally appeared in three contrasted ballets, dancing them at every performance throughout the season. Unlike most star dancers, who prefer to appear at most two or three times a week, Nureyev always said that the more he danced, the better he was. In 1980, at the age of 42, he again astounded New York audiences and critics by dancing James in *La Sylphide*, with great success, seven times a week.

As a choreographer, Nureyev adapted some of the classics as well as creating new ballets of his own. His versions of *Raymonda* and *Don Quixote* mainly used the original choreography, though he expanded the leading male roles and eliminated a great deal of mime and story-telling. He introduced some original dramatic ideas in his *Swan Lake* in Vienna in 1964, while his versions of *The Nutcracker* and *Romeo and Juliet* are more personal. *Don Quixote* is recorded, with Nureyev's own performance as Basilio, in an excellent film made by the Australian Ballet. His first original ballet, *Tancredi* to music by Henze, was made in Vienna in 1966. None of his original works have yet been as successful as his stagings of the classics. His performances can be seen in numerous films and television programmes which provide a permanent record of his artistry and virtuosity.

Nureyev is unusual among dancers for his wide range of interests, keeping abreast of developments in the related arts of theatre and cinema. He also has an unusually catholic taste in dance. This should make him uniquely qualified to be the director of a ballet company when he gives up dancing.

Nureyev has written two autobiographies, and there are sympathetic critical books about him by Alexander Bland, John Percival and Clive Barnes, among others. There are also numerous picture books and magazine articles devoted to him and his work.

Valery Panov (b.1938) and Galina Panova (b.1949)

Valery Panov and his wife Galina achieved world fame with their struggle to be allowed to leave the Soviet Union. They were persecuted by the Soviet authorities for several years, prevented from dancing or leaving the country, but finally allowed to emigrate to Israel in 1974 after demonstrations and protests on their behalf in Britain and the United States and after Valery's hunger strike in Leningrad.

Panov was a leading dancer of the Kirov Ballet, specializing in humorous and dramatic roles. He had a particularly strong stage personality and technique, and was considered by critics who saw him to be the outstanding interpreter of acting roles. He was a Mercutio rather than a Romeo, a jester or a tragedian rather than a poet or a prince. His wife, previously Galina Rogozhina, was one of the youngest ballerinas ever appointed at the Kirov. An attractive and petite blonde, she was originally regarded in the West as primarily a soubrette. She has developed into a versatile ballerina who has been praised in a wide variety of roles, including Giselle.

When they first came to the West, the Panovs had problems of adjustment, accentuated by the fact that they were out of practice as a result of not being allowed to dance or even take classes in the Soviet Union. Panov's first appearances in London, as a guest with Festival Ballet, were not particularly successful. His acting in *Giselle* was thought old-fashioned and exaggerated, and his *Petrouchka* was widely condemned for altering Fokine's choreography. Since then, however, he recovered much of his old technical brilliance and found a repertory to suit him, especially in the works he created for the Berlin Ballet. His combination of melodramatic acting and virtuoso dancing was particularly well displayed as Rogozhin in his Dostoievsky ballet, *The Idiot*. His version of *Cinderella* was also highly praised in Berlin.

Panov has written his life-story, including a harrowing account of his and Galina's experiences in the Soviet Union. It was published in 1978.

Natalia Makarova (b.1940)

Makarova, the second Soviet star to 'defect' to the West, was a ballerina of the Kirov Ballet. Her Giselle was particularly admired in London when she performed it with the Kirov and it was in London, in 1970, that she left the Kirov and started her successful freelance career in the West. She is now generally acclaimed as the greatest present-day classical ballerina.

Natalia Makarova in the first act of the Kirov's production of Giselle

Makarova danced regularly with American Ballet Theatre and with the Royal Ballet. At first she was partnered by Nureyev, but there were temperamental clashes between them. Later Makarova danced very successfully with Baryshnikov and more recently, in a regular partnership with Anthony Dowell. They appeared together to much acclaim in a wide variety of ballets in London and New York.

In addition to Giselle, her most famous role, Makarova excels in humorous, high-spirited parts like Kitry in *Don Quixote* and Lise in *La Fille mal Gardée*. She also danced romantic roles in the modern repertoire, scoring particular successes with the Royal Ballet in MacMillan's *Romeo and Juliet* and as Natalia Petrovna in Ashton's *A Month in the Country.*

Makarova has been criticized for her use of music, sometimes having it slowed down to accommodate her lengthy balances or slow phrasing. Her admirers, on the other hand, felt this to be legitimate for a great dancer; it is certainly in the tradition of many Russian ballerinas, including Pavlova. There is no argument about Makarova's charm, dramatic ability, romantic style, and technical skill.

In 1974, Makarova successfully staged the Kingdom of Shades scene from *La Bayadère* for American Ballet Theatre and in 1980 she surprised everyone by making a success of the full ballet, never before staged in the West, for the same company. Later in 1980 she launched her own group, Makarova and Company, with famous guest artists, in a short Broadway season. In 1979 she published her autobiography, much praised for her insights about ballet and about being a ballerina.

Mikhail Baryshnikov (b. 1948)

Baryshnikov, the third Kirov star to leave for the West, is undoubtedly the greatest male dancer of his generation. His brilliant technical virtuosity and humorous, boyish charm were much admired on the Kirov's visits to the West. He was also seen as a skilful dramatic artist in *Vestris*, a solo created for him by the Soviet choreographer Leonid Jacobsen. He created the title role in Sergeyev's *Hamlet* in Leningrad in 1970. His known interest in Western ballet and lifestyles prevented him from leaving the Soviet Union in the early 1970s and he feared he might never be allowed out. In 1974, however, he was sent to Canada with a concert group of dancers led by Irina Kolpakova; he left the group in Toronto, requesting asylum in Canada.

Since then, Baryshnikov has danced regularly with American Ballet Theatre. At first, he partnered Gelsey Kirkland, who left New York City Ballet to join American Ballet Theatre at that time. Later he appeared regularly with Makarova. He has also guested from time to time with the Royal Ballet, appearing with enormous success in *Giselle, Romeo and Juliet*, and *La Fille mal Gardée.* One of his greatest successes with American Ballet Theatre was in Twyla Tharp's *Push Comes to Shove*, which provided full opportunities to display the comic and show-business sides of his talent.

In the classics, Baryshnikov is famous for his sincere, romantic manner and for his very pure yet spectacular technique, with very high jumps and complicated spins performed as if they were the easiest thing in the world. Critics have sometimes tried to compare Baryshnikov and Nureyev to the detriment of one or the other. Such comparisons, apart from being invidious, are also futile. Both dancers had extraordinary techniques and personalities, but they were quite different in style. Nureyev was the more flamboyant, sexy and charismatic, Baryshnikov being cooler and seemingly more 'innocent'. The difference in their ages meant that Baryshnikov could still perform difficult virtuoso steps at a time when Nureyev was beginning to rely more on his artistry; people sometimes forgot the sensational jumps and spins which Nureyev had displayed to astonished audiences earlier.

146

Like Nureyev, Baryshnikov has appeared with modern dance companies and as a guest with classical companies all over the world. He joined New York City Ballet for a year in 1978. Although Jerome Robbins created some rewarding new roles for him, Balanchine did not, and the repertory in general failed to exploit Baryshnikov's special talents.

Baryshnikov produced the full-length *Nutcracker* and *Don Quixote* for American Ballet Theatre. He also appeared on American television in a Broadway spectacular, performing specially arranged dances from hit musicals, introduced by Liza Minelli. He sang and acted delightfully, as well as dancing, in Herbert Ross's movie, *The Turning Point*. In 1980 he became director of American Ballet Theatre, with whom he intends to continue dancing.

Other 'defectors' from the Soviet Union include Vladimir Gelvan, a young *premier danseur* who joined American Ballet Theatre and then went to the Berlin Ballet. He scored a particular success as Myshkin, a role he created in Panov's *The Idiot*. In 1979, principal dancers from the Bolshoi Ballet defected for the first time. During their tour of the USA, Alexander Godunov and Leonid and Valentina Kozlov decided to stay in the West. Godunov, a handsome blond with a striking stage presence, had been hailed as an outstanding interpreter of the title-role in *Spartacus*. He joined American Ballet Theatre. The Kozlovs appeared as guest artists with various companies and then decided to run a small regional ballet company near New York.

British Ballet Yesterday

Anton Dolin (b.1904)

Born Patrick Healey-Kay, Dolin studied with Astafieva and Nijinska, and became a child actor before he joined the Diaghilev ballet in 1921. Nijinska made *Le Train Bleu* specially for him. He was one of Diaghilev's last protégés; after Diaghilev's death, he appeared in revues and then as a regular guest with the Vic-Wells Ballet, partnering Markova and creating the role of Satan in *Job*. His career as a dancer was closely linked with Markova's; their partnership became world famous. In addition to classic roles like Albrecht in *Giselle*, Dolin performed several solo specialities of his own, notably Ravel's *Bolero*. He was the first British *danseur noble*, gifted with a distinguished stage presence and a strong technique. In later years, Dolin staged revivals of the classics, especially *Giselle*, all over the world, appeared as an actor, playing Cecchetti in Herbert Ross's *Nijinsky* film

Anton Dolin, the first great British male dancer, recreates Petrouchka, one of Nijinsky's most famous roles

Alicia Markova, the first great British ballerina, as Taglioni in Dolin's Pas de Quatre, *a recreation of a work first danced in 1845*

and doing his own one-man show about Diaghilev. He wrote several books, about himself, Markova and Spessivtseva, whom he helped to transfer from an insane asylum to the Tolstoi Home. As artistic director of Festival Ballet in its early years, he was responsible for the coaching and development of many new British stars, notably John Gilpin. Dolin received a knighthood in 1981.

Alicia Markova (b.1910)

Born Lillian Alicia Marks, Markova was the first British ballerina of international status. She was trained by Russians and Italians—Astafieva, Legat, Cecchetti and Celli—and joined the Diaghilev ballet in 1925. She was the Vic-Wells Ballet's first ballerina, staying with the company till 1935. She danced the leads in the first English productions of the nineteenth-century classics, and also created roles in early ballets by Ashton and de Valois. She and Anton Dolin then formed their own company, which toured Britain till 1938. They then went to the United States, dancing mainly with American Ballet Theatre. Markova and Dolin reappeared in England, as guests with the Sadler's Wells Ballet at Covent Garden, in 1948, and in 1949 they formed their own British company again, which developed into Festival Ballet. She continued to dance until 1962. Markova was particularly noted for her ethereality and lightness; her most celebrated role was Giselle, in which she was sometimes compared to Pavlova. She was made a Dame of the British Empire in 1963.

Frederic Franklin (b.1914)

Franklin was a British dancer who had most of his career abroad. Trained by émigré Russian ballerinas in London, he danced in various revues before joining the Markova-Dolin company in 1935. He joined Ballet Russe de Monte Carlo in 1938, and worked in the United States most of the time since then. He created roles in a number of Massine's ballets, partnered Mia Slavenska and Alexandra Danilova, directed regional companies including the National Ballet of Washington, and staged revivals of the classics for numerous companies throughout the States.

Margot Fonteyn (b.1919)

Born Peggy Hookham, Fonteyn became the second British ballerina of international reputation. At the end of her long career, in partnership with Rudolf Nureyev, she toured the world becoming the most famous and most admired ballerina since Pavlova. Like Pavlova and Nijinsky, Fonteyn and Nureyev

became household words, well-known even to people who knew and cared nothing about ballet.

Fonteyn started her training in Shanghai, with George Goncharov, and continued it in London

Margot Fonteyn in the title-role of Ashton's three-act Ondine, *once described as 'a concerto for Fonteyn'*

with Astafieva and at the Sadler's Wells School. She joined the Vic-Wells Ballet in 1934, speedily succeeding Markova in all the major classical roles and creating roles in the new ballets. Most of Ashton's works were created for her. She stayed with the Sadler's Wells Ballet till 1959, after which she continued to appear with the company regularly as a guest. She led the first Sadler's Wells visit to New York, in 1949, when she played a crucial part in winning acceptance for the company as one of the world's great classical troupes. Her Aurora in *The Sleeping Beauty* was for many years her most famous classical role, closely followed by her Odette-Odile and succeeded later by Giselle, which came into full fruition in her partnership with Nureyev. Her earlier regular partners were Robert Helpmann, Michael Somes and David Blair. In the final years of her dancing career she danced with a long list of partners and companies, all over the world.

Fonteyn was famous for her musicality, 'line', and interpretative powers, which were helped by her perfect physique and remarkably expressive eyes. She shared with Pavlova the special gift of imprinting her image and personality on most of her roles, so that those who saw her always remembered her and used her as a standard of comparison for subsequent interpreters. Also like Pavlova, she had comparatively weak feet and elevation. Neither ballerina was a sensational technical virtuoso, though both had much stronger techniques than was sometimes realized by their critics.

Fonteyn continued dancing till 1979 making her dancing career one of the longest on record. She was President of the Royal Academy of Dancing from 1954 and was made a Dame of the British Empire in 1956. She has appeared in several ballet films and television features, mostly with Nureyev. Her autobiography was published in 1975, numerous books about her include James Monahan's thoughtful, critical biography in 1957 and Keith Money's picture books about her in 1965 and 1973. Fonteyn was without any doubt the most popular and successful dancer of her time, a great artist and is much admired as a person—especially for the way she looked after her husband, Dr Roberto Arias, after he was shot and paralysed.

John Gilpin (b.1930)

Trained at the Cone-Ripman and Rambert schools, Gilpin became the outstanding British virtuoso of his time, with a big following and reputation throughout Europe. He started his career with Ballet Rambert, but it was with Festival Ballet, which he joined in 1950, that he made his name.

He led the company on its many tours and eventually became its artistic director (1962–65). He also had a brief period with the Royal Ballet, but was never assimilated into the company or its repertoire. He specialized in fast, yet perfectly controlled pirouettes, shown at their best in Lander's *Etudes*, in which his natural brio and *joie de vivre* also stood out in the 'finger clicking' solo towards the end. He was a poetic Albrecht in *Giselle* and memorably moving and dramatic in the title-role of Jack Carter's *Witch Boy*. A leg injury forced him to give up dancing around the age of 40; after that he fought with ill-health but staged ballets in various parts of the world, including the Irish Republic, Japan and the United States.

There have been many other stars of British ballet, though not with quite such big international reputations. The Royal Ballet's distinguished ballerinas over the years included June Brae, Pamela May, Beryl Grey, Violetta Elvin, Moira Shearer, Nadia Nerina, Svetlana Beriosova, Antoinette Sibley and Doreen Wells. Robert Helpmann was a leading star of the company for many years, though his fame rested more on his dramatic abilities and partnering skills than on his actual dancing. Harold Turner, Alexis Rassine, Brian Shaw, and Graham Usher were among the company's male virtuosi; Alexander Grant was an outstanding and remarkable character dancer, while Christopher Gable brought a sincerity and sensitivity to leading roles which remain unequalled. Other companies too have had their stars. These include Rambert's Walter Gore (who also created the Rake with the Sadler's Wells Ballet), his wife Paula Hinton, and Sally Gilmour, both fine, dramatic ballerinas. Rambert also produced two brilliant soubrette ballerinas, Belinda Wright and Lucette Aldous, who both went on to stardom with Festival Ballet. Aldous later had further successes in Australia, notably in the full-length *Don Quixote*. It is impossible to mention more than a few of the outstanding dancers who have helped to make British ballet what it is.

British Ballet Today

Merle Park (b.1937)

With the premature retirement of Antoinette Sibley, Park became the undisputed leading ballerina of the Royal Ballet. Born in Rhodesia and trained partly there and partly at the Elmhurst School in Surrey before joining the Sadler's Wells School, she was first regarded as a soubrette, a lively, bouncy dancer destined to excel in vivacious and

Galina Samsova in a typical Soviet-style jeté

Galina Samsova (b.1937)

Originally called Samtsova, and born and trained in Kiev, where she started her professional career, Samsova married a Canadian and was allowed to leave the Soviet Union with him. She joined the National Ballet of Canada in 1961, danced in Paris in 1963, and joined London Festival Ballet in 1964. Most of her subsequent career has been in England, first with London Festival Ballet and later with the New London Ballet, which she formed with her partner and second husband, André Prokovsky. They became one of the most popular and gifted dancing partnerships in Britain, dancing all the classics and a number of modern ballets together. When Prokovsky gave up dancing, and the New London Ballet closed, Samsova started guest appearances with the Royal Ballet, which she joined as a ballerina in 1979. She is only the second Soviet-trained ballerina to settle in Britain (the first was Violetta Elvin, née Prokhorova) and she brought a welcome touch of Russian warmth to what is often the rather cooler style of British ballerinas.

humorous roles. Later however she changed her style and personality, becoming much thinner and more 'tragic' looking, and taking over the major classical ballerina roles. She danced regularly with Nureyev after Fonteyn left the Royal Ballet, and was the first ballerina to star in his Covent Garden production of *The Nutcracker*. In 1981 she created the title-role in MacMillan's full-length *Isadora*.

Lynn Seymour (b.1939)

A Canadian who received her first training in Vancouver, Seymour entered the Sadler's Wells School in 1954. She danced her first full-length *Swan Lake* soon after joining the company, and rapidly became known for her intense dramatic personality and her highly individual style of dancing. She created roles in numerous ballets by Kenneth MacMillan, most notably the young girl who is raped in *The Invitation*. He designed Juliet in his *Romeo and Juliet* for her, though it was first danced by Fonteyn. She also

Antoinette Sibley and Anthony Dowell in the Meditation pas de deux *(to music from Massenet's* Thaïs*), specially created for them by Frederick Ashton*

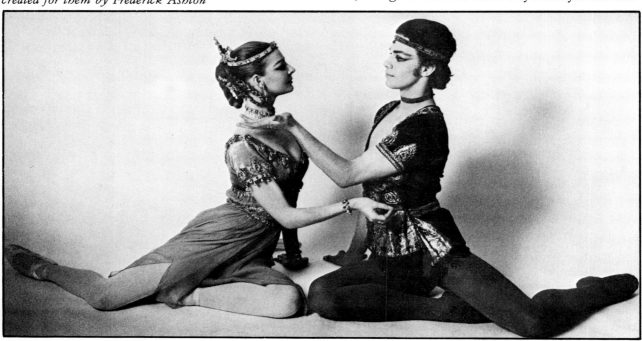

created the ballerina role in Ashton's *The Two Pigeons*. Her partnership with Christopher Gable in those ballets was memorable. For many years she specialized in playing unhappy teenage girls; in recent years she gave powerful performances in the title-role of MacMillan's *Anastasia* and as Natalia Petrovna in Ashton's *A Month in the Country*. Ashton also created some dances in the style of Isadora Duncan for her. She left the Royal Ballet to be leading ballerina in Berlin when MacMillan directed the company there and again in 1978 to direct the company in Munich. She has guested with various other companies, creating the role of Janis Joplin in Alvin Ailey's *Flowers*, and choreographed ballets for the touring section of the Royal Ballet and for the London Contemporary Dance Theatre. She returned to the Royal Ballet briefly in 1980 but found it difficult to resume her old repertoire and did not give any performances. Instead, in 1981 she attempted to launch a new company, to specialize in ballets set to rock music.

Anthony Dowell (b.1943)

Trained almost entirely at the Royal Ballet School, Dowell was the first international male star it produced. He joined the Royal Ballet in 1961 and made an immediate impression with his good looks and strong technique in a small solo role in the *Napoli divertissement*. At first he was more notable for his technical finesse than for his acting ability, but his dramatic powers were gradually developed in a series of created roles, notably Oberon in Ashton's *The Dream*, the Boy with Matted Hair in Tudor's *Shadowplay* and Belyaev in Ashton's *A Month in the Country*. His partnership with Antoinette Sibley in the full-length classics, and in *The Dream*, became celebrated. It was abruptly terminated by Sibley's injuries and subsequent retirement. Later Dowell formed a new partnership with Makarova. In 1978 he left the Royal Ballet to join American Ballet Theatre, to dance more frequently with her and to widen his experience and repertoire. Hailed as a star in the United States, Dowell rapidly developed a stronger and more charismatic stage personality. He also found a comic side to his interpretative abilities, most notably as Basilio in the full-length *Don Quixote*. In recent years, Dowell has divided his time between American Ballet Theatre and the Royal Ballet, and in 1980 he also partnered Makarova in the first Broadway season of her own company.

David Wall (b.1946)

Since Dowell's decision to spend the greater part of his time in the United States, Wall has been the leading male dancer of the Royal Ballet. Like Dowell, he was trained at the Royal Ballet School, joining the company in 1963. At the beginning of his career, he was for many years the leading dancer of the touring company, dancing all the principal roles, mostly partnering Doreen Wells. He has a strong dramatic presence, and the ability to invest even the most cardboard roles with interest and significance. He is always a reliable partner, a gripping performer, and a strong dancer.

He is an outstanding interpreter of the title-role in de Valois' *The Rake's Progress*, and Tudor made *Knight Errant* for him. At Covent Garden he has become a reliable and popular star, dancing the classical princes, Albrecht, Romeo, the hero of *The Two Pigeons*, both principal male roles in MacMillan's *Manon* and the title-role in his *Mayerling*. His warm, attractive personality has made him a favourite with audiences everywhere.

Elisabetta Terabust (b.1946)

Trained at the Rome Opera, Terabust has become a popular international ballerina who appears regularly with London Festival Ballet. She has been successful both in romantic roles like Giselle and soubrette ones like Swanilda in *Coppélia*. She has a charming stage manner, and a light, precise technique; she is similar in many ways to Carla Fracci, the most famous Italian ballerina of our day. Terabust has also appeared with Roland Petit's company and in the first Broadway season of Makarova and Company.

Eva Evdokimova as Odette in Swan Lake, *displaying her high 'extension' in an arabesque*

Eva Evdokimova (b.1948)

The most cosmopolitan of all ballerinas, Evdokimova was born in Switzerland, trained in Munich and at the Royal Ballet School, has an American passport, and started her career with the Royal Danish Ballet! She now divides her time mainly between Berlin and London Festival Ballet. Her most famous role is Giselle; she also dances the other classics and created a leading role in Panov's *The Idiot*. She has also danced with Nureyev on numerous tours.

Peter Schaufuss (b.1949)

Schaufuss, a Danish dancer, is an international star, who is equally well-known in London, New York, Toronto and his native Copenhagen. Born of distinguished dancing parents—Frank Schaufuss and Mona Vangsaae (the first Juliet in Ashton's *Romeo and Juliet*)—Schaufuss was trained at the Royal Danish Ballet School. After about a year in the company, however, he left to join the National Ballet of Canada and then London Festival Ballet. From the beginning, he was much admired for his virtuoso technique and strong personality, which in many ways seemed more Russian than Danish. He now divides his time mainly between the National Ballet of Canada and London Festival Ballet, with guest appearances in Copenhagen and all over the world. His performance in his own production of *La Sylphide* for Festival Ballet has been particularly highly praised, as has the production.

Lesley Collier as Lise in Ashton's La Fille mal Gardée. *The ribbon is a recurring 'leitmotiv' throughout the ballet*

The Royal Ballet's leading dancers in 1980 also included Lesley Collier and Jennifer Penney, who shared the leading ballerina roles at Covent Garden with Merle Park, and Stephen Jefferies, Wayne Eagling and Mark Silver, who shared the leading male roles with David Wall. Collier and Jefferies excelled in dramatic roles, Penney and Eagling in pure dance, while Silver had an exceptionally sympathetic and romantic stage manner, recalling dancers like Christopher Gable and Paul Clarke. Margaret Barbieri, Galina Samsova, David Ashmole and Carl Myers led the touring section of the company with versatility and distinction. Wayne Sleep, though too small for leading classical roles, was one of the Royal Ballet's brightest and most ebullient stars, specializing in comic character roles created for him by Ashton and MacMillan. He also appeared in a musical, and in 1980 staged his own dance revue. His show-business personality could make him a star in the commercial theatre. Michael Batchelor, Stephen Beagley and Roland Price led the Royal Ballet's hopes for the next generation of male principals; Bryony Brind, Fiona Chadwick, Allesandra Ferri and Karen Paisey were considered potential ballerinas.

American Ballet Yesterday

André Eglevsky (1917 – 1977) and Igor Youskevitch (b.1912)

These Russian-born dancers both studied with émigré teachers in Paris and started their careers with Ballets Russes companies in Europe. (Youskevitch was an athlete before he was a dancer.) Both of them were true *danseurs nobles* of the traditional type—tall, thin and aristocratic of bearing, with strong techniques and good partnering ability. They were dancers and partners rather than actors, and gave American ballet in its early days much-needed male technical strength. Eglevsky was with Ballet Theatre in the mid-1940s and with New York City Ballet in the 1950s. Youskevitch was with Ballet Theatre from 1946 to 1955. He was for a long time Alonso's regular partner. Eglevsky retired in 1958, and taught first at the School of American Ballet and then at his own school in Long Island, eventually forming the Eglevsky Ballet which later became the Long Island Ballet. Youskevitch retired in 1962 and also taught in Long Island.

Nora Kaye (b.1920)

Born in New York of Russian parents (her family name was Koreff), Kaye trained at the Metropolitan

Opera Ballet School and started her career there. She joined the *corps de ballet* of Ballet Theatre on its foundation in 1940, created the role of Hagar in Tudor's *Pillar of Fire*, and soon danced the classical leads, including *Giselle*. She and Alonso were the principal ballerinas of the company for many years. Kaye transferred to New York City Ballet in 1951, when Robbins made *The Cage* for her special combination of technical and dramatic strength. She returned to Ballet Theatre in 1954 and retired from dancing in 1961. She became Baryshnikov's associate artistic director of the company in 1980. Kaye is married to Herbert Ross, the choreographer, film producer and director.

Rosella Hightower (b.1920)

Trained in Kansas, Hightower was a ballerina of American Indian origin. She started her career with various Ballets Russes companies, joining Ballet Theatre in 1941. After the second world war she went to Europe, joining the Nouveau Ballet de Monte Carlo which later became the Cuevas Ballet. She was the leading ballerina of this company from 1947 to 1961, appearing with them regularly all over Europe, including Covent Garden. She was particularly admired for her remarkable technical virtuosity in showpieces like the *Black Swan pas de deux*. She founded an important ballet school in Cannes in 1962, directed ballet companies in Marseilles and Nancy between 1969 and 1974, and became director of the Paris Opéra Ballet in 1980.

Alicia Alonso (b.1921)

Born in Cuba, Alonso was partly trained there and partly at the School of American Ballet in New York. She joined Ballet Theatre in 1941 and was a principal ballerina with the company throughout the 1940s and 1950s. She was one of the company's two leading ballerinas when it came to Covent Garden for the first time in 1946. She had a strong classical technique and was a much admired Giselle; she also created the role of the murderess Lizzie Borden in de Mille's *Fall River Legend*. In 1948 she formed her own company in Cuba, which became the Cuban National Ballet in 1955. Alonso appeared as a guest ballerina in the Soviet Union and at the Paris Opéra, staging *Giselle* there in 1972. Despite failing eyesight causing near-blindness, she continued to dance throughout the 1970s and into the 1980s, leading the Cuban Ballet on tours to the Metropolitan Opera, New York and to the Edinburgh Festival. She was also director of the ballet school in Havana, which produced many technically gifted dancers for the Cuban Ballet.

Rudolf Nureyev watches Rosella Hightower demonstrating at her school in Cannes

Melissa Hayden (b.1923)

Born in Canada but trained in New York, Hayden joined Ballet Theatre in 1945, moving to New York City Ballet in 1950 and staying there till she retired in 1973. During her long career as a ballerina, she created roles in a large number of new ballets. She combined dramatic and technical strength, used to good effect in William Dollar's *The Duel*; she was also a moving Odette in *Swan Lake*. Hayden and Leclerq were particularly popular with British critics and audiences when New York City Ballet came to Covent Garden in the 1950s. Since 1974, Hayden has taught in New York.

Maria Tallchief (b.1925)

Another ballerina of American Indian descent, Tallchief was partly trained at the School of American Ballet, and partly by other Russian teachers including Nijinska and Lichine. From 1942 to 1947 she was with the Ballet Russe de Monte Carlo. She married George Balanchine in 1946, danced in his ballets at the Paris Opéra in 1947, and then became the principal ballerina of his New York City Ballet. She created roles in numerous Balanchine ballets and danced the leads in his versions of the classics. Her marriage to Balanchine ended in 1952, but she stayed with New York City Ballet till 1965. When she resigned she was quoted as saying that she did not mind

Marjorie Tallchief and George Skibine, American dancers who led the Cuevas Ballet for many years and then became stars of the Paris Opéra, seen here in Daphnis and Chloe

being listed alphabetically but she was not going to be treated alphabetically! She eventually retired to Chicago, where she taught and in 1980 started to launch a new ballet company.

Marjorie Tallchief (b.1927)

Maria Tallchief's younger sister started her career with Ballet Theatre in 1944, but spent most of her professional life in Europe. She married George Skibine in 1947 and they both became leading dancers with the Cuevas Ballet. She remained with Cuevas till 1957, alternating with Hightower in the classics and creating roles in Skibine's ballets. She was a leading ballerina at the Paris Opéra from 1957 to 1962, and guested with various other companies. She was much admired for her technique and dramatic ability. She gave up dancing in the mid 1960s, and retired to teach in the United States.

Tanaquil Leclerq (b.1929)

Trained at the School of American Ballet, Leclerq became one of the founder members of New York City Ballet. She created leading roles in a large number of Balanchine's ballets, and is particularly remembered for the charm and humour she brought to some of them, notably *Bourrée Fantasque*. She was married to Balanchine from 1952 to

1969 and was stricken with poliomyelitis in 1956, which left her paralysed and tragically cut short her career.

Violette Verdy (b.1933)

Verdy, who was trained in Paris and started her career there with Roland Petit's companies, joined American Ballet Theatre in 1957 and New York City Ballet in 1958, staying with that company till 1970. She had a distinguished career in Europe, including seasons with Festival Ballet, Ballet Rambert and the Royal Ballet in London. She created roles in several of Petit's ballets, notably *Le Loup*. During her long period with New York City Ballet, however, she came to be regarded as an American ballerina, bringing her Gallic warmth and personality to numerous roles by Balanchine and Robbins. She was director of the Paris Opéra Ballet from

Violette Verdy dancing in the Balanchine Tchaikovsky Pas de deux. *She became director of the Paris Opéra Ballet, and then associate director of the Boston Ballet*

1977 to 1980, when she became an artistic director of the Boston Ballet.

Jacques d'Amboise (b.1934)

Graduating from the School of American Ballet into New York City Ballet in 1950, d'Amboise excelled in roles requiring good looks and a strong, extrovert manner. He was outstanding in the lighter Balanchine works, notably *Western Symphony, Stars and Stripes,* and *Union Jack.* His physical presence also made him a memorable Apollo, and equally successful in Robbins's *Afternoon of a Faun.* He was in many ways a particularly American dancer, having a brash, likeable personality. He danced in several film musicals. In the 1970s he did some choreography, was for a time Dean of Dance at the State University of New York in Purchase, and continued to appear occasionally in character roles.

Carla Fracci (b.1936) and Erik Bruhn (b.1928)

Fracci, an Italian ballerina, and Bruhn, a Danish *danseur noble*, both had distinguished careers in their own countries and appeared as guest artists all over the world. Fracci was hailed in Italy as the new Taglioni and was famous for her soft, romantic style. Bruhn brought nobility and strength to the Bournonville ballets and the other nineteenth-century classics, and great dramatic force to modern ballets like Birgit Cullberg's *Miss Julie.* Nevertheless, they both reached the height of their fame when they appeared together with American Ballet Theatre in the late 1960s and early 1970s. Their Giselle and Albrecht became as popular and famous as the Fonteyn-Nureyev partnership. Since then Fracci has mostly appeared in Italy, and Bruhn has staged classical revivals for various companies, especially the National Ballet of Canada and the Royal Swedish Ballet. He has also appeared occasionally in character and mime roles.

Edward Villella (b.1937)

Trained at the School of American Ballet, Villella became New York City Ballet's first home-produced male virtuoso. He joined the company in 1957, and soon became known for his humour, vitality and technical skill. He shone particularly in Balanchine's *Tarantella* and *Tchaikovsky Pas de Deux.* He also became a famous interpreter of *The Prodigal Son.* He danced in the Broadway musical *Brigadoon* in 1962. Injury brought his dancing career to a premature end, but he continued to appear in character and mime roles throughout the 1970s.

Suzanne Farrell, a leading ballerina of New York City Ballet for many years and one of Balanchine's favourite dancers. She also spent some years with Béjart's Ballet of the Twentieth Century

18
Full-length classics

The Royal Ballet *corps* balancing in arabesques in
La Bayadère. This is one of the best showpieces for
the classical *corps de ballet*, and usually earns a big
ovation. A white *corps* of this kind is a standard
feature of all the 19th-century Russian classics.

La Fille mal Gardée

The first version of this ballet was choreographed by Jean Dauberval in Bordeaux in 1789, to a musical score consisting of popular French melodies. It was given in London in 1791. Hérold wrote a new score for a Paris Opéra production in 1828, and Hertel yet another for Berlin in 1864. Petipa and Ivanov used the Hertel score for their St Petersburg version in 1885, and this was the basis for the productions subsequently toured by Pavlova and later Ballets Russes companies. It was also performed by the Marquis de Cuevas Ballet and by American Ballet Theatre.

The most successful and established present-day version goes back to the Hérold score, arranged by John Lanchbery and augmented, in the traditional manner, with melodies by Rossini and Donizetti. This score was created for the production at the Royal Opera House, Covent Garden, in 1960, with décor by Osbert Lancaster and choreography by Sir Frederick Ashton. It is now in the repertoire of the Royal Ballet, the Australian Ballet, the National Ballet of Canada, and many other companies.

All the versions preserve the essentials of the original scenario, with comic characterizations and business which have been handed down over the years. Ashton's version is remarkably successful in integrating this comic business with exciting and lyrical dancing, so that one scarcely notices when acting and dancing merge into each other. The story is clearly and simply told, provoking both laughter and tears.

It opens in a farmyard, with a delightful comic dance, a bit like a can-can, for four hens and a cockerel. It is dawn, and soon we see young Lise and her handsome lover Colas, a farmer. Lise's mother, Widow Simone, is arranging her engagement to Alain, the simpleton son of a rich vineyard owner. In the second scene, sometimes played as a separate act, there are harvest festivities; Alain makes a fool

Above, *Christopher Gable and Lynn Seymour in the roles they created in Ashton's* The Two Pigeons. *This tender* pas de deux, *which closes the ballet, is one of Ashton's supreme evocations of young love and,* **below,** *Brenda Last and Desmond Kelly in* La Fille mal Gardée

of himself trying to dance with Lise, who prefers to dance a joyous and technically difficult *pas de deux* with Colas. The Widow enters into the spirit of the festivities, and dances a lively and amusing clog dance, something like a tap dance. During an ensemble dance around the maypole, a storm breaks out, Colas protects Lise, and Alain is swept up into the air, on invisible wires, apparently being carried by his umbrella.

In the last act, inside the Widow's house, Lise tries to steal a key while her mother is asleep, so as to let Colas in or herself out. She fails, but Colas is smuggled into the room hidden in some bales of corn. Lise, left alone, has a charming day-dreaming scene, in which she imagines herself married and with small children. In the middle of her mime, the bales of corn burst apart and Colas emerges, causing Lise to burst into embarrassed tears. All is soon happily mended, the Widow agrees to the lovers' wedding, and even Alain seems happy when he retrieves his lost umbrella, a surprise touch for the final curtain.

Alain can be appealing and touching as well as comic: Alexander Grant, who created the role in Ashton's version, had considerable pathos in his clumsy attempts to do classical ballet steps, and his bashful hiding behind his huge red umbrella. The Widow, created by Stanley Holden, is a fine role for a comedian who must tread a delicate borderline between obvious, crude humour, and refinement. Colas and Lise, in addition to their dancing, have a lot of business with ribbons and lovers' knots. They usually get a round of applause when they make a cat's cradle with the ribbons in their dance in the first scene. Ribbons recur throughout the ballet, emphasizing its folksy nature. A lot of Ashton's choreography, too, is based on traditional English folk-dance, notably the clog dance for Widow Simone.

The Two Pigeons

This is another old French ballet which has been given a new lease of life in our time by Sir Frederick Ashton. It was first choreographed in Paris in 1866 by Louis Mérante, with a story based on a fable by La Fontaine and with music by Messager. Ashton has preserved the music but changed the story and created new choreography. It has not achieved such great popularity as *La Fille mal Gardée* but those who appreciate its simple story, melodious music and energetic gypsy dancing like it at least as much.

The original version of the ballet had a dual role for the ballerina, an innocent girl abandoned by her lover and also the gypsy who seduces him. Ashton's ballet has two contrasted ballerinas in these roles. He has also ingeniously used live pigeons, or doves, to link the scenes of the ballet and his two human love-birds.

The story opens in a young artist's attic studio in late nineteenth-century Paris, a beautiful set, with a huge window open to the sky and the birds outside, designed by Jacques Dupont. The artist is painting his girl-friend, who wriggles about in her chair, making faces and exasperating him. A band of gypsies is heard in the street below and they are invited up. They dance, and the artist is attracted by the chief gypsy girl. Ashton has devised rival solos for the two girls, with the gypsy doing dynamic, slightly vulgar steps and the heroine imitating them in a softer style and causing amusement by her attempts to be brazen.

The heroine—the characters have no names—drives the gypsies out of the house, but the artist follows them. She is left alone, watching a pigeon fly past the window, leaving her as her boy-friend has done.

The second act opens in the gypsy camp, with a little gypsy boy picking the pockets of rich sightseers and with a host of lively gypsy dances. The artist dances with the gypsy girl, has a trial of strength with her boy-friend, and is beaten-up and thrown out of the camp by the gang. A pigeon flutters down on to his wrist and leads him home to his patiently waiting girl-friend. They dance a *pas de deux* of love and reunion, during which a second bird flies on to the stage and settles with its mate on top of the chair they are dancing around. Human and feathered birds are reunited as the curtain falls.

Ashton has used the birds, not merely to symbolize the action, but to suggest actual choreography. In the first act the lovers play at being birds, using their elbows and shoulders like wings, and strutting around the stage together in a playful flirtation. The ballet as a whole can be described as a danced operetta, not to be taken too seriously but none the worse for that. Its charm and its unpretentiousness give it a special appeal.

La Sylphide

This ballet, not to be confused with Fokine's much more recent *Les Sylphides*, was first produced at the Paris Opéra in 1832, with music by Schneitzhoeffer and choreography by Filippo Taglioni; another version of the same story, using music by Løvenskjold, was created by Bournonville in Copenhagen in 1836. Although this production has remained in the permanent repertory of the Royal Danish Ballet, the work fell into neglect elsewhere till comparatively recently. However Bournonville's version is now in the repertory of several companies, including London Festival Ballet, Scottish Ballet, American Ballet Theatre and the National Ballet of

Canada. French companies have occasionally staged new versions of the ballet to the Schneitzhoeffer score, notably a reconstruction by Pierre Lacotte at the Paris Opéra in 1972. This production was also mounted in Buenos Aires in 1974 and by the Boston Ballet in New York in 1980.

The action is set in Scotland, making this the only classical ballet in which the human characters wear kilts instead of tights or tutus. The first act is realistic, while the second is concerned with spirits and magic in the woods, a formula used in *Giselle* even more successfully.

James, a young laird, is engaged to Effy, and they are about to celebrate their wedding. But a mysterious Sylphide floats in through a window, hovers around James who is asleep in a chair, and dances with him. She reappears later, when James and Effy are leading a celebratory reel. He becomes obsessed with her, and rushes out of the house after her, leaving Effy and the other guests bewildered as the curtain falls on the first act.

The plot is complicated by Madge the Witch, an old hag who visits the house during the celebrations, begging for alms and telling fortunes. She is snubbed by James and predicts that Effy will never marry him but will have children by Gurn, her unsuccessful suitor. James furiously throws her out of the house.

In the second act Madge makes her plot come true. First, she and other witches are seen boiling a magic shawl in an enormous cauldron. Then the scene changes to a romantic forest, where James joins the *corps de ballet* of white-clad sylphs. When the other humans come looking for James, Gurn finds some of his things but Madge throws them away, telling Gurn to say there is no trace of James. She then pretends to help James, offering him the shawl as a way of preventing the Sylphide from constantly flying away from him. In fact, when he wraps the shawl around the Sylph, her wings drop off and she dies. The ballet ends with Madge triumphant and James desolate, as Effy and Gurn cross the stage in a wedding procession and the sylph floats up to heaven.

Ballerinas with a mysterious fey expression and a light, romantic style have been very successful as the Sylphide. Madge the Witch is a powerful mime role, which can be taken by either a man or a woman. James has exciting, bounding solos which have been particularly well performed in recent times by various Danish dancers from Erik Bruhn to Peter Schaufuss, as well as by the Russian, Rudolf Nureyev.

The dancing is varied, including ensemble folk-dances, male classical solos, and delicate romantic steps for the sylphs. The production traditionally includes various trick effects—the Sylphide flying down from a window, disappearing from an apparently solid chair, and floating up a chimney. Peter Schaufuss, in his production for London Festival Ballet, has restored some forgotten music and dances, including one from the Taglioni version, and has given James more dancing, so that the ballet is choreographically and dramatically stronger.

However good the production, the story of *La Sylphide* can never be made very moving. The human characters are too fickle and the sylph is too cool and remote for any of them to arouse much sympathy. The ballet relies on charm, occasional humour, its tuneful score, and the personality and dancing skill of its principal interpreters. It is important, historically, as the first ballet of its kind, and the immediate precursor of *Giselle*.

Other full-length works by Bournonville, notably *Napoli*, (1842), *Kermesse in Bruges* (1849) and *A Folk Tale* (1854) have remained in the repertory of the Royal Danish Ballet and are popular attractions for foreign ballet-goers visiting Copenhagen. They are folksy works, full of vivacious dancing and charming mime. Brief extracts from *Napoli* are performed by several other companies, including the Royal Ballet and New York City Ballet, and the full-length *Napoli* has been staged in Sweden, Scotland and Canada. But none of these works has yet won international acceptance as 'classics'.

Giselle

This is regarded by many people as the greatest and most effective of all ballets. Unlike *Fille*, *Pigeons* and *La Sylphide*, *Giselle* has survived in the repertoire of virtually every ballet company, in something like its original form.

It was created at the Paris Opéra in 1841, and revised by Petipa in St Petersburg. The music is by Adolphe Adam, a French composer who wrote many ballet scores, with an interpolated 'peasant' *pas de deux* by Friedrich Burgmüller and with later additions, made for Petipa's production, by Minkus. While not sufficiently distinguished to hold a place in the concert hall, the music is tuneful and appropriately dramatic. There are recurrent themes, like Giselle's solo which is repeated in slower, broken measure when she goes mad.

The story, devised by Théophile Gautier from a book by Heine, is more dramatic than *La Sylphide* but still does not bear close examination. Despite the efforts of modern producers to make *Giselle* consistent and rational, all sorts of questions must always remain unanswered in what is essentially a romantic fantasy.

The role of Giselle is a great test of the acting

Left, upper, *Yuri Soloviev of the Kirov Ballet as Albrecht in* Giselle. **Above,** *Antoinette Sibley as Giselle, being honoured as queen of the vine festival, with Anthony Dowell as Albrecht admiring her. Sibley and Dowell were a famous Royal Ballet partnership.* **Left, lower,** *Baryshnikov and Makarova in American Ballet Theatre's* Giselle

and dancing abilities of a ballerina. She must impersonate a peasant girl who falls in love with Albrecht, a nobleman who is engaged to Bathilde but who presents himself to her and to her village as a peasant boy, Loys. The deception is exposed by Hilarion, a jealous villager who wants Giselle for himself. The shock drives Giselle mad, and she dies, only to be transformed in the second act into a spirit or Wili, haunting the woods at night, luring men to dance to their death. The Wilis kill Hilarion in this way and then turn on Albrecht. Giselle tries to save him, but Myrtha, the icy queen of the Wilis, insists on revenge. Giselle's efforts in playing for time are successful; Albrecht is just about to die when he is saved by the dawn, which brings the end of the power of the Wilis. Giselle returns to her grave, and Albrecht is left alone to mourn and repent—in some productions he is shown reunited with his aristocratic friends and relations.

There is room for a great variety of interpretation and dramatic detail in productions of *Giselle*. Sometimes Albrecht is portrayed as genuinely in

Marguerite Porter and David Wall of the Royal Ballet in the second act of Giselle

love with Giselle from the beginning; sometimes he is a philanderer who is only converted to true love by her death. Hilarion can be presented sympathetically as a wronged lover or as a jealous boor. Giselle herself can be so frail and nervous that she dies of shock, or so grief-stricken that she stabs herself. At the end of the ballet, she usually returns to her grave alone, as if driven by an invisible force, but sometimes Albrecht carries her to rest, or even takes her to a new resting place, presumably to escape the eternal fate of being a Wili.

However these details are decided, *Giselle* almost always works in the theatre. It is the epitome of romanticism, the search for ideal love, the battle of love and faith against class distinctions, jealousy, the mystic forces of evil, and death itself. The title-role has been danced by nearly every ballerina and would-be ballerina since Grisi, who created it in Paris. Famous interpreters have included Pavlova, Karsavina, Spessivtseva and other Russians in the early years of this century, and their successors—the Russian Ulanova, the British Markova

and Fonteyn, the French Chauviré, the Italian Fracci, and the Cuban Alonso—in more recent years. The most recent great exponent of Giselle is Natalia Makarova.

In the first act, the ballerina has to suggest totally trusting infatuation with Albrecht, and should ideally have the nervous intensity and frailty to make her subsequent heartbreak and death credible and moving. She must also be lively and vivacious in leading the other peasant girls in their dances and must radiate the sheer physical joy of dancing, even while performing a very difficult solo balancing on the points of one foot. The mad scene can be largely mimed, but is more effective when it is danced, especially in view of the musical repetition of steps done earlier, when Giselle was happy. In the second act, the ballerina has to be light and rapid, jumping high and landing silently, and doing neat little foot movements, suggesting a spirit, not a human. While being ethereal, she must also suggest devotion to Albrecht. The role has been called the Hamlet of the dance.

As with Hamlet, one problem is to find an artist young enough to look the part but mature and experienced enough to convey the emotions. Some young dancers do the steps easily but without expressing much meaning; older dancers sometimes give powerful dramatic performances even when they can no longer manage the steps. In general, ballerinas in their 40s seem to suit the role best, being still able to dance and look young.

The ballerina role is obviously crucial to the success of *Giselle*, as it is to all the big nineteenth-century ballets. But the role of Albrecht is more interesting and more difficult than most of the principal male roles in these works. A skilled actor can portray Albrecht's conflicting emotions, his embarrassment and shame when caught cheating Giselle, and his remorse when she dies. He can also suggest his own exhaustion and approaching death while still dancing brilliantly in the second act. Even

John Gilpin as Franz in Festival Ballet's Harald Lander production of Coppélia, *with Dianne Richards as Swanilda and John Auld (right) as Dr Coppélius*

Margaret Barbieri as Swanilda in the Sadler's Wells Royal Ballet's production of Coppélia

Albrecht's walk to Giselle's grave at the beginning of that act can be hypnotically moving; a great Albrecht can dominate the stage with his anguish at the final curtain.

The role of Myrtha is also important. She is now generally danced by a taller ballerina, to give her more authority. She should exude coldness and power, but of course her dancing should be as light and airy as Giselle's. Her first appearance, crossing the stage silently on the points of her feet and then turning around while balancing on one foot in the centre of the stage, are immediate tests of her skill and assurance.

Coppélia

This eternally popular folk-tale ballet, designed for children of all ages, is in the realistic tradition of *La Fille mal Gardée*, rather than the romantic style of *La Sylphide* and *Giselle*. It owes its popularity partly to its story and partly to its delightful, melodious score by Delibes, one of the first specially written ballet scores by a distinguished composer. The first production was at the Paris Opéra in 1870. The scenario by Charles Nuitter and Arthur Saint-Léon is based on one of Hoffmann's tales about a toymaker who tries to make his dolls come to life. The original choreography was by Saint-Léon. Since then there have been many different productions all over the world. Most versions seen today are based on Petipa's St Petersburg production of 1884 though the Danish Ballet has preserved a rather more realistic version, derived from Hans Beck's production of 1896. The last act, which is the weakest choreographically and dramatically, has been re-arranged by many hands, most notably by Balanchine for his New York City Ballet version in 1974.

Coppélia is a fairly straightforward tale of a peasant girl, Swanilda, and her boy friend, Franz. Swanilda spots Franz blowing kisses to Coppélia, a curiously impassive girl sitting up on the balcony of the house belonging to old Dr Coppélius, the toy-maker. (Coppélia's impassivity is not surprising as she is, in fact, a doll.) Swanilda is jealous and Franz taunts her further by dancing national dances with another village girl.

Dr Coppélius crosses the square from his house to the inn, is jostled and mocked by the village boys, and drops his key in the confusion. Swanilda finds the key and leads her girl friends into the house to explore. Dr Coppélius, having missed his key, also returns, while Franz climbs into the house by a step-ladder, in an effort to meet Coppélia.

The second act takes place in Dr Coppélius's house. The girls are startled by Dr Coppélius. They all escape, except Swanilda who hides in the doll cupboard, puts on Coppélia's clothes and fools Dr Coppélius into believing that he has actually succeeded in bringing his pet doll to life. He does this by 'transferring' bodily functions from Franz, whom he has doped with drugged wine, to the supposed doll. Swanilda dances like a robot, then becomes more human, doing a Spanish and a Scottish dance as Dr Coppélius gives her a fan and a tartan scarf. She eventually succeeds in waking Franz and shows Dr Coppélius his lifeless doll. He is left miserable while the two lovers cheerfully escape.

The last act is simply their wedding celebration, with a *divertissement* of various dances and a classical *pas de deux* for the hero and heroine. Dr Coppélius is mollified with a bag of gold from the local seigneur.

The most popular act is the middle one, with Swanilda's doll impersonations and with a number of other dancers impersonating mechanical dolls around the room. A skilled actress and comedienne can suggest a doll while clearly reminding the audience that she is a human being all the time. Swanilda's solos give her an opportunity to show virtuosity in various styles. The first act is notable mainly for the national dances, and for some jealous flirtations between the lovers. Franz is an uninteresting role, originally danced by a girl as was the fashion at the Paris Opéra at that time.

There is also a version of *Coppélia* by Roland Petit, in which Franz becomes a soldier stationed in the town barracks, Swanilda becomes a flirt and a vamp, and Coppélius becomes a tail-coated conjurer and roué, in love with Swanilda. His 'dolls' are mostly broken bones which he brings to life by

magic. Some of the music is played on a barrel-organ. It has considerable theatricality and inventiveness, but it lacks the happy folksiness of the original ballet, and is less suited to Delibes' music. It is no longer a ballet for children.

The Sleeping Beauty

Two of the major Tchaikovsky-Petipa classics are definitely suitable for children. They also contain enough good music and virtuoso dancing to delight adults, though they are not particularly dramatic. *The Sleeping Beauty* was produced at the Maryinsky Theatre, St Petersburg, in 1890. Subsequent famous productions included Diaghilev's at the Alhambra Theatre, London in 1921, which lost a fortune, and the Royal Ballet's, with which the company started its tenure of the Royal Opera House, Covent Garden, in 1946. It was also the ballet with which the Royal Ballet first conquered New York, at the Metropolitan Opera House in 1949. This production, like the Royal Ballet's other Russian classics, is mainly based on Petipa's original, as brought to England, in notation, by Nicolai Sergeyev.

The story is of course the famous Perrault fairy-tale. It lends itself perfectly to spectacular staging and to the display of classical virtuosity in which Petipa specialized.

The first act, more correctly called the prologue, is the baby Princess Aurora's christening. It is mainly an excuse for a succession of fairies to dance solos as they present their gifts. The Lilac Fairy is just about to present her gift when the fairy Carabosse appears, uninvited and in a fury, and puts a curse on Aurora, that she will prick her finger and die on her sixteenth birthday. The Lilac Fairy cannot totally undo the curse, but she can modify it, so that Aurora will sleep for 100 years instead of dying. Carabosse (often played by a man) has a strong mime scene and an evil little dance, surrounded by her creatures, and is then taken aback when the Lilac Fairy advances on her with a deceptive, mildly mocking bow. The solos for the fairies are all technically difficult, but must be made to seem simple and natural, not like gymnastic exercises. They should also look gentle and feminine, not the forced aggressive displays they sometimes become. Even today, the Kirov Ballet of Leningrad usually masters this style better than any other company.

The next act is Aurora's sixteenth birthday party. Four princely suitors each present her with roses and she dances the celebrated 'rose adagio', one of the most famous showpieces for a ballerina. She should look like an innocent young girl having her first experience of being wooed, and should not

The Royal Ballet's
Sleeping Beauty. **Left,**
the production of 1968
with sets by Henry
Bardon. **Above,** the
corps de ballet *with*
Vergie Derman as the
Lilac Fairy and, **below,**
Lesley Collier dances
the rose adagio

167

show the strain of the technically demanding dance, a strain made worse by the fact that the ballerina has to perform it 'cold', almost immediately after her first entry in the ballet. The dance arouses mounting excitement, as Aurora moves from one suitor to another. Each prince partners her in turn, helping her to balance on the points of one foot, and then removing his hand so that she can stay balanced, unsupported, till she lowers her hand to receive the next suitor. When this is performed without wobbling and without strain showing on the face, but with a joyous youthful smile, it is not merely exciting but also seems to epitomize the happiness of youth.

At the end of this act, Carabosse sneaks into the party in disguise, fascinates Aurora with a spindle, something which the young princess has never been allowed to see before, and then gives it to her. Aurora dances with the spindle in her hand, pricks herself, quickly recovers from the initial pain and shock, and tries to continue dancing, getting dizzier and dizzier and finally collapsing into her 100-year sleep. The Lilac Fairy appears, supervises while Aurora is carried off to bed, and then puts the whole court to sleep with the princess. Finally she conjures up a magic forest to protect Aurora and the court while they sleep. Trees and plants grow up in a spectacular transformation as the curtain falls.

Lynn Seymour as Carabosse, the wicked fairy in the Royal Ballet production of Sleeping Beauty. *This role is frequently taken by a man*

A hundred years later, a young Prince is out hunting. He is melancholy and asks to be left alone; then the Lilac Fairy appears to him and shows him a vision of Aurora. He is immediately captivated and dances with the vision, who keeps escaping his embrace, in a romantic scene which is closer to the style of the second acts of *Giselle* and *La Sylphide* than the rest of this ballet. The style also anticipates the celebrated second act of *Swan Lake*. Aurora is accompanied by a *corps de ballet* of girl friends, whose dramatic justification at this point is not clear!

A fine opportunity for spectacular staging and a big transformation scene is provided by the Prince's journey to the castle where Aurora sleeps. The Lilac Fairy leads him, sometimes on foot, sometimes in a magic boat, through various woods. In some productions they encounter and frighten away the lurking Carabosse. The whole scene is similar to the transformation scenes which used to be familiar in the traditional British Christmas pantomimes.

The last act of *The Sleeping Beauty* shows the awakening of Aurora, with a kiss, and the ensuing wedding celebration. For some revivals at Covent Garden, Sir Frederick Ashton interpolated a romantic 'awakening' *pas de deux* for Aurora and her Prince, a kind of dream sequence before the actual wedding celebrations. This was glorious choreography, but some people felt it stylistically and dramatically inappropriate. The wedding celebration is a big formal *divertissement*, which Petipa included in virtually every ballet. Fairy-tale characters come to the wedding and dance. The most famous of these dances is the 'Blue Bird' *pas de deux*, strictly speaking a duet for a male blue bird and his princess, but often danced nowadays as if it were for two blue birds. The male solo, with its diagonal movements across the stage with the arms beating like wings and intricate beats of the feet at the same time, is one of the most famous male solos in classical ballet and requires a brilliant virtuoso dancer.

The grand climax of the celebration is the *pas de deux* for Aurora and her Prince. Such a *pas de deux* is also the grand climax of every Petipa *divertissement*. It takes a standard form: the ballerina and her partner first dance together, with him supporting her in various lifts and balances at adagio speed, then each of them dances brilliant solos, called 'variations', and finally they dance a fast-moving and breathtaking finale, or 'coda', together. The final *pas de deux* in *The Sleeping Beauty* is generally known as the 'Aurora' *pas de deux*. Like the 'Blue Bird' *pas de deux*, it is often performed on its own at gala performances and dance concerts.

Tchaikovsky's music for *The Sleeping Beauty*, written to Petipa's specifications, contains many dance melodies which are often performed in concerts. The complete score, however, is virtually never performed in concert, and like most major ballet scores is only known from performances in the theatre and from recordings.

There is not a great deal of scope for dramatic ability in *The Sleeping Beauty*, except in the role of Carabosse. The ballerina dancing Aurora may succeed in suggesting her development from an inexperienced teenage girl into a mature princess, but the main requirements for the role are an attractive appearance and a strong classical technique.

The Prince is a small role, even by the standards of the nineteenth-century Russian classics. He does not appear till half-way through the ballet, and then only does a little stately dancing with the ladies at the hunting party. His only classical dancing is in the Aurora *pas de deux*, and he is often eclipsed by the Blue Bird, who has a much more exciting solo. However recent productions have enlarged the Prince's role, by giving him an elegiac, melancholy solo when he is left alone, before seeing the vision of Aurora, by adding a *pas de deux* after Aurora's awakening, and sometimes by giving him further dancing during the hunting scene. Rudolf Nureyev's production, especially, gives the Prince so much to do that he almost becomes the central figure of the ballet.

A toy soldier, danced by Michael Coleman, in Nureyev's production of The Nutcracker *for the Royal Ballet; Nureyev (right) is seen as Dr Drosselmeyer, who is later transformed into the Prince*

Finale of the divertissement in the second act of Festival Ballet's production of The Nutcracker *with Marilyn Burr and Flemming Flindt*

The Nutcracker

This ballet has even less dramatic action than *The Sleeping Beauty*. It is essentially two acts of dancing, in various styles, held together mainly by Tchaikovsky's extremely popular and melodious music. The 'Nutcracker Suite', often performed at concerts, is mainly part of the *divertissement* from the second act.

The Nutcracker, also often known by its French title *Casse-Noisette*, was first performed in St Petersburg in 1892. Petipa devised the scenario but illness forced him to hand over the details of the production to his assistant, Lev Ivanov. Very little of Ivanov's choreography survives; the best known item is the big *pas de deux* from the second act, known simply as the 'Nutcracker' *pas de deux*. Like the 'Aurora' and 'Blue Bird' *pas de deux*, it is often performed on its own at gala concerts. Although it is by Ivanov, it is very similar to Petipa's style.

The original story, based on another of Hoffman's tales, is about a small girl whose toys, including a nutcracker doll, come to life and fight among themselves. The nutcracker, transformed into a victorious prince after his duel with a rat-king, takes her on a magic journey through the snowflakes to the Kingdom of Sweets. Children are usually used in the opening Christmas party scene, at which the little girl is given presents, and the children often impersonate the toys as they come to life. The snowflakes scene is an excuse for the entry of the white-clad *corps de ballet*, as in the second acts of *Giselle* and *La Sylphide*, while the Kingdom of Sweets is the setting for the standard Petipa-style *divertissement*, with the various sweets doing Indian, Chinese and Spanish dances, and the Prince dancing a final *pas de deux* with the Sugar Plum Fairy. Originally the ballerina only appeared in the second act, as the Sugar Plum Fairy.

All sorts of attempts have been made to make this story more dramatic, and to enlarge the principal dancers' roles. Many productions now introduce the ballerina in the first act, as the Queen of Snow, and some present-day versions also make her

impersonate the child-heroine. The usual way of doing this is to have the child fall asleep at her party, and then dream the rest of the action, including her own transformation into a ballerina. John Neumeier, for his production in Hamburg, carried this idea to its logical conclusion by revising the whole story, and making it a ballet about a would-be ballerina. Earlier, John Cranko in Stuttgart also devised a totally new scenario.

One of the more interesting recent productions is Rudolf Nureyev's for the Royal Ballet at Covent Garden and other companies. This introduces some psychological ideas like having the little girl's relations return in various nightmare disguises in her dream. Nureyev also expanded the principal male role—as he does in all his classic productions—by making the dancer who plays Drosselmeyer, the mysterious figure who gives the little girl her nutcracker doll, become transformed into the Prince who takes her on her journey. The ballerina also impersonates the little girl at the beginning.

Very successful traditional versions, using lots of children, have been given every Christmas for years by London Festival Ballet and by New York City Ballet. The Festival Ballet production has been revised by different choreographers and producers, but always uses children from The Arts Educational Schools. NYCB's version is of course by Balanchine, with children from the company's School of American Ballet. It is entirely traditional, with a realistic recreation of a nineteenth-century children's party, and with the ballerina's role restricted to the final *pas de deux*.

The Nutcracker is now often regarded as a Christmas ballet. In the United States, it is staged at Christmas in virtually every city, by companies ranging from American Ballet Theatre, with their big production by Baryshnikov, to small school and amateur groups. In the last twenty years it has become an American tradition. In addition to the music, its appeal is based on its nostalgic period charm—and on the opportunities for children to get

Jennifer Penney and Mark Silver of the Royal Ballet in Act 2 of Swan Lake

their first stage experience. However, there is no reason why performances should be limited to Christmas, merely because the ballet starts with a Christmas party, and indeed major companies from the Bolshoi to American Ballet Theatre and the Royal Ballet keep *The Nutcracker* in their general repertoire.

Swan Lake

Tchaikovsky's score was written for a production of this ballet in Moscow in 1877, which was not a success. Ivanov's version of the second act, which has become a classic, was not seen until 1894, in St

Petersburg, where the full four-act version was staged the following year. For a long time the whole ballet was credited to Petipa, but recent research suggests that the second and fourth acts were by Ivanov.

As in *The Sleeping Beauty* and the original version of *The Nutcracker*, the ballerina does not appear in the first act, which takes place on Prince Siegfried's coming of age. Various folk and classical dances are performed as part of the celebrations. The Prince's mother, the reigning Queen or Princess, comes to tell him to face his responsibilities and choose a wife from various would-be fiancées at the coming ball. The Prince, depressed by his mother's reproaches, is more enthusiastic about her gift—a cross-bow, and decides to go out hunting a flock of swans which fly overhead. They lead him to the lakeside, and to the famous second act, which is often performed on its own in mixed programmes with other one-act ballets.

The swans at the lakeside are young girls—in other words, they are the white-clad female *corps de ballet*. They are led by Odette, the ballerina Swan-Queen. They have all been transformed into swans by Rotbart, an evil magician, but resume their human form in the moonlight. The spell can only be broken when a man swears faithful love to one of them, and keeps his vow. (The plot is unclear at this point. It is uncertain how long the Prince must be faithful to Odette before the spell is broken, or whether her release would automatically release all the other swan-maidens.) Needless to say, the Prince duly falls in love with Odette, protects the other swans from his fellow-huntsmen, and dances a romantic and lyrical *pas de deux* with the ballerina. There are also various group dances for the swans, including a famous number for four 'cygnets', little swans dancing together in unison with linked arms. At the end of this act, Odette and the other maidens are forced to resume their swan-like existence. They depart, leaving a disconsolate Prince alone on the stage.

Odette's role in the second act is the epitome of pure classical dancing. In addition to her *pas de deux* with the Prince, she has a more energetic solo, involving a lot of quick, neat footwork. Her fluttering arm movements and the gentle curving of her neck suggest her ambiguous status as part human, part bird. There is a mime passage in which she explains her plight to the Prince, and throughout the act her dancing should express her love and trust for him. She should never appear to be showing off; all her dancing is soft, poignant and lyrical. Some interpreters now do elaborate snake-like ripplings and huge wing-like movements of the arms to enhance the bird-effect. This was not part of Ivanov's original choreography. The *pas de deux* was originally a *pas de trois*, in which Odette seemed to swoon away from the Prince, only to be caught by his friend Benno. Benno is omitted from this act in most productions today.

There was no male solo for the Prince in either of the first two acts, but this too is frequently remedied nowadays. The Ballets Russes companies used to give the Prince, and sometimes Benno, a solo in the second act. Nureyev started the custom of giving the Prince a sad, elegiac solo in the first act, after his mother has instructed him and before he goes off to the hunt, and many productions also make the Prince dance in the first act *pas de trois*, which is normally presented for his entertainment.

The third act takes place in a ballroom. It is the party at which the Prince is supposed to choose a bride, and it is also the inevitable Petipa *divertissement*. As usual, there are national dances, in this case Spanish, Polish, Hungarian, Neapolitan and Russian, though the latter is sadly often omitted. There is also a waltz for the fiancées, during which the prince usually dances for a few moments with each of them, in a desultory uninterested way. The Prince seems quite uninterested in the proceedings until a mysterious stranger arrives with his sophisticated, glamorous daughter. (In some productions the stranger brings the national dancers with him in his entourage, so the Prince has to take an interest in them too.) The daughter resembles Odette, which is not surprising as she is generally danced by the same ballerina, making this a challenging dual role. Odile is hard, glittery, and a show-off, the exact opposite of Odette, but she performs some of the same swan-like gestures, to captivate the Prince. She is in fact an evil enchantress, conjured up by Rotbart, who is of course her mysterious 'father'. In some productions both Rotbart and Odile look so sinister that one wonders how any Prince could be fooled. The contrast is more effective when it is done with more subtlety and restraint.

Odile and the Prince dance the famous 'Black Swan' *pas de deux*, so-called because Odile traditionally wears black as opposed to Odette's white. This is yet another of the Petipa *pas de deux* which are often used as showpieces at galas and in mixed programmes. It is flashy, and full of virtuosity and difficulty. Odile's most famous stunt is the series of 32 *fouettés*, a step in which she spins around rapidly, balancing on the point of one foot, while 'whipping' the other foot around at knee level. The spins are supposed to be done in the centre of the stage, without the ballerina travelling sideways or down towards the footlights, and should end precisely, with the ballerina facing the audience. These *fouettés* were first introduced into *Swan Lake* by the Italian ballerina Legnani who created the dual role of Odette-Odile. In the twentieth-century the *fouettés* became a commonplace, and it was generally assumed that all ballerinas could easily achieve them. However that is not the case; some ballerinas nowadays find them difficult and prefer to substitute some other step, which is often better than muffing the *fouettés*.

The national dances in the third act have not survived in Petipa's original choreography and are generally newly staged for each new production of *Swan Lake*. Sir Frederick Ashton's version of the Neapolitan Dance, a fast-moving duet for dancers with streamers flying from their costumes, and with the dancers shaking tambourines and constantly changing direction towards and away from each other, has become a minor classic in its own right and is always included in Royal Ballet revisions of *Swan Lake*.

After the Prince and Odile have danced the 'Black Swan', he swears eternal love to her, a vision of Odette appears looking frantic at the back of the stage, Rotbart and Odile disappear, laughing triumphantly, and the Prince runs off in search of Odette, leaving the ballroom a desolate shambles.

In the last act, the ballerina is Odette again, heartbroken by the Prince's betrayal and doomed to be a swan forever. She dances woefully with her fellow swans. Then the Prince rushes in, looking for her. Odette forgives him, they dance together, and then make a suicide pact, with Odette drowning herself in the lake, closely followed by the Prince. This proof of their true love destroys Rotbart's power. In a final apotheosis, we see Odette and the Prince sailing away, reunited in a better world.

At least that is the ending which is now generally accepted in the Western world and is performed by the Royal Ballet. In the original Petipa production, Odette and the Prince simply indicated their readiness to die; this was enough to break Rotbart's spell and restore all the swan maidens to human form. In most Soviet productions, the Prince fights with Rotbart and kills him, so as to be happily reunited with Odette in the dawn. The trouble with this ending is that the audience wonders, if it was so easy to defeat Rotbart, why it had not happened earlier. Another trouble is that Tchaikovsky's music for the apotheosis seems to many listeners to suggest something less prosaic than a mere continuation of everyday life. Yet another alternative ending, which some people find even more appropriate to the music, is to have the Prince drowned and Odette remain a swan, without any happy ending at all, as John Cranko did in his Stuttgart production, and also Nureyev in Vienna.

There are all sorts of other versions, dramatic and choreographic. There is a Moscow tradition, probably started by Gorsky at the beginning of this century, of having a jester bounding about in the first and third acts. Though there is no jester in the Petipa-Ivanov version, he has now leapt and spun his way into many Western productions.

The first serious attempt to rethink *Swan Lake* in modern years was by another Russian ballet master, Vladimir Bourmeister. Staging the ballet for the Stanislavsky Theatre (Moscow's second ballet company) in 1953, he went back to Tchaikovsky's original score, abandoned by Petipa, and made the ballet much more dramatic. The French were so impressed by this production when it was taken to Paris in 1956 that they persuaded Bourmeister to mount it for the Paris Opéra in 1960. He was due to mount it also for London Festival Ballet but was refused permission to leave the Soviet Union. His version was very influential on other Western productions, both in its specific ideas and in encouraging producers and choreographers to take a new look at the classics.

Swan Lake is a much deeper and more satisfying ballet intellectually than *The Sleeping Beauty* or *The Nutcracker* because its story can be taken either at its face value or as an allegory. It is based on a German fairy-tale, and like all the best fairy-tales it has many psychological truths concealed in its fantasy.

Some critics have suggested that Tchaikovsky himself may, consciously or unconsciously, have seen it as a tale of his own homosexuality and his unsuccessful search for happiness in love. The young man who does not want to marry, but is under pressure from his mother to do so, is almost a stereotype of every young homosexual male. Even the heterosexual male, however, is often brought up with a romantic picture of what a woman should be, which makes it impossible for him to find happiness with ordinary women as they really are.

The dual role of Odette-Odile clearly represents two aspects of womanhood, especially as seen in a conventional male chauvinistic view. Odette is the soft, elusive, romantic figure, too good to be true and too remote to be available; Odile is the scheming, aggressive woman, anxious to get a man in her clutches.

If one prefers to take *Swan Lake* as a psychological allegory, it is better for the animal and magical aspects of the story to be played down. An Odette who is almost a woman is clearly more appropriate than one who is forever rippling her arms like a bird. Similarly, a Rotbart who is just a sinister presence is preferable to a man in a grotesque owl's costume and make-up, engaging in unarmed combat with the Prince at the end. Personally I sometimes wish that Rotbart did not appear at all, but was just an unseen force, at any rate in the lakeside scenes. At most his appearances in these scenes should be limited to the background. Such a treatment of *Swan Lake* need not prevent children and others who prefer to do so from regarding it as a mere fairy-story. It is precisely because *Swan Lake* can be taken at so many different levels, and because it contains such a variety of dancing styles and possible dramatic interpretations, that many people think it the most interesting and successful of all ballets, including *Giselle*.

Don Quixote, La Bayadère, and Raymonda

These three Petipa ballets were totally neglected in

Left, *the Kirov Ballet production of* Raymonda. **Below, left,** *the Apotheosis—finale of the Royal Ballet* Swan Lake. **Below,** *the Vienna State Opera Ballet production of* The Prince of the Pagodas *by Vaslav Orlikowsky*

Above, *Galina Samsova and Karl Musil in the Festival Ballet* Swan Lake. Right, *Johan Renvall as the Bronze Idol in* La Bayadère. Below, *David Wall and Genesia Rosato in Kenneth MacMillan's* Mayerling

the West for many years, perhaps because they did not have the benefit of Tchaikovsky's music. A *pas de deux* from *Don Quixote* was regularly performed in *divertissements* and galas, as a showpiece for virtuoso dancers; the other two ballets did not even have that much exposure. However they all remained in the permanent Soviet repertoire, and have recently been discovered in the West.

Don Quixote, a full-length work based on Cervantes' famous story, has now had several Western productions. The first was by the old Ballet Rambert, a production later revised for London Festival Ballet. The most successful versions have been Nureyev's in Vienna, Australia and Zurich and Baryshnikov's for American Ballet Theatre. The Australian Ballet production is permanently recorded in one of the most successful ballet films yet made, starring Lucette Aldous, Sir Robert Helpmann and Nureyev himself.

The music for *Don Quixote* is by Leon Minkus, Austrian-born of Polish family, whose original name was Ludwig Minkus. He composed ballet music—notably for *Paquita* and *La Source*—in Paris, before becoming an official ballet composer in Russia, where he worked from 1864 to 1886. His music has often been derided as 'hack' or 'trash' but it is eminently tuneful and danceable. John Lanchbery, who rearranged and orchestrated the score for Nureyev's production, has described it as 'instant melody'. He has pointed out that

Nadia Nerina and Rudolf Nureyev in the Laurencia pas de six *staged for the Royal Ballet by Nureyev in 1965*

although Minkus tended to supply lilting waltzes for all occasions, regardless of geographical or dramatic situation, the *Don Quixote* score has some fairly authentic-sounding Spanish numbers. The score as performed today includes various interpolations by other composers. Patrick Flynn, who arranged the score for Baryshnikov's production, even composed new music of his own for the scene-changes, and the curtain-calls, and arranged a piano-solo medley for the brief prologue which Baryshnikov invented to introduce the characters.

Both Nureyev and Baryshnikov have eliminated most of the mime and story-telling from this ballet, making it virtually an abstract series of rousing Spanish and gypsy dances. It includes numerous flashy solos and duets for the principals, young lovers called Kitry and Basilio, in addition to the famous *pas de deux*. There is also a typical romantic white ballet, the flimsy pretext for which is that it is Don Quixote's vision in a dream. Don Quixote and Sancho Panza are purely acting roles, which can be made interesting by older dancers with strong personalities but which inevitably remain subsidiary to the dancing roles. The ballet is enjoyable in much the same way as a revue or an operetta, making no claims to dramatic or artistic consistency.

Petipa's *Don Quixote* was created in Moscow in 1869 and revised in St Petersburg in 1871. There is another full-length *Don Quixote* ballet created by Balanchine for New York City Ballet in 1965 to music by Nicolas Nabokov. There have also been numerous one-act treatments of the subject, including one by Dame Ninette de Valois for the Royal Ballet in 1950, with specially written music by Roberto Gerhard. None of these *Don Quixote* ballets has been very successful.

La Bayadère, a four-act ballet created in St Petersburg in 1877, also has music by Minkus. It has remained in the Leningrad repertoire, was scheduled for production in England by International Ballet in the 1940s, but was not in fact seen in the West till Leningrad's Kirov Ballet performed 'the kingdom of shades' extract from it in Paris and London in 1961. Nureyev staged this same extract for the Royal Ballet in 1963, with enormous success, and since then it has had several other Western productions, including one by Makarova for American Ballet Theatre. In 1980, Makarova staged her own version of the complete work for American Ballet Theatre, abridging it to three acts. This was the first production of a complete *La Bayadère* in the West.

The story is complicated and, like *Don Quixote*, originally contained a lot of mime. Makarova's version retains enough naturalistic acting to make the story clear, but concentrates mainly on dancing.

The action takes place in a romanticized India. Solor, a successful warrior, is torn between love for Nikiya, a temple dancer, and Gamzatti, the Rajah's daughter. In a plot that starts off with striking similarities to *Aida*, the Rajah and Gamzatti try to make Solor forget Nikiya and finally have her killed by a poisonous snake. Nikiya returns to Solor as a vision in his opium dream, and then returns again, as a spirit, to disrupt his wedding to Gamzatti, blowing up the palace and leading Solor off to another world. This finale, omitted in recent Soviet productions but restored by Makarova, gives the ballet an almost Wagnerian apotheosis. Indeed the whole ballet is rather like a danced opera, not only recalling *Aida* but also Bizet's *The Pearl Fishers*.

Stylistically, *La Bayadère* has many similarities to the Bournonville ballets: the exotic setting, the naturalistic acting of the human characters, mixed with magic and fantasy, and even the female solos which suddenly stop with the dancer 'freezing' in a balanced pose. *La Bayadère* also resembles *La Sylphide*, having a *pas de deux* with a scarf and also having the human wedding preparations interrupted by a spirit, invisible to all except the bridegroom. Indeed *La Bayadère* includes a *pas de trois* for Solor, Nikiya and Gamzatti which is very similar to one staged by Peter Schaufuss and taken from Filippo Taglioni's original version of *La Sylphide*.

The vision scene, known as the 'kingdom of shades', is the extract which has become widely known. Performed in isolation, it is an abstract 'ballet blanc', robbed of the dramatic significance it has in the complete ballet. Its appeal consists in its difficult and unusual choreography. There are four effective female solos, the famous 'scarf' *pas de deux*, and very exciting male solos, one of which is more correctly placed by Makarova in the first act. In recent years, nearly all great male dancers have attempted Solor in this extract. It has become as familiar a showpiece for virtuosity as the 'Blue Bird' or 'Black Swan' *pas de deux*.

The most original and remarkable section of the 'kingdom of shades' is the opening, when the female *corps de ballet* enters, one by one, down a ramp at the back of the stage, each girl echoing the other's movements as the line moves sideways, backwards and forwards across the stage. Between each step forward, they all hold balances in the arabesque position. When performed by a secure and skilled *corps de ballet*, this has a remarkably beautiful and hypnotic effect. In the complete ballet, it represents a multiplicity of Nikiyas in Solor's drugged mind. Similarly, the *corps de ballet*, which starts by dancing very slowly and demurely and then moves into much more rapid and lively steps, echoes the change in the personality of Nikiya that

takes place during the ballet.

The two ballerina roles in *La Bayadère* seem to represent the antithesis between pure self-sacrificing love and selfish, scheming lust, rather like Odette and Odile in *Swan Lake* or like the rivals for the young artist in *The Two Pigeons*. Nikiya's personality is complex, however, as she changes from a virginal temple dancer into a vengeful spirit, and hers is generally regarded as the principal role. Nevertheless, leading ballerinas are often cast in both roles.

John Lanchbery has recalled that when he was asked to arrange the music for the Royal Ballet's production of the 'kingdom of shades', he was at first 'appalled' by what seemed to be its poor quality. 'Yet the music of Minkus has a way of endearing itself bit by bit', and many ballet-goers now hum tunes from *La Bayadère* as readily as themes from *Swan Lake* or *The Nutcracker*. For Makarova's full-length production, Lanchbery wrote new music, copying Minkus's style, for the interludes covering scene changes and for a substantial part of the last act. He also cut some of Minkus's more banal numbers from the score.

Raymonda, first performed in St Petersburg in 1898, has music by Glazunov, a much more respected composer. It also has a very complicated story, about knights of the crusades and their loves, and is set in Hungary. Nureyev has staged the complete ballet for various western companies, including the Royal Ballet (1964), but it has never found a regular audience. A *divertissement* from it is still performed by the Royal Ballet, however, and Balanchine has arranged at least three different *divertissements* to sections of the music: *Pas de Dix* (1955), *Raymonda Variations* (1961) and *Cortège Hongrois* (1973). These are performed by New York City Ballet and by other companies. In 1980, Baryshnikov made another *Raymonda divertissement* for ABT. The music has a lot of Hungarian and gypsy character, and the ballet abounds in both classical and folk-dancing.

After Petipa

No new full-length ballets of any importance were created between the Petipa-Ivanov works of the late nineteenth-century and the middle of the twentieth-century. Indeed in the 1920s and 1930s it was generally assumed that full-length ballets were out-of-date, superseded by the more compact, more 'artistic' and much more economical short ballets created for Diaghilev and the various Ballets Russes companies which succeeded him. In Britain, the Sadler's Wells Ballet was one of the few companies anywhere in the western world performing authentic versions of the Petipa-Ivanov classics. The company had neither the financial nor the artistic resources at that time to attempt to make new ballets of the same kind. New full-length ballets were still produced in Russia, which had become the Soviet Union, but these were heavily propagandistic in content and were not exported. It was, however, the Soviet Union which did eventually re-export full-length ballets to the west, with the Prokofiev scores for *Romeo and Juliet* and *Cinderella*. These are now performed by many western companies and may be said to have attained 'classic' status.

Western choreographers began creating their own full-length works in the 1950s, commissioning scores or special arrangements of existing music. Benjamin Britten wrote *The Prince of the Pagodas* (1957) for John Cranko and the Royal Ballet, and Hans Werner Henze wrote *Ondine* (1958) for Sir Frederick Ashton and the same company. Cranko also created two popular new full-length works in Stuttgart: *Eugene Onegin* (1965) to an assortment of specially arranged pieces by Tchaikovsky (though not from his opera of the same name) and *The Taming of the Shrew* (1969), one of the few long comic ballets, to a similar arrangement of pieces by Scarlatti.

Kenneth MacMillan created a series of dramatic and spectacular new full-length works for the Royal Ballet. *Anastasia* (1971) recounted the events of the Russian Revolution in romanticized form, using two symphonies by Tchaikovsky and a symphonic poem by Martinu, as well as some electronic music. *Manon* (1974) had a special orchestration of music by Massenet (but, like Cranko's *Onegin*, not from the opera), *Mayerling* (1978), another fantasized slice of history, to music by Liszt, was followed by *Isadora* (1981) about the notorious 'modern' dancer Isadora Duncan, to specially written music by Richard Rodney Bennett.

In Germany, the American choreographer John Neumeier produced several new full-length ballets and also, like John Cranko, invented new stories and choreography for some of the Tchaikovsky classics. His version of *The Lady of the Camelias*, based on the novel by Dumas and set to music by Chopin, was extremely highly praised when first staged in Stuttgart in 1978 but found little favour with American critics and audiences when the company brought it to the United States.

There are now a very large number of new full-length ballets scattered around the world, though few of them have won a permanent place in the repertoire and even fewer have been accepted internationally. In Britain, the Soviet choreographer Vladimir Bourmeister made a *Snowmaiden* to music by Tchaikovsky for London Festival Ballet (1961), while Vaslav Orlikowsky, a Soviet emigrant, staged his *Peer Gynt* to Grieg's music for the same company (1963), revising the ballet from

his earlier version made in Basle, Switzerland (1956). Jack Carter made *Beatrix*, an attempt to recreate the French nineteenth-century ballet *La Jolie Fille de Gand*, for Festival Ballet in 1966. Peter Darrell made *Sun into Darkness* in the same year for Western Theatre Ballet, with a scenario by the playwright David Rudkin, specially composed music by Malcolm Williamson and a production by the stage and opera director Colin Graham. Later Darrell made two further full-length ballets with specially written scores for Scottish Ballet: *Beauty and the Beast* (1967) with music by Thea Musgrave and *Mary Queen of Scots* (1979), with music by John McCabe. His *Tales of Hoffman* (1972) to music from the Offenbach opera, made for Scottish Ballet, was also for a time in the repertory of American Ballet Theatre.

Ronald Hynd made *The Merry Widow* (1975) to Lehar's music, as a vehicle for Fonteyn with the Australian Ballet. He later recreated *Le Papillon*, a nineteenth-century work to music by Offenbach, for the Houston Ballet in the USA (1979) and subsequently for the Sadler's Wells Royal Ballet, and also made *Rosalinda* (1979), closely based on Johann Strauss's operetta *Die Fledermaus*, for London Festival Ballet.

In France, Roland Petit made *Cyrano de*

Vaslav Orlikowsky checking the costumes for his production of Peer Gynt *by London Festival Ballet*

Roland Petit rehearsing Fonteyn and Nureyev in Paradise Lost

Bergerac (1959), based on Edmond Rostand's play and to a score by Marius Constant, for his Ballets de Paris; it was also for a time in the repertory of the Royal Danish Ballet. At the Paris Opéra, he made *Notre Dame de Paris* (1965), based on Victor Hugo's novel and with music by Maurice Jarre, *Turangalila* (1968), an abstract work to music by

Messiaen, and *Phantom of the Opera* (1980), based on the novel by Gaston Leroux and to music by Marcel Landowski. *Notre Dame* was subsequently performed by Petit's own Marseilles company and by the Kirov Ballet of Leningrad; *Turangalila* was performed by the National Ballet of Canada, for whom Petit made a further full-length abstract work, *Kraanerg* (1969) to music by Xenakis.

For his Ballet de Marseille, Petit made: *Marcel Proust Remembered* (1974), a two-hour work consisting of abstract and dramatic dances inspired by Proust to music by composers including Wagner, Debussy, Fauré and Reynaldo Hahn; *La Dame de Pique* (1978), based on Pushkin and using specially orchestrated music from Tchaikovsky's opera; and *La Chauve-Souris* (1979), a very free adaptation of Johann Strauss's *Die Fledermaus*.

Denmark also became the home of several new full-length works. Apart from importing *Notre Dame*, Flemming Flindt made *The Three Musketeers* (1966), based on Alexandre Dumas' novel and with music by Georges Delerue. It was later performed by the Munich Ballet. Flindt also created full-length works in a more deliberately popular, quasi-revue style: *The Triumph of Death* (1971) to an electronic pop score, and *Salome* (1979), to a specially written score by Peter Maxwell Davies, the British composer. Both these works achieved a certain notoriety by including nudity; *Salome* was staged in Copenhagen's circus building.

In Brussels, Maurice Béjart and his Ballet of the Twentieth Century have also staged spectacular, revue-style works in the circus building. Béjart often uses a collage of classical and pop music, mixed with the spoken word, as a sound

Maurice Béjart with some of the props for his Clown of God, *a spectacular ballet about Nijinsky*

background for his works, which appeal to a mass audience. Folk-music composed and performed by The Chieftains was used by Joan Denise Moriarty and the Irish Ballet for their version of J.M. Synge's play, *The Playboy of the Western World* (1978).

The most popular literary sources for full-length ballet scenarios have been French and Russian classics. In 1979, two choreographers of Russian origin ventured to use two of the greatest nineteenth-century Russian novels, and both were remarkably successful. André Prokovsky's *Anna Karenina*, based on Tolstoi and using Tchaikovsky, was staged for the Australian Ballet and Valery Panov's *The Idiot*, based on Dostoievsky and using Shostakovitch, by the West Berlin Ballet. In 1981, Panov also turned to Tolstoi, using music by Tchaikovsky for his *War and Peace*.

Strangely enough, there have not been many full-length Shakespearian ballets, apart from innumerable versions of *Romeo and Juliet*. Vladimir Vasiliev staged a two-act *Macbeth* at the Bolshoi in Moscow in 1980. *A Midsummer Night's Dream* was Balanchine's first full-length ballet, in 1962, using Mendelssohn's music. John Neumeier has also done a full-length *A Midsummer Night's Dream*, created in Hamburg and also taken into the repertoires of the Royal Danish Ballet and the Paris Opéra Ballet. There are several Soviet versions of *Hamlet*, and Panov considers doing one of his own. *The Tempest* recently attracted two American choreographers: Glen Tetley who did a 'modern' version for Ballet Rambert in 1979, using music by Arne Nordheim, and Michael Smuin, who used a specially commissioned score by Paul Chihara (after Purcell) for a classical ballet staged by the San Francisco Ballet in 1980. This can be regarded as the first American full-length ballet to have its own original music; Balanchine's *Don Quixote* was produced in 1965 but some of Nicholas Nabokov's music had been written and published previously.

There has been comparatively little demand for new full-length works in the United States, where critical and public taste has tended to prefer one-act and abstract works. Balanchine's *Jewels* (1967), although described as a three-act ballet, is actually three separate abstract ballets, to music by Fauré, Stravinsky and Tchaikovsky. The demand for new dramatic full-length works developed in Britain and West Germany, and has spread to much of western Europe, and to Australia and Canada. It is a demand that is exceedingly difficult to meet. None of the post-Petipa full-length works listed has won general acceptance as an international classic, though several of them have found permanent places in the repertoires for which they were created, and some of them have been performed elsewhere. The difficulty is to find scenarios and music which work well for dancing, stand the test of time, and cross the frontiers of international taste.

Romeo and Juliet

This was the first full-length twentieth-century work which did establish itself as an international classic. It now seems to be almost as frequently performed, in various versions, as *Giselle* or *Swan Lake*. The secret of its success is partly Shakespeare's foolproof story and partly Prokofiev's atmospheric, melodious and danceable score.

The first production of this ballet was not in Russia, as is often assumed. The music was originally banned there on ideological grounds, and the world première was in Brno, Czechoslovakia, in 1938, with choreography by Vania Psota. However the production which established the ballet *was* Russian, choreographed by Leonid Lavrovsky at the Kirov Theatre, Leningrad, in 1940, with the young Galina Ulanova as Juliet. Lavrovsky restaged his version at the Bolshoi Theatre, Moscow, in 1946 and it was this production which was brought to Covent Garden in 1956 when the Bolshoi Ballet made its first visit to the west. It has twice been filmed, the first time with Ulanova in the role she created in 1954. Another version of the ballet, by Margarita Froman, had already been performed in London at the old Stoll Theatre by the Zagreb Ballet of Yugoslavia in 1955, but had made little impact. Sir Frederick Ashton also made his own version for the Royal Danish Ballet in 1955, a version which has lapsed from the repertoire for many years.

Since then countless choreographers have reset the ballet, most notably John Cranko in Venice (1958) and Stuttgart (1962), Kenneth MacMillan at Covent Garden (1965), John Neumeier in Frankfurt (1971), Hamburg (1973) and Copenhagen (1974) and Rudolf Nureyev for London Festival Ballet (1977). Cranko's and Neumeier's versions have also been staged by other companies, Neumeier's replacing Ashton's in the Royal Danish repertoire.

A recent trend in Soviet productions of this ballet, as of other full-length classics, has been to eliminate a lot of the acting and story-telling, making it even more obviously a dance work. A production of this kind by Oleg Vinogradov, staged by the Novosibirsk company in 1965, was followed by similar ones by Yuri Grigorovitch, first for the Paris Opéra in 1978 and then for the Bolshoi Ballet. This production was so controversial, and unpopular with the older Bolshoi dancers, that the company made the unusual decision to retain both the Lavrovsky and the Grigorovitch versions in the repertoire!

There is general agreement that Prokofiev's music is of very high quality; some people—for example the perceptive American critic Jack Anderson—think it too powerful in its own right, dwarfing any choreography that can be set to it. That is a minority view. The majority view, put simply, is that it is the best ballet score since Tchaikovsky.

The story, with its doomed young lovers, its fights, and its lively crowd scenes, is a 'natural' for ballet. It is almost impossible to fail completely when producing it—though Serge Lifar did, in his short-lived version for the Paris Opéra (1955). Lavrovsky must be credited with devising new-style *pas de deux* for the lovers which seem to flow naturally from the action, and to express the complex feelings of the protagonists, and which were not merely excuses for technical display in the old Petipa style. He also choreographed exciting fights, with Mercutio and Tybalt dying dramatically but in quite different ways.

The most difficult moment in the score occurs after Tybalt's death, when Prokofiev provides very melodramatic funeral music, staged by Lavrovsky as a scene of grief for Lady Capulet, tearing at her bosom as she rides on Tybalt's bier in the funeral procession. This suggests too strong an emotional involvement between Lady Capulet and Tybalt. Rudolf Nureyev solved this problem neatly in his production by having Juliet rush in and mourn Tybalt; her grief seems especially poignant because of her knowledge that the killer was Romeo, her lover.

The best-known version in Britain is MacMillan's, which has been regularly in the repertoire of the Royal Ballet since its creation. The principal roles were originally devised for Lynn Seymour and Christopher Gable, though they were actually danced at the première by Margot Fonteyn and Rudolf Nureyev. Since then all the principals of the Royal Ballet have appeared in them, making *Romeo and Juliet* as much a part of the standard classical repertoire as *Swan Lake* or *The Sleeping Beauty*. Guest ballerinas Natalia Makarova and Gelsey Kirkland have also appeared as Juliet, and guest *premier danseur* Mikhail Baryshnikov as Romeo.

It is fairly widely agreed that the most successful parts of MacMillan's version are the *pas de deux* for the lovers and the danced fights for Mercutio and Romeo against Tybalt. The crowd scenes, with the repetitive appearances of a group of three whores, are generally thought to be less inventive. Apart from the hero and heroine, the best role in the ballet is Mercutio, originally created with style and wit by David Blair. There is also an energetic mandolin dance for a group of boys, which has been particularly excitingly led by the diminutive Wayne Sleep. The character roles—Lord and Lady Capulet, the Nurse, Friar Laurence—are fairly conventional

Above, *Fonteyn as the young Juliet, playing with her doll, in Kenneth MacMillan's* Romeo and Juliet *and,* **right,** *Margot Fonteyn and David Blair in a* pas de deux *from Ashton's* Cinderella

stereotypes, which can be made interesting by experienced artists. This production was filmed, with Fonteyn and Nureyev, in 1966.

Cinderella

Despite another attractive Prokofiev score and its well-known fairy-tale story, based on Perrault, *Cinderella* has not attained the universal popularity of *Romeo and Juliet*. The original production, with choreography by Rostislav Zakharov, was at the Bolshoi Theatre, Moscow, in 1945. The following year Konstantin Sergeyev did a version at the Kirov, and in 1948 Sir Frederick Ashton made it his very first full-length ballet, at Covent Garden. Although the Kirov has performed its version in London, Ashton's is the best-known version in the West. It has also been mounted by the Australian Ballet. The original fantasy designs by Jean-Denis Malclès were later replaced by more conventional, realistic sets and costumes by Henry Bardon and David Walker.

The highlights of Ashton's version are the *pas de deux* for Cinderella and her Prince in the ballroom scene, one of the most beautiful of his many beautiful *pas de deux*, and the comic roles of the Ugly Sisters, played by men—originally Sir Robert Helpmann and Ashton himself. Helpmann played a bossy, aggressive sister, while Ashton was an intimidated and excessively shy one. They continued to play these roles for many years, inventing new comic business as they grew older and could manage less strenuous dancing; none of their successors have ever quite equalled them.

There is not much drama in the ballet, and the ballerina's role dwindles away at the end. Ashton omitted a long journey around the world, in which the Prince looks for Cinderella, which is included in Soviet versions. Either way the last act is something of an anti-climax. This may account for the comparative lack of success of the ballet.

Various other choreographers have set the Prokofiev score. Ben Stevenson, a British choreographer and ballet-director who has worked in the United States for many years, mounted his *Cinderella* for the National Ballet in Washington, DC, in 1970 and re-staged it for London Festival Ballet in 1973. He has since also mounted it in Houston, Texas.

In 1979, two other British choreographers made full-length versions of *Cinderella*, using quite different music. Peter Darrell's version for Scottish Ballet used music from Rossini's opera of the same name, and from other Rossini works. Robert de Warren's version for Northern Ballet Theatre in Manchester used long-forgotten music by Johann Strauss, originally composed for a German *Cinderella* ballet, Aschenbrödel.

Frederick Ashton as the shy, unhappy sister (left) and Robert Helpmann as the bossy one, with David Blair as the Prince — trying on the slipper in the last act of Ashton's Cinderella

19
Choreographers and their ballets

Frederick Ashton rehearsing Margot Fonteyn and
Michael Somes in his *Ondine*. This ballet, to
specially written music by Hans Werner Henze,
provided Fonteyn with one of her most successful
roles as a flirtatious water-sprite

The choreographers included in this section are the major figures of world ballet, whose works have stood the test of time or are internationally accepted today. There are now probably more choreographers producing new ballets all over the world than at any other time in history. Many of them are talented and some will be remembered and performed in years to come. It is impossible to list them, though many of them are mentioned or discussed elsewhere in this book, and it is difficult to predict which of them will eventually qualify to rank with those discussed here. Some of them are mentioned at the end of this chapter.

Marius Petipa (1818–1910)

Petipa was born in Marseilles, France, and trained in Belgium by his father, Jean Antoine Petipa, a French ballet-master. He danced in various companies run by his father in Belgium and France, toured North America, and studied Spanish dance in Madrid. He and his father moved to St Petersburg in 1848, and Marius became principal male dancer. He made his first ballet there in 1855, and was appointed ballet-master in 1869. He choreographed about 50 ballets in Russia, including *Don Quixote, Bayaderka* (*La Bayadère*), *Le Corsaire, The Sleeping Beauty, Raymonda* and *Les Millions d'Arléquin*. He planned, supervised, and partly choreographed *Swan Lake* and *The Nutcracker*. He is remembered mainly for his choreography of the Tchaikovsky classics, though *Don Quixote, Raymonda* and *La Bayadère* have recently been revived and become popular in the west as has the *pas de deux* from *Le Corsaire*. Modern productions of *Giselle* are largely based on Petipa's. They incorporate some of his choreographic additions and revisions; he had worked as assistant to Jules Perrot, one of the original choreographers of *Giselle*. Petipa was the founder of what we now think of as 'classical' choreography. He was not much concerned with drama or realism, but used music and story as pegs for dancing and spectacle. He was a master of displaying dancers to their best advantage and showing off their technical skills, which were increasing rapidly during his lifetime. His ballets included a wide variety of dancing styles: the white female *corps de ballet* of swans or spirits, lively folk-dances based on the styles of many lands, and displays of virtuosity for both men and women in the formal *pas de deux* which provided the climaxes of his works. He perfected the *divertissement* in which dances of many kinds were performed in swift succession, usually on the pretext of a celebration of a wedding or birthday.

Lev Ivanov (1834–1901)

Ivanov is now believed to have choreographed the 'white' acts of *Swan Lake,* originally credited to Petipa, and the whole of *The Nutcracker,* which was planned by Petipa. Recent Soviet research suggests that Petipa deliberately kept Ivanov in comparative obscurity, partly out of jealousy and partly because native Russians were not thought fit for the highest positions in ballet at that time. There is still some doubt about the precise division of labour between Petipa and Ivanov, but it seems that the famous *corps de ballet* of swans in *Swan Lake,* and the equally famous adagio *pas de deux* for Odette and the Prince, were Ivanov's invention. He was also the original choreographer of the Polovtsian Dances in Borodin's opera *Prince Igor;* Fokine's staging of these dances, which became internationally famous, was based on Ivanov's.

August Bournonville (1805–1879)

Bournonville was born, and died, in Copenhagen. His father, Antoine Bournonville, was a French ballet-master working there; his mother was Swedish. He studied at the Danish ballet school and in Paris, where he danced for a time, partnering Taglioni. He joined the Royal Danish Ballet as a dancer, becoming its director and choreographer in 1830. He worked in those capacities till his death, though he officially retired two years before that. He travelled extensively in Europe, and many of his ballets were set abroad, incorporating folk-steps and local colour he had absorbed.

He was an intellectual, a friend of the leading Danish composers of his time and of Hans Christian Andersen, who had briefly studied ballet and even appeared in one. He was also a great Danish patriot and took some part in politics. He had a strong social conscience, and considerably raised the standing and respectability of Danish ballet dancers. His ballets were happy and uplifting, telling credible stories about real people, though mixed with fantasy and humour.

La Sylphide, Bournonville's most famous work, is not typical, being a remake of a French ballet in the style of *Giselle. Napoli, Kermesse in Bruges, A Folk Tale, La Ventana, Flower Festival in Genzano, Far From Denmark, The Life Guards of Amager,* and *From Siberia to Moscow,* with their firm roots in real places, are among his most distinctive works. Several of them survive in their entirety, while extracts are still performed from the others.

Bournonville's dancing style is softer and less flashy than Petipa's. It is characterized by light, bouncy jumps and by *joie de vivre. Pas de deux* are less formal than Petipa's; the man and woman often dance side by side, doing the same steps. Bournonville gave the principal men in his ballets much more dancing than Petipa, rarely using them as 'porters' to lift their ballerinas. Characteristics of

Bournonville dancing are soft, relaxed arms, often held out welcomingly towards the audience, quick sideways movements with sudden reversals of direction, and a 'freeze' in a balance during a female solo. Instead of drawing attention to their technical skill and virtuosity, as Petipa dancers often do, Bournonville dancers seem to be saying how easy and pleasant it is to dance. The difficulty of steps is concealed, as indeed it is by the greatest Petipa dancers.

Bournonville's ballets contain a great deal of naturalistic acting and mime, not the formal artificial mime gestures of nineteenth-century French and Russian ballet. He provided older dancers with a wealth of rewarding roles in which they could continue to appear on the stage.

After years of neglect outside Denmark, Bournonville's works are now being staged by most western companies. Nearly every company, from the largest and most famous to small student groups, now includes at least one Bournonville *pas de deux* in its repertoire. Dancers in Britain and America are being taught something of his style and technique.

Mikhail (Michel) Fokine (1880–1942)

Born in St Petersburg, Fokine trained as a dancer at the famous school there, and joined the Imperial Russian Ballet, becoming a principal soloist. He made his first ballet for a student group in 1905. He danced regularly with Pavlova, and made her famous solo, *The Swan* (better known as *The Dying Swan*) for her in 1907. In the same year he also made *Chopiniana,* which he revised many times and which became world-famous as *Les Sylphides,* and *Le Pavillon d'Armide,* his first major production at the Maryinsky Theatre.

From the beginning Fokine was full of new ideas and theories about the nature of ballet. When

Michel Fokine, Diaghilev's first choreographer, at rehearsal

he made *Eunice,* based on *Quo Vadis,* for a charity performance in 1907, he wanted it danced barefoot, in the style of Isadora Duncan, who had recently appeared in St Petersburg. This was forbidden by the management of the Imperial Ballet, so toes, complete with coloured toe-nails, as well as heels and knees were painted on the dancers' tights! When he made *Chopiniana,* he wanted the dancers just to interpret the music, without trying to win applause or show off flashy steps, a big change from the Petipa tradition.

His unconventional ideas were not appreciated or encouraged by the Imperial Theatre, so it was natural that Fokine should join Diaghilev in taking Russian ballet to western Europe. In addition, Fokine and Pavlova were leaders of a group in the ballet company which organized protests against the management. They wanted better conditions of work, and also pleaded for the return of Petipa, who had fallen out of favour. They even organized a one-night strike. Although they were not punished and were allowed to continue working, both Pavlova and Fokine thought their future prospects at the Maryinsky would be affected.

Fokine was Diaghilev's principal choreographer from 1909 till 1914. He also produced ballets for Pavlova. He did not return to Russia after the Revolution, working in Scandinavia and then settling in New York in 1923. He worked as a freelance choreographer with Ballets Russes companies, and then with American Ballet Theatre.

His most famous ballets, however, date from the Diaghilev era. These include *Les Sylphides,* the *Polovtsian Dances* from *Prince Igor, The Firebird, Schéhérazade, Petrouchka, Le Spectre de la Rose* and *Carnaval.*

These are all one-act works, mostly telling a story in a specific setting, period and atmosphere. They marked Fokine's reaction against elaborate full-length ballets, with their unrealistic settings and stories, which Fokine thought would soon die forever. The shorter, more compact works he developed set the pattern for most of the ballets created in the west during the first half of the twentieth century. Fokine's works were not intended to be abstract, however; even *Les Sylphides,* which can easily look like an abstract ballet in a bad performance, was intended to show sylphs and a poet in a moonlit wood.

Because of the importance Fokine attached to exact characterization, even of small roles, and the amount of detailed rehearsal required to achieve the illusion of naturalness he required, his ballets are difficult to revive. They depend on décor, lighting, music and acting as much as on actual dancing. The dancing is not just a matter of technique, but of using the whole body and face expressively to recreate the atmosphere and the characters of the ballet.

For many years, *Les Sylphides* was the most frequently performed of all ballets, being used to open almost every mixed programme. A few other Fokine ballets are also constantly revived, and also often fail to recreate the mood and impact they had in Fokine's day. In a bad performance, it is hard to see what all the excitement was about; a good performance can still be a magical theatrical experience.

Les Sylphides in something like its present form was first produced in Paris in 1909. *Chopiniana*, the earlier version produced in Russia, had a more specific dramatic content, some realistic sets, and some dancers in Polish national costumes. *Les Sylphides* simply has a female *corps de ballet* of sylphs, with three female soloists and one man, a poetic figure in their midst. It is a series of ensemble dances, solos and just one *pas de deux* for the poet and a female soloist. Similarly the *Polovtsian Dances* from Borodin's opera *Prince Igor* also produced in Paris in the same year, is a suite of dances for warriors, their ladies and their captive slaves. There is a particularly athletic solo, with big jumps over the crouched figures of the other warriors, for the Polovtsian Chief.

Le Spectre de la Rose and *Carnaval* tell very slight stories, and also depend mainly on the evocation of an atmosphere. *Carnaval*, first produced in Paris in 1910, to music by Schumann, shows meetings and flirtations between the harlequinade characters—Columbine, Harlequin, Pierrot and so forth. The flirtation between Columbine and the nimble, high jumping and mocking Harlequin (originally danced by Karsavina and Nijinsky) provides one of the high points of the ballet. The sad-faced Pierrot, always being ignored and rebuffed, provides its dramatic content. The dances require elegance and the ability to convey emotion and mood; they also require some prior understanding of the traditional harlequinade characters on the part of the audience. Modern revivals of *Carnaval* rarely make much effect. The blame can probably be divided between the dancers and the audience, both ignorant of the style and significance of the characters.

Spectre de la Rose works better. It is simply a *pas de deux*, to Weber's well-known 'Invitation to the Waltz', first danced by Karsavina and Nijinsky in Paris in 1911. The girl falls asleep on returning from a ball; she dreams that her rose comes to life and dances with her. Finally the rose leaps out of the window and she wakes up. Nijinsky brought the Rose his celebrated elevation—his final jump through the window has become such a legend that no dancer today can hope to fulfil the audience's ex-

Margot Fonteyn as Fokine's Firebird, *in which she was coached by Karsavina, the role's creator*

pectations. Nevertheless, with a good virtuoso male dancer and a stylish romantic ballerina, who can make the audience believe she really is dreaming, the work can still be charming and effective.

Schéhérazade, *The Firebird* and *Petrouchka* all tell much more specific stories and rely more heavily on mime and décor. *Schéhérazade*, to Rimsky-Korsakov's colourful music, was first produced in Paris in 1910. It is an exotic oriental spectacle, with a plot about a handsome negro slave who makes love to one of the Emperor's wives while he is out hunting, and then is caught and executed. The slave was one of Nijinsky's famous roles, ending with a sensational spin upside down on the back of his neck, which—like most of Nijinsky's stunts—has not been repeated by his successors. Nowadays the ballet is less sensational, but can still work if well staged, as by the Dance Theatre of Harlem.

The Firebird and *Petrouchka* are more popular. They both have colourful folksy music by Stravinsky, and they both tell Russian folk-tales. *The*

187

Firebird, also produced in Paris in 1910—a prolific year for Diaghilev and Fokine—is about a young prince who captures a magic firebird in the woods, releases her in exchange for her magic feather, is captivated by a beautiful princess, captured by the evil magician who keeps the princess prisoner, and finally, using the feather to summon the help of the firebird, kills the magician, and marries the princess. The firebird, half woman, half bird, was created by Karsavina; more recently it provided Fonteyn, who was coached by Karsavina, with one of her best roles. There is a charming scene for the enslaved princesses, wearing long white gowns and throwing golden apples to each other in a kind of ball game, and the evil magician has a bizarre retinue of colourful monsters and creatures. The only virtuoso dancing role is the Firebird, though the princess does some gentle lyrical dancing. The ballet is more of a pantomime than a danced work.

The same is true of *Petrouchka,* first produced in Paris in 1911. It opens during a fair in a big square in St Petersburg, where a showman is demonstrating his puppets—Petrouchka, a Blackamoor and a Ballerina. The puppets—played by humans of course—dance in jerky doll-like movements; the two men both try to flirt with the ballerina, but Petrouchka is so nervous and intense that he frightens her. The Blackamoor is macho and aggressive, chases Petrouchka with a scimitar, and finally kills him in the town square. An angry crowd gathers around Petrouchka's body, which is quickly replaced by a straw dummy so that the showman can tell the crowd it was only a puppet. However the live Petrouchka appears on the roof-tops, gesticulating vainly towards the audience before he collapses as the curtain falls. Nijinsky had another of his big successes as Petrouchka, as did Karsavina as the Ballerina. The artist playing Petrouchka has to be half-human, half-doll, so that the audience is never quite certain which he is. The Ballerina is vacant and stupid, the Blackamoor virile and equally stupid. The crowd scenes provide opportunities for Russian folk-dancing and for a colourful spectacle.

Fokine made a number of other ballets, most of which have not survived. He was by far the most important choreographer of his time, and influenced all his successors, but his works can now easily seem dated. It is sometimes hard for a modern audience to see why they roused so much enthusiasm.

One of Fokine's ballets, *The Legend of Joseph* (1914), though long forgotten, was recently reborn in new choreography by John Neumeier (1977).

Left, *Fonteyn as the ballerina-puppet in Fokine's* Petrouchka

This version of the biblical story, created in Vienna, with Kevin Haigen in the role originally performed by Massine, has been extremely popular. It is also in the repertoire in Hamburg and Munich.

Vaslav Nijinsky (1888 or 1889–1950)

Nijinsky is mainly famous as a dancer; his choreography was forgotten for many years. Only one of his ballets—*L'Après-midi d'un Faune*—is now remembered and performed. Diaghilev aimed to develop Nijinsky as Fokine's successor and in his very short career Nijinsky made four ballets, which were evidently ahead of their time. They were deliberately revolutionary and experimental.

L'Après-midi d'un Faune, Nijinsky's first ballet, was produced in Paris in 1912, to a well-known piece of music by Debussy. The ballet was controversial in style and content. Nijinsky played a faun who watches a group of nymphs, is sexually aroused by one of them, and lies down on her scarf after her departure. People were shocked by the ending, when Nijinsky jerked his pelvis to suggest orgasm, though not simulating orgasm in the much more realistic way adopted in Herbert Ross's *Nijinsky* film of 1980! There was no dancing of the brilliant classical kind expected from Nijinsky, in fact scarcely any dancing in the conventional sense at all. The movements for the faun and the nymphs were stylized, like figures on a frieze, moving sideways across the stage with their arms and heads in profile, but their bodies facing the audience. There was applause and booing at the Paris première; Diaghilev had the ballet repeated immediately. It created a scandal and the theatre was sold out for all performances. The reception in London the following year was less excitable, and the ballet was better appreciated.

There have been other choreographic versions of this music since, notably by Lifar and by Jerome Robbins. The Nijinsky version disappeared for many years, but was revived by Ballet Rambert in the 1960s by the Joffrey Ballet (with Nureyev) in 1979 and by Ballet Theatre in 1980. *Jeux* and *Le Sacre du Printemps (The Rite of Spring)* had their premières in Paris in 1913 within a few weeks of each other. *Jeux,* to a specially commissioned score by Debussy, was the first Diaghilev ballet about modern people—tennis-players flirting with each other. Nijinsky gave the dancers arm-swinging movements which were supposed to represent tennis, and stylized poses. There was little dancing, and little obvious relationship to the music. Some of the audience found it funny, and laughed.

The première of *The Rite of Spring* created a scandal and an uproar which have become famous.

Tamara Karsavina as a tennis-player in Nijinsky's Jeux

Stravinsky's music and Nijinsky's choreography, with the dancers crouching, clenching their fists, and turning in their feet, were thought by many people to be barbaric and coarse. The ballet was intended to show a primitive ritual, and probably succeeded.

Nijinsky was still only in his early 20s, and might have gone on to become one of the world's great choreographers, as well as being a legendary dancer, if he had not gone insane. He did make one more ballet, to Richard Strauss's *Till Eulenspiegel,* in North America, in 1916. It was popular with the public and the critics but, like *Jeux* and *The Rite of Spring,* is now forgotten.

Bronislava Nijinska (1891–1972)

Nijinsky's sister, unlike her brother, lived long enough to see herself recognized in Britain and America as a great choreographer. Her principal works, created in the 1920s, had also been ahead of their time.

Nijinska danced with Diaghilev's company in Paris before the First World War, but returned to Russia in 1914, staying there till 1921, when she rejoined Diaghilev. She choreographed a Russian folk-dance for 'the three Ivans' and the dances in the hunting scene in Diaghilev's production of *The Sleeping Beauty.* She revived this choreography for the Cuevas company in 1960, and a 'three Ivans' dance of one kind or another has featured in many productions of the ballet since Diaghilev's.

Her most famous ballets, both made for Diaghilev, are *Les Noces* (1923) and *Les Biches* (1924). She also made *Les Fâcheux* and *Le Train Bleu* in 1924. Although she made numerous fur-

Above, *Svetlana Beriosova as the bride, with her friends, in the Royal Ballet's production of Bronislava Nijinska's* Les Noces *and,* **right,** *Georgina Parkinson as the ambiguous girl in blue, or page-boy, in Nijinska's* Les Biches

ther ballets for other companies after Diaghilev's death, none established themselves in a permanent repertoire. Even *Les Noces* was forgotten for many years but was revived by the Royal Ballet in 1966. *Les Biches* was staged by the Cuevas company in 1947 and by the Royal Ballet in 1964.

Les Noces is a semi-abstract version of a Russian village wedding ceremony, set to a percussion and vocal score by Stravinsky, who first had the idea for the ballet. The dancing and costumes are stylized and formal, not realistic, and the choreography is notable for the various sculptural groupings formed by the dancers. Jerome Robbins's version of *Les Noces* (1965) is more realistic and folksy. A choice between the two is a matter of personal preference—both are distinctive and memorable.

Les Biches, to jolly tuneful music by Poulenc, shows a rather decadent house-party in the 1920s. It is really a loosely connected suite of dances, involving muscle boys from the beach, an androgynous page boy (danced by a girl), a sophisticated hostess with a long cigarette-holder and two young girls who dance together and kiss. Oddly enough, this kiss—which was clearly erotic in the original production—became a much chaster peck on the cheek in the Royal Ballet's revival. 'Les Biches' means 'the does' or—in French slang—'the young darlings'. It was translated as *The House Party* when performed in 1937 by the Markova-Dolin company but is now given under its

original French title. It is a nostalgic reminder of an age which, for certain classes, was almost as permissive as our own.

Les Fâcheux is famous for giving Dolin a solo on point and *Le Train Bleu* for having a book by Jean Cocteau, who was inspired by Dolin, costumes by Chanel, a curtain by Picasso, and music by Milhaud, and for depicting various sports and beach games in a lighthearted and not in a classical ballet way. There is no blue train. As Diaghilev put it the train 'has already reached its destination and disembarked its passengers'.

Léonide Massine (1895 – 1979)

Massine, whose name in Russian is pronounced 'Myassine', was dancing in Moscow when discovered by Diaghilev. He succeeded Nijinsky as Diaghilev's lover and protégé. He became one of the outstanding character dancers of all time, and continued dancing into the 1950s. As a choreographer, he developed two new genres—a comedy ballet akin to operetta and a symphonic ballet which was abstract, but with strong emotional implications. Both these genres fell out of fashion in the 1950s and 1960s, though more recently there have been signs that they might come back into favour. Roland Petit's *La Chauve-Souris* and *Coppélia,* and even Eliot Feld's *Scenes for the Theatre* for example, recall Massine's comic style, while John Neumeier's ballets to Mahler are in the Massine symphonic tradition.

Massine's most famous comic ballets are *La Boutique Fantasque, Le Beau Danube, Gaieté Parisienne* and *Mam'zelle Angot.* The principal symphonic ballets are *Les Présages, Choreartium* and *Symphonie Fantastique.* Other well-known Massine ballets include *Le Tricorne (The Three-Cornered Hat), The Good-Humoured Ladies, Parade,* and *Ode,* produced in 1928, which was one of the first ballets to use film sequences and what we now call psychedelic lighting effects.

La Boutique Fantasque has music by Rossini, arranged by Respighi—music which has become very popular in the concert-hall and on the radio. It was first performed in London in 1919. There is a slight story about a toy shop where the toys perform amusing dances for the customers—two English spinsters, an American family with a horrid spoiled boy, and a Russian family with five children. The toys include a pair of tarantella dancers, poodles (one of whom misbehaves on the American boy's trousers), cossack soldiers, an elegant snob, and the famous can-can dancers, originally played by Massine himself with Lopoukhova. Massine also danced this role in the Covent Garden revival of 1948–49, with Moira Shearer. *Boutique* is the most famous and popular of all Massine's ballets.

Léonide Massine teaching

The basic idea, toys coming to life, recalls *Coppélia* and *The Nutcracker.* But Massine made this idea the central point of his ballet. The climax comes when the can-can dancers are threatened with separation, one being bought by the Americans, the other by the Russians. During the night the toys come to life and get the can-can dancers out of their wrappings. In the morning the toys chase the customers out of the shop and attack the shop-owner and his assistant.

As in other Massine ballets, the human characters are caricatured, moving almost like puppets, making exaggerated gestures and wearing unrealistic facial make-up. Fokine criticized Massine for making the humans and the toy dolls too much alike. But audiences are not worried by such things, and simply enjoy the humour and the dancing.

The series of toy dances is reminiscent of the *divertissement* in Petipa's *The Sleeping Beauty.* The most famous dance is the can-can, but the dance for the Snob and the Melon Hawker and the *galop* ensemble for all the live toys are also particularly successful. Like all Massine's comedy ballets, *Boutique* requires artists who are vivacious, full of personality, and good actors as well as technically accomplished dancers.

La Boutique Fantasque has been revived at in-

191

(1928), now called simply *Apollo,* and *The Prodigal Son* (1929). Stravinsky's music for *Apollo* was first choreographed by Bolm in Washington two months before Balanchine's version in Paris, but it is Balanchine's which has survived and become accepted as a classic of our time. The title-role was created by the sensationally handsome young Lifar; the ballet showed the birth of Apollo, who was unwrapped from swaddling clothes in front of a floral drop curtain, followed by a long scene in which Apollo danced with the muses of poetry, mime and dance, giving them each symbols of their art. Finally Apollo led the muses up a staircase towards heaven, being met by a chariot drawn by horses.

The slight story was always told mainly through dance, and the ballet is usually cited as marking the birth of Balanchine's neo-classical style. Over the years he simplified Apollo further, reducing the scenery to a staircase, and most recently eliminating the birth and the ascent to heaven altogether. Thus it became more and more of an abstract ballet, with vestigial hints of its original scenario in the presentation of the gifts to the muses and in the way the muse of mime puts her fingers to her lips to indicate her silence. The task of the dancers to indicate something of the nature of their roles is now all the harder. The interpreter of the title-role needs considerable personality and acting ability, as well as good looks, to hold the work together and give it meaning.

Apollo is regularly in the repertory of New York City Ballet, and of many other companies in the West, notably the British Royal Ballet and the Royal Danish Ballet. While *Apollo* was the precursor of Balanchine's later style, *The Prodigal Son* often now seems like a relic of an old one. It tells the biblical story in a series of short scenes, with spectacular costumes and scenery by the painter Georges Rouault. The music is by Prokofiev. Once again, the title-role was created by Lifar; famous interpreters with New York City Ballet have included Edward Villella and, for one season, Mikhail Baryshnikov. Baryshnikov later danced it with American Ballet Theatre. Nureyev has been its most distinguished exponent with the Royal Ballet. The role requires dramatic ability at least as much as dancing skill, and certainly does not need a virtuoso dancer. Stephen Jefferies, an outstanding actor-dancer, has been one of the Royal Ballet's best interpreters.

The Prodigal Son is often dismissed as 'old-fashioned', mainly because people do not expect Balanchine ballets to tell stories. Actually, Balanchine continued to make story ballets from time to time, and never restricted himself entirely to the 'abstract' style for which he became best known. Moreover *The Prodigal Son* was ahead of its time in some ways: the scene between the hero and the seductive siren, and the antics of two drunken men at an orgy, were remarkably erotic, and the use of a simple wooden prop to represent in turn a fence, a table and a boat, anticipated later stage techniques. When well acted and staged this ballet can still be exciting and moving.

Seventeen years later, in 1946, Balanchine made two ballets which can roughly be described as continuing the style of *Apollo* and *The Prodigal Son. The Four Temperaments,* created for Ballet Society in New York, does not tell a story but does indicate the 'temperaments' or moods of Hindemith's music, so that the ballet is not totally abstract. (*Orpheus,* made in 1948, was even more like *Apollo,* having music by Stravinsky.) *Night Shadow,* for Ballet Russe de Monte Carlo in New York, tells a dramatic story about a jealous husband, his coquettish mistress, his wife, and a poet who dances with her while she sleep-walks. (The ballet has also been called *La Somnambule* and *La Sonnambula*; it has music arranged by Rieti from Bellini's opera of that name.) The story is romantic, and not precise, though it ends precisely enough with the husband killing the poet, who is carried off in the sleep-walker's arms. The ballet follows a traditional pattern—even including a brief and highly original *divertissement*—and has been a popular feature of many repertoires, including the Cuevas, the Royal Danish Ballet, and London Festival Ballet, as well as New York City Ballet.

Right, *Suzanne Farrell in Balanchine's* Union Jack, *a light-hearted tribute to Britain and,* **below,** *Robert La Fosse as* The Prodigal Son *in American Ballet Theatre's production of Balanchine's ballet*

Margot Fonteyn as the Sleepwalker with John Gilpin as the Poet in Festival Ballet's production of Balanchine's Night Shadow (La Sonnambula)

Many distinguished and famous dancers have done the leading roles.

The first of Balanchine's totally abstract ballets to remain in the present-day repertoire is *Serenade,* to Tchaikovsky's Serenade in C Major for String Orchestra. Originally created for a student group in New York in 1934, it has become an international classic, performed by most major companies. One seemingly 'dramatic' touch in the ballet, when a girl enters late to join the *corps,* was the result of a girl accidentally coming late during rehearsals! There is a hint of drama when a man enters with a girl behind him, covering his eyes with her hand like a figure of fate. But despite these hints of emotion and of personal relationships, there is no story, or rather, as Balanchine himself has put it, '*Serenade* tells the story musically and choreographically, without any extraneous narrative'. The choreography contains some of Balanchine's happiest and most lyrical inventions, including a 'signature' device, a line of girls curling and unfolding around a single man—which Balanchine repeated in several other abstract ballets, most notably *Concerto Barocco* (Bach).

Balanchine was a most prolific and hard-working choreographer, producing about two new ballets each season for his New York City Ballet. Most of them were 'abstract', though this category can be sub-divided into works in pure classical style, more romantic and lyrical pieces, 'modern' settings of contemporary scores, and brash pieces of joyous 'Americana' with chorus-line high kicks. He even combined the first three of these styles in one so-called full-length ballet, *Jewels* (1967) which has sections by Tchaikovsky, Fauré and Stravinsky.

Among his best known formal classical display pieces are *Ballet Imperial* (1941, later retitled, after its music, *Tchaikovsky Piano Concerto No 2*), *Le Palais de Cristal* (1946, later retitled *Symphony in C,* its Bizet music), *Theme and Variations* (Tchaikovsky, 1947), *Bourrée Fantasque* (Chabrier, 1949—this ballet also has touches of humour), and three pieces with music from Glazounov's *Raymonda: Pas de Dix* (1955), *Raymonda Variations* (1961) and *Cortège Hongrois* (1973).

The 'romantic' pieces include three stylish and dramatic arrangements of waltzes: *La Valse* (Ravel, 1951), *Liebeslieder Walzer* (Brahms, 1960) and *Vienna Waltzes* (Johann Strauss, Lehar, Richard Strauss, 1977).

The more 'modern' pieces, in which Balanchine developed new staccato movements to match the percussive scores, include *Episodes* (Webern, 1959) and a whole series of Stravinsky ballets: *Agon* (1957), *Monumentum pro Gesualdo* (1960), *Movements for Piano and Orchestra* (1963), *Symphony in Three Movements* (1972), *Stravinsky Violin Concerto* (1972), and *Duo Concertante* (1972).

Highlights of Balanchine's light-hearted 'Americana' output are: *Western Symphony* (Hershy Kay, 1954), *Stars and Stripes* (Sousa, 1958), and *Who Cares?* (Gershwin, 1970). He also transferred his national sympathy to Britain in *Union Jack* (traditional music arranged by Hershy Kay, 1976), which includes sailors' hornpipes, massed guards marching, and a comic coster-monger *pas de deux.*

Balanchine's 'abstract' style has had an enormous influence on other present-day choreographers, especially in the United States but also in western Europe. Choreographers everywhere, young and old, experienced and inexperienced, now produce plotless ballets to various pieces of concert music, sometimes with a hint of emotion or of personal relationships. Unfortunately many of these ballets are simply exercises in technique, displaying a series of academic, classroom steps, more or less fitted to the music but lacking the originality and inspiration with which Balanchine often surprised and delighted us. Even Balanchine, however, in his enormous output, sometimes produced works which were mere run-of-the-mill, and which did not survive.

There are also numerous Balanchine ballets of other types—some of which do not fit neatly into any category. His own revisions of well-known classics are often surprisingly disappointing. *Swan Lake,* in a one-act version incorporating part of the last act as well as most of the second, made very little dramatic or musical sense. *The Nutcracker* is traditional in style, but lacks interesting dancing roles for the principals. Most critics prefer Fokine's original to Balanchine's various revisions of *The Firebird,* though the version presented in 1980, with the collaboration of Jerome Robbins, had a certain folksy and science-fiction charm of its own. *Don Quixote* and *A Midsummer Night's Dream* were only partially successful attempts to make new full-length ballets—the second act of *Dream* is virtually an independent 'abstract' ballet. *Bugaku* was an attempt to translate Japanese marriage ritual into western ballet while *Variations pour une porte et un soupir* was a derivative piece of 'avant-garde minimalist' choreography to some electronic sounds.

The more theatrical and show-business side of Balanchine's talents led him to do successful choreography for various Hollywood musicals, Broadway shows and opera ballets.

In addition to his influence on other choreographers, Balanchine has also had an enormous influence on dancers. He tended to prefer young, tall girls, capable of fast movement, athletic jumps and very high kicks and leg extensions. His abstract ballets were mainly choreographed for women. Indeed Balanchine has repeatedly said that, for him, ballet is about women. He prefers them to be super-efficient technicians rather than to have individual personalities or acting styles of their own. He also prefers them to be very young and still in their teens. Balanchine's best roles for men tended, on the other hand, to involve acting and personality—as in *Apollo, The Prodigal Son* and his recent creation of a comic role for Nureyev in *Le Bourgois Gentilhomme,* based on Molière. But it is the speed, strength and coolness of his female dancers which has come to be thought of as typically Balanchine, and thus, indeed, typically American.

Ninette de Valois (b.1898)

De Valois not only created the British Royal Ballet company. She also provided it, especially in its early years, with several of the staple works in its repertoire. Her ballets stressed drama and atmosphere rather than pure dance, both because those were useful works for a young company, still short of vir-

tuoso dancers, and because her inclinations ran in that direction. If Frederick Ashton laid the basis for the English classical and lyrical style, de Valois established a tradition of distinguished actor-dancers, whom the Royal Ballet has always developed and displayed to advantage.

As well as dancing with the Diaghilev company in its last years, de Valois also danced in Massine's company in 1922. The style of character dancing she developed in her ballets was clearly influenced by Massine. Her first ballet was a setting of Mozart's *Les Petits Riens,* as a curtain-raiser to the opera *Hansel and Gretel* at the Old Vic in 1928. Three of the ballets she created in the 1930s for the Vic-Wells Ballet—*Job, The Rake's Progress* and *Checkmate*—still feature regularly in the Royal Ballet's repertoire. Two others—*The Haunted Ballroom* and *The Prospect Before Us*—were revived in the 1950s but have recently been neglected.

Job, The Rake's Progress and *Checkmate* may be regarded as classics of the English repertoire. They had English composers and designers, while *Job* and *The Rake's Progress* took their artistic inspiration from English sources.

Job was described as 'a masque for dancing' rather than a ballet; distinctions between ballet and other forms of theatrical dance were more precise in the 1930s. The original idea for the work came from Geoffrey Keynes, an expert on the art of William Blake. He persuaded Gwendolen Raverat to prepare stage designs based on Blake's illustrations to the biblical Book of Job. Vaughan Williams then wrote the powerful score. Keynes suggested the work to Diaghilev, who rejected it as 'too English' and 'too old-fashioned'. It still had no choreographer! Then Ninette de Valois became interested in the project, and choreographed it in 1931. Anton Dolin played Satan, the only virtuoso role; it was later taken for many years by Robert Helpmann. *Job* was a staple of the Sadler's Wells repertoire throughout the 1930s and into the 1950s. Then it did indeed begin to seem 'old-fashioned'. With the changing cycles of fashion, and the revival of interest in all forms of dance, not just classical ballet, it was revived again, with great success, in the 1970s. It is a spectacular and moving work, which combines religious sincerity with theatricality.

The Rake's Progress is also based on pictures, in this case the series of the same name by Hogarth. Like *Job, The Rake's Progress* relies more on mime, acting and stagecraft than on dancing, though there is a touching solo on point for the Betrayed Girl. Seven scenes depict the rise and fall of the Rake, from riches to the mad-house, a shocking final scene full of horrifying grotesques. The dancer playing

Robert Helpmann in the mad-house scene which concludes Ninette de Valois' The Rake's Progress

the Rake has to range from elegance and period style at the beginning to frenzied dementia at the end. The role was created by Walter Gore; Robert Helpmann was one of its most famous interpreters. Markova created the Betrayed Girl, which was later danced for many years by Fonteyn. Outstanding recent interpreters of the Rake included David Wall and Stephen Jefferies.

De Valois was as successful in recreating the atmosphere of eighteenth-century London, and bringing Hogarth's paintings to life, as she had been with Blake and the Bible. The ballet was a success from its first performance in 1935 and has been in the Sadler's Wells/Royal Ballet repertoire ever since. Important ingredients in its success are the designs (after Hogarth) by Rex Whistler and the effective atmospheric music by Gavin Gordon.

Checkmate, created in 1937, is in some ways the most 'dated' of these three ballets, though it is still performed fairly regularly. It brings to life a game of chess. The black players, led by a strong and treacherous Queen, represent Death. They at-

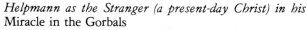
Helpmann as the Stranger (a present-day Christ) in his Miracle in the Gorbals

tack the gentler and weaker red forces, who represent Love. The Black Queen seduces and kills the Red Knight, so that she can kill the senile and doddering Red King. The Black Queen requires a tall, authoritative ballerina, strong on her points, the Red Knight is a virtuoso dancer, and the Red King must be a convincing mime. These roles were created by June Brae, Harold Turner and Robert Helpmann. Helpmann continued to play the King off and on, into the early 1970s. The Black Queen

Artists of the Royal Ballet in the Waltz from Ashton's
Façade

provided Beryl Grey with one of her best roles in the 1940s and 1950s.

The music by Bliss is powerful and dramatic but the sets by E. McKnight Kauffer now seem rather too typical of the commercial art of the 1930s. When strongly danced and acted, however, *Checkmate* is still very effective and exciting.

De Valois also choreographed a number of other ballets, most of which now seem to be forgotten. Her works were extremely influential in developing the acting skills of British dancers and the tastes of British audiences. They provided the repertoire with much-needed dramatic contrast to the classics and were its principal ballets before Ashton got into his stride as the country's leading choreographer.

Ninette de Valois became a Dame of the British Empire in 1951 in recognition of her services to British ballet. These are immeasurable. Without her, British ballet might never have developed and flourished. It would certainly have been different.

Robert Helpmann (b.1909)

The only one of Helpmann's ballets which is still performed from time to time by the Royal Ballet is *Hamlet*. His *Comus* and *Miracle in the Gorbals* were in the regular repertoire in the 1940s and, like the de Valois ballets, provided dramatic and theatrical works at a time when the company was short of classical dancers. In the 1960s, Helpmann also choreographed some ballets which were in the repertoire of the Australian Ballet for several years; two of them, *The Display* and *Yugen*, were performed by the company at Covent Garden in 1965. Also for the Australian Ballet, he directed Ronald Hynd's *The Merry Widow*.

Helpmann's link with Russian ballet is not with Diaghilev but with Pavlova. He was 'hooked' on ballet when he first saw her dance on one of her Australian tours, and he studied with members of her company there. He came to London in 1933 and was promptly accepted by de Valois for the Sadler's Wells Ballet. He soon became its leading male dancer, and Fonteyn's partner until 1950.

Hamlet, to Tchaikovsky's fantasy-overture of the same name had its première in 1942, with Helpmann himself in the title-role. In 1981 Dowell and Jeffries almost equalled his success in it. The ballet tells the events of Hamlet's life in jumbled, flash-back form, as remembered by him in his dying dream. It includes the Freudian notion that Hamlet confused Gertrude and Ophelia, cleverly conveyed to the audience by having the two dancers replacing each other constantly in front of him. It is an effective piece of theatre, which depends to a large extent on Helpmann's magnetic personality.

Miracle in the Gorbals, first produced in 1944, was also a powerful theatrical work. It seemed more like a mime play than a ballet, and told the story of a present-day Christ (played by Helpmann) visiting the slums of Glasgow and being destroyed because of his involvement with a prostitute. It has music by Bliss. It fell out of the repertoire when the emphasis shifted towards more pure danced works, and against mime. It might find renewed popularity as it is akin to many modern dance works, and more effective than most of them.

Helpmann was knighted in 1968.

Frederick Ashton (b.1904)

For at least 35 years (1945–1980), Ashton was the most important choreographer in Britain and was generally acknowledged to be—with Balanchine—one of the two great choreographers of our time and one of the greatest of all time. The roles he created for Margot Fonteyn helped her to establish her status as the leading ballerina of the western world and his style—sometimes described as 'the English style'—equally played a crucial role in establishing the Royal Ballet as the western world's leading classical company.

Like Helpmann, Ashton was first 'hooked' on ballet by Pavlova, in Peru where he was brought up. Soon after, his family moved home to England, where he saw performances by the Diaghilev company. In 1924 he started having weekly ballet lessons with Massine. After six months, when Massine left London, Ashton transferred to Rambert's school, and it was Rambert who encouraged him to try choreography. His first work was *The Tragedy of Fashion* (1926), which was included in a revue at the Lyric Theatre, Hammersmith. None of the numerous ballets Ashton made for Rambert survive; his earliest ballet in the present repertoire is *Façade,* made for the Camargo Society in 1931. He made *Les Rendezvous* for the Sadler's Wells Ballet in 1933, joining the company as a choreographer and dancer in 1935. Since then he made a continuous stream of ballets for the company, interrupted only by the Second World War, when he served in the Royal Air Force. He became associate director of the company in 1952 and succeeded de Valois as director in 1963, retiring in 1970. He continued to make occasional ballets for the company after that. He was knighted in 1962.

Façade and *Les Rendezvous* are similar, being chic and amusing suites of dances, loosely linked together. *Façade* originally consisted of poems by Edith Sitwell recited to music by William Walton. Later Walton wrote a concert suite, without the poems, which Ashton used for the ballet, though there have been occasional performances at which the poems were also recited. The numbers are mainly gentle parodies of the ballroom dances of the '20s', with a Scottish dance thrown in for good measure. The highlights are 'popular song', a soft-shoe shuffle for two men, and 'tango', in which an exaggeratedly sexy dago hurls a debutante to the ground and twirls her upside down in the air, a parody which has since had many imitators. Ashton himself created the role of the dago, and continued to dance it at intervals throughout his career. Helpmann also had a big success in the role, which provides opportunities for larger-than-life comic acting.

Les Rendezvous, to music by Auber, provokes relaxed smiles rather than loud laughter. It starts with the dancers crossing the stage and shaking hands as they meet, and it ends with various couples departing through iron gates at the back of the

Left, *Deanne Bergsma (as the Hostess) with Bronislava Nijinska and Frederick Ashton at a rehearsal of Nijinska's social comedy* Les Biches *and,* **right,** *The Royal Ballet in Ashton's* Les Patineurs, *his ever-popular skating ballet*

stage. There is a charming and delicate ballerina role, created by Markova, and a virtuoso male role, created by Idzikowski. A particularly distinctive number is the *pas de trois* for two men and a girl, in which their arms bob up and down, almost like clockwork, and the girl is twisted quickly from side to side, an effect Ashton repeated many years later in his brilliant Neapolitan Dance for *Swan Lake.* There is also an energetic precision *pas de quatre* for men, which ends with them half lying on the floor supporting their heads on their hands, waiting for the girls to join them. Both *Façade* and *Les Rendez-vous* have been in the repertoire regularly since their creation and continue to be very popular. They are also performed by various foreign companies.

Les Patineurs (1937) has probably been performed even more frequently and is even more popular. It might be called the English answer to *Les Sylphides.* Set to lilting music by Meyerbeer, it did for a skating rink what Fokine's ballet did for moonlit glades. Like *Les Sylphides,* it has regularly been used as an opening ballet in triple-bill programmes. It has remained constantly in the British repertoire, and is also performed by foreign companies. It's a suite of lively dances, including a virtuoso role for the principal male, the Blue Skater, who closes the ballet with a seemingly endless series of pirouettes as the curtain falls. The ballet also has its occasional touches of comedy, provided by simulated falls on the 'ice'.

Another Ashton ballet from 1937 that is still in the Royal Ballet repertoire, and also performed by

the Joffrey Ballet in the United States, is *A Wedding Bouquet,* a strange caricature of a French wedding, with nonsense verses by Gertrude Stein recited by an increasingly drunk narrator at the side of the stage. The verses occasionally bear some haphazard relationship to the characters and actions on the stage, but mostly do not. Originally they were sung by a chorus, but later they were spoken by Constant Lambert, the Vic-Wells Ballet's first musical director. Robert Helpmann was a very successful narrator in later years and so, most recently, was Anthony Dowell. Ninette de Valois gave her farewell performance as a dancer with the company in this ballet. The music and décor are by Lord Berners.

The other Ashton ballets performed today were all created in his most prolific and mature period, after the Second World War, when the Sadler's Wells Ballet had moved to the larger stage of Covent Garden. His first ballet there was the very successful *Symphonic Variations* (1946), an abstract work for six dancers to the music by César Franck. It provided Fonteyn with one of her most famous roles, in which she was hailed by her biographer James Monahan as a supreme example of musicality and 'line'. The ballet is still revived, with new casts, from time to time.

Other outstanding 'abstract' ballets made by Ashton since then include *Scènes de Ballet* (Stravinsky, 1948), *Homage to the Queen* (Malcolm Arnold, 1953), *Birthday Offering* (Glazunov, 1956), *Monotones* (Satie, 1965–66), and *Rhapsody* (Rachmaninov, 1980). The first two of these were classical display pieces, created for gala occasions, while *Rhapsody* was primarily a vehicle for Baryshnikov, who was appearing as a guest with the company. *Monotones* is a unique work consisting of two *pas de trois,* one created in 1965 and the second, which is now performed first, the following year. The original trio consisted of two men and a woman in white, moving and balancing slowly as if floating in outer space. It is generally regarded as a masterpiece, and certainly the more interesting of the two sections; it is still often performed on its own. The later section is for two women and a man, originally dressed in green, later changed to brown. It provides a more 'earthly' contrast to the white trio.

Jazz Calendar (1968) is a semi-abstract ballet to symphonic jazz by Richard Rodney Bennett. It's based on the rhyme beginning 'Monday's child is fair of face', and lightheartedly illustrates the seven days of the week in dance. Friday's child, 'loving and giving', is an erotic *pas de deux,* first danced by Antoinette Sibley and Nureyev, while Saturday's child, who 'works hard for his living', is a ballet class for a group of boys who are worked to dropping point by their ballet-master. It's also performed by the Joffrey Ballet.

The principal one-act 'story' ballets by Ashton which have been performed recently are *Daphnis and Chloe, Marguerite and Armand, The Dream, Enigma Variations,* and *A Month in the Country.*

Wendy Groombridge dancing the role of Monday's child ('fair of face') in Ashton's Jazz Calendar

Daphnis and Chloe (1951), to Ravel's music, provided Fonteyn with one of her most touching roles as Chloe, and has an interesting modern Greek setting by John Craxton. *Marguerite and Armand* (1963), to music by Liszt, is virtually a *pas de deux*—with a few extra characters—for Fonteyn and Nureyev as Marguerite Gautier and Armand Duval from Dumas' *La Dame aux Camélias*. Fonteyn and Nureyev performed it all over the world and it is not certain if it will be performed by other dancers.

The Dream (1964), one of Ashton's most popular ballets, is a version of Shakespeare's *A Midsummer Night's Dream*, using the music by Mendelssohn, arranged by John Lanchbery. It has a wonderful lyrical *pas de deux* for Titania and Oberon, created by Sibley and Dowell, and comic roles for Bottom and the human lovers. It is remarkably successful in capturing the mood and humour of Shakespeare's play, provides several dancers with rewarding roles, and has alternative and equally effective décors by Henry Bardon and Peter Farmer.

Enigma Variations (1968), marked a new departure for Ashton. Using Elgar's very well-known music, he showed Elgar himself, surrounded by his wife and various friends. A slight plot is provided by the arrival of a telegram, which causes general rejoicing at the end of the ballet. (A programme note explains that the telegram informs Elgar that Richter has agreed to conduct his music.) The *pas de trois* for Elgar, his wife and his friend Jaeger is an acknowledged masterpiece, conveying the ideas of trust and friendship. Derek Rencher, the first interpreter of Elgar, used make-up to achieve a remarkable resemblance, and Svetlana Beriosova was deeply moving as Lady Elgar, accepting her husband's occasional flirtations with younger girls. The sets and costumes by Julia Trevelyan Oman are extremely realistic, and Ashton succeeds in devising a great deal of dancing in Edwardian period clothes.

A Month in the Country (1976) is a continuation of this style, a danced version of Turgenev's play. Julia Trevelyan Oman again did the realistic set and costumes. Lanchbery again arranged the score, this time using music by Chopin. Lynn Seymour had a big personal success as Natalia Petrovna, the first middle-aged role created for her, after her series of convincing teenagers in ballets by MacMillan. Dowell also had a big success as Belyaev, the young tutor. *Les Illuminations,* made

*Above, **right**, Marion Tait and Carl Myers in the Sadler's Wells Royal Ballet's production of Ashton's* The Two Pigeons *and,* **below,** *David Wall as Belyaev, the tutor, and Wendy Ellis as Vera in Ashton's version of Turgenev's* A Month in the Country

Left, *Annette Page, David Blair, Anya Linden and Margot Fonteyn (kneeling) in Ashton's abstract masterpiece,* Symphonic Variations *and,* **below,** *Vyvyan Lorrayne and Robert Mead as Isobel Fitton and Meath Baker in Ashton's* Enigma Variations, *a ballet about Sir Edward Elgar and his friends*

Left, *Ashton's* Monotones, *an abstract 'space-age' ballet with Michael Coleman (left), Vyvyan Lorrayne and Anthony Dowell*

for New York City Ballet in 1950, used music by Benjamin Britten to tell episodes based on the writings of Rimbaud. It was revived by the Joffrey Ballet in 1980.

Ashton's full-length works are *Cinderella* (1948), *Sylvia* (1952), *Romeo and Juliet* (1955), *Ondine* (1958), *La Fille mal Gardée* (1960) and *The Two Pigeons* (1961). Three of these—*Cinderella, La Fille mal Gardée,* and *The Two Pigeons*—are regularly in the repertoire, and are discussed in the previous chapter. *Sylvia* has been abandoned; *Romeo and Juliet,* made for the Royal Danish Ballet, was presumed 'forgotten' for many years. *Ondine,* based on a story about a water-sprite and her human lover by Friedrich de la Motte Fouquet, was regarded by most critics as mainly a vehicle for Fonteyn. The solo in which she danced with her own shadow was particularly memorable. The ballet was occasionally performed by other ballerinas, and is due for revival.

Ashton also did the crucial choreography for the original production of Britten's opera, *Death in Venice,* and choreographed the fantasy film, *Tales from Beatrix Potter,* in which the dancers wear elaborate animal masks.

Antony Tudor (b.1908)

Tudor is regarded by connoisseurs as one of the great choreographers of our time, on a level with Ashton and Balanchine. He is comparatively unknown to the general public; his output is extremely small—it is a matter of quality, not quantity—and there were long periods when his ballets were not performed in Britain. His best-known works are *Jardin aux Lilas* and *Dark Elegies.*

Born in London, Tudor began his studies with

Rambert and choreographed his first ballets for her. His works have often been described as 'psychological', because they deal with human relationships. He dislikes this label, arguing that any work about human beings must inevitably deal with their relationships.

Jardin aux Lilas was made for Ballet Rambert in 1936 and remained in the Rambert repertoire till the company abandoned the classical style. It has also been performed by many other companies, including American Ballet Theatre and the Royal Ballet. It is sometimes called *Lilac Garden,* but Tudor prefers the original French title. Set to haunting and atmospheric music by Chausson, it shows a wedding party attended by the bridegroom's mistress and the bride's former lover. There is a series of interrupted meetings and dances; the ballet ends with the bride reluctantly leaving with 'the man she must marry'. There is a famous tableau in which the four principal characters 'freeze', looking at each other. Tudor himself originally danced the bridegroom; his friend and regular collaborator Hugh Laing danced the lover.

Dark Elegies (1937), also made for Rambert, was revived by that company in 1980 after many years neglect. It was also staged for the first time by the Royal Ballet in the same year. It has long been in the repertoire of Ballet Theatre. Set to Mahler's *Kindertotenlieder,* it shows a group of villagers in an unspecified place, mourning after some unspecified disaster. The style is more akin to 'modern dance' than to classical ballet. In addition to Tudor and Laing, the original cast included the

Antony Tudor rehearsing Merle Park and Anthony Dowell in his Shadowplay, *an allegorical tale about a jungle boy*

Above, *from left to right, Rudolf Nureyev, David Wall, Ann Jenner, Anthony Dowell and Laura Connor in the Royal Ballet's production of Jerome Robbins's* Dances at a Gathering *and,* **below,** *The Royal Ballet in John Cranko's* Card Game. **Right,** *Scottish Theatre Ballet in Darrell's full length* Beauty and the Beast

young Agnes de Mille, who later became a famous American choreographer of folk ballets and Broadway shows.

In 1938 Tudor and Laing formed their own London Ballet, for which Tudor made *Gala Performance,* to music by Prokofiev. This ballet was later performed by Ballet Rambert for many years, and also by Ballet Theatre. It is a satire on the exaggerated antics of star ballerinas. First the dancers are shown preparing and practising before a gala; then we see the gala itself. Ballerinas from Moscow, Milan and Paris compete with each other, each showing some of the typical traits of their national styles and temperaments. Their efforts to upstage each other are extremely funny, and there is also some brilliant virtuoso dancing to excite the audience. It is one of the few successful comic ballets, and has had many imitators.

Also in 1938, Tudor made another comic ballet, *Judgement of Paris.* Set to music from Kurt Weill's *Threepenny Opera,* it shows a sleazy bar where three tired whores rob a rich, drunken patron. It is slight, but amusing, and provides good opportunities for mime and character dancing.

In 1940, Tudor and Laing moved to New York, seeking greater opportunities. It is sometimes argued that Tudor should have been engaged for the Sadler's Wells Ballet, but de Valois could not afford or find opportunities for a further choreographer, in addition to herself, Ashton and Helpmann. Britain's loss was America's gain, as Tudor joined the newly formed Ballet Theatre as it was then called and worked with it more or less continuously ever since. His principal works for American Ballet Theatre are *Pillar of Fire* (1942), *Romeo and Juliet* (1943), *Undertow* (1945), *The Leaves are Fading* (1975) and *The Tiller in the Fields* (1979).

When Laing gave up dancing, Tudor lost his inspiration. He did very little creative work in the 1950s. His 'come-back' was *Echoing of Trumpets,* made for the Royal Swedish Ballet in 1963. He made *Shadowplay,* his first work for the Royal Ballet, in 1967 and *Knight Errant* for the Royal Ballet's touring section in 1968.

Pillar of Fire, to music by Schoenberg, provided Nora Kaye with one of her most famous dramatic roles as Hagar, a woman who is jealous of her younger sister's flirtations with her lover and so gives herself to a stranger. Tudor's *Romeo and Juliet* used music by Delius and was first danced by Markova and Laing. *Undertow,* another highly dramatic work, has music by the American composer William Schuman. It is about a murderer, originally danced by Laing, and the background events which led up to his crime. All these ballets were regularly performed by American Ballet Theatre for many years.

The Leaves are Fading and *The Tiller in the Fields* showed a new Tudor, more concerned with abstract classical dancing and less with drama or humour. They are not completely abstract, however. Both are danced to music by Dvorak. *Leaves* suggests various relationships, while *Tiller* has a slight plot about a shy village boy and a girl who seduces him and actually becomes pregnant—a surprising and possibly jarring realistic touch—at the end of the ballet. The ballet mainly consists of charming pastiche folk dances.

Shadowplay, to music by Charles Koechlin, is a strange allegorical work, about a jungle boy 'with matted hair', who seems to be learning about life from bird and monkey-like creatures, a female seductress and a powerful male figure. The exact nature of these characters, and their relationships, is not made explicit. The ballet ends with the boy crouching and scratching himself, like the monkeys. It is not clear whether he has learned anything or not. The ballet is curiously effective and engrossing, and provided Anthony Dowell with a created role exceptionally well suited to his talent and personality. He later danced it with American Ballet Theatre.

Knight Errant, to music by Richard Strauss, similarly provided David Wall with a remarkable role, as a rake who seduces three women and then surprises them by arranging secret rendezvous—with their husbands! It is a bawdy comedy, with a complicated plot, which failed to win a permanent place in the repertoire though many critics admired it and feel it should be revived.

In addition to his choreography, Tudor worked regularly as a ballet master and director with American Ballet Theatre. He taught at various New York ballet schools, and was director of the Royal Swedish Ballet for the 1949–50 season.

Jerome Robbins (b.1918)

Robbins is a more controversial choreographer than Ashton, Balanchine or Tudor. Most experienced and distinguished critics would place him in the same élite category, but some still think that his talent depends more on theatricality and slickness than on original creativity. His reputation as a serious choreographer has been affected for some people by his enormous success as a choreographer and director of Broadway shows. Nevertheless, at least one of his ballets—*Dances at a Gathering*—is generally accepted as a masterpiece and so, in its very different and more modern way, is *Fancy Free.*

Robbins was born in New York, of partly Russian Jewish parentage. He studied acting as well as dancing, and made his stage debut as an actor with a

Yiddish theatre in New York. He appeared as a dancer in Broadway musicals before joining Ballet Theatre in 1940. *Fancy Free,* his first ballet, was made for the company in 1944 and was an immediate hit. To specially written music by Leonard Bernstein, it shows three US sailors on shore leave, visiting a bar and picking up girls. The dancing is clearly in Broadway rather than classical ballet style, though some of the sailors are given difficult balletic jumps and spins. *Fancy Free* was the basis of the very successful movie, *On the Town,* also choreographed by Robbins, which starred Gene Kelly and Frank Sinatra as two of the sailors.

Interplay, made for a revue in 1945, is a lively abstract work, with hints of human relationships, to jazzy music by Morton Gould. It has been performed regularly by both American Ballet Theatre

Above, *Jerome Robbins, choreographer of classic ballets and of* West Side Story

Below, *Ballets U.S.A., Robbins's own company, in* The Concert, *his hilarious parody of classical ballet and of concert audiences*

and New York City Ballet, and is an ideal ballet for displaying the talents of young dancers, snapping their fingers, wiggling their hips, and almost jiving as they dance.

Robbins transferred to New York City Ballet in 1949, staying with the company for ten years. During that period he made several ballets. *Age of Anxiety,* an interesting work based on W.H.Auden's poem and set to music by Leonard Bernstein, has not been performed for some time. *The Cage, Fanfare, Afternoon of a Faun* and *The Concert,* however, remain in the NYCB repertoire; *Fanfare* was also performed by the Royal Danish Ballet, while *Faun* and *The Concert* have been frequently performed by the Royal Ballet.

The Cage (1951), a dramatic work to music by Stravinsky, gave Nora Kaye another of her powerful roles, this time as the leader of a female insect-like society which captures, seduces, castrates and kills male intruders. *Fanfare* (1953) is a comedy work set to Britten's 'The Young Person's Guide to the Orchestra', or Variations on a Theme by Purcell. The instruments of the orchestra are introduced by a narrator and amusingly impersonated by dancers. There are several character roles for older dancers, which were particularly well played by the Royal Danish Ballet.

Afternoon of a Faun (1953), to the Debussy music used by Nijinsky, shows a male and a female dancer practising in a ballet studio, totally self-absorbed except when the man surprises the girl with a brief kiss. It is as successful an interpretation of the music as Nijinsky's, and has a great appeal to present-day dancers and audiences.

The Concert (1956), to music by Chopin, is one of the funniest of all ballets. It satirizes an audience at a piano recital, showing them fighting for seats, disturbing each other with their late arrivals and paper rustling, and then fantasizing to the music. The fantasies include a hilarious balletic spoof, a little like Tudor's *Gala Performance,* a husband 'murdering' his bossy wife, and a charming sequence with umbrellas in imaginary rain.

In 1958 Robbins formed his own Ballets U.S.A., for which he made *Moves,* an abstract ballet performed in silence, and *New York Export: Opus Jazz,* a lively work to music by Robert Prince. Both these works were later taken into the repertoire of the Joffrey Ballet.

In 1965, Robbins made a new version of Stravinsky's *Les Noces* for American Ballet Theatre. It was more realistic and more obviously folksy than Nijinska's version, and is preferred by some people.

He returned to New York City Ballet in 1969, and has remained there since. His major ballets during this period were *Dances at a Gathering, In the Night, The Goldberg Variations, Watermill, Dybbuk Variations, Mother Goose Suite, Other Dances,* and *The Four Seasons.* These remain in the current repertoire, and *Dances at a Gathering* is also performed regularly by the Royal Ballet.

Dances (1969) is a suite of loosely linked dances set to piano music by Chopin. There are ten dancers, meeting and parting; there is a mock contest of skill between two male dancers, a lonely girl who tries vainly to find a partner, and a strange, haunting finale when one of the men touches the ground, as if to say farewell to the earth or to seek reassurance that it is still there, and the couples walk off into an unknown future. It is possible to see the ballet as a ritual gathering of old friends, or as a tribute or farewell to their country—there are hints of Polish national dance steps to match Chopin's music. Some episodes can be played for laughs, and some almost draw tears. Yet essentially it is an 'abstract' ballet, with no plot but with a great deal of beautiful and difficult dancing.

In the Night (1970) is in a sense a continuation of *Dances,* using more Chopin pieces, showing three couples meeting and parting in the starlight. *Goldberg Variations* (1971) is a long abstract ballet to Bach's famous music.

Watermill (1972), by contrast, is an exercise in Japanese style, with music by Teiji Ito, using the techniques of Noh drama to show a man recalling the phases of his life. It is a difficult and not a popular work, but it is much admired by people who can accept its deliberately slow and understated style and its Japanese feeling. *Dybbuk Variations* (1974) was an attempt to illustrate the Jewish legend of a girl possessed by the soul of her lover in a series of dances, to music by Leonard Bernstein. It was later shortened into a series of dances for men, still containing hints of Jewish folk-steps, and was retitled simply *Suite of Dances.*

Mother Goose Suite (1975) is a charming series of fairy-tale stories, acted out by a group of dancers who pick costumes out of a hamper and adopt the various roles required. It is set to Ravel's music of the same name, and contains pastiches of classical ballet.

Other Dances, to still further piano music by Chopin, 'left over' from *Dances at a Gathering* and *In the Night,* is a *pas de deux,* created for a gala for Makarova and Baryshnikov, and later performed by various other couples, including Makarova and *Dowell, who gave the London première.*

The Four Seasons (1979), to ballet music by Verdi, followed Verdi's original scenario, interpreting the seasons in dance. The 'autumn' bacchanale seemed at first like a deliberate parody of the Bolshoi Ballet's *Walpurgisnacht,* especially as Baryshnikov made fun of his extravagant leaps.

Later the role was danced with slightly different choreography and in a completely serious manner by Peter Martins. The ballet contains numerous opportunities for virtuoso dancing and is a very effective setting of the music.

Robbins also conceived and directed the musical *West Side Story* and directed and choreographed many other musicals, including *Fiddler on the Roof.* He also directed some plays. His combination of Broadway and classical ballet skills has made him the most widely popular of the leading American choreographers.

John Cranko (1927–1973)

Although born in South Africa, Cranko's work was mainly in Britain and Germany, where he came to be regarded as the outstanding choreographer of his generation. He created the bulk of the repertoire of the Stuttgart Ballet, as well as training and coaching its dancers, enabling the company to achieve world fame and to undertake tours to major foreign opera houses. Although there were some critical reservations about his choreography in the United States, the Stuttgart Ballet was immensely popular there and enjoyed regular successful seasons at the Metropolitan Opera. It also had successful seasons in London. Several of Cranko's works remain in the regular repertoire of the Royal Ballet.

Cranko arrived in London and started studying at the Sadler's Wells School in 1946. He soon began choreography, and did several ballets for the Sadler's Wells Theatre Ballet and then for the main company at Covent Garden. Those for the SWTB included a *Beauty and the Beast pas de deux* to Ravel's music (1949), *Harlequin in April* (1951) a complex symbolical ballet about Harlequin and Columbine, to music by Richard Arnell and *Bonne-Bouche* (1953) a comedy about a smart London girl who marries an African cannibal, to music by Arthur Oldham. Those for Covent Garden included *The Shadow* (1953), a mysterious and effective work to music by Dohnányi about a man torn between a cheerful extrovert girl and an elusive romantic one who mysteriously disappears—a role memorably created by Svetlana Beriosova. Another of his Covent Garden successes was *Antigone* (1950), a modern version of the Greek tragedy with another powerful role for Beriosova and some male dances which were unusually athletic and virile for the company at that time, set to music by Theodorakis. The work packed a powerful anti-war punch. In 1957, Cranko made his first full-length work, *The Prince of the Pagodas,* at Covent Garden. Unfortunately none of these works has survived in the present repertoire, though *Beauty and the Beast* was revived several times, most recently

John Cranko at a rehearsal of his Card Game

by Northern Dance Theatre in 1977. *The Shadow* and *Antigone* might well be popular again today.

Two ballets from that period have not only survived, however, but have been popular and hardy perennials in the Royal Ballet's repertoire: *Pineapple Poll* and *The Lady and the Fool.*

Pineapple Poll was produced by the Sadler's Wells Theatre Ballet in 1951. Cranko's scenario is *based on one of W.S. Gilbert's Bab Ballads*, and the music is selected and arranged by Charles Mackerras from various operas by Sullivan. The amusing décor is by Osbert Lancaster. It is a tale of a handsome naval captain in Portsmouth, his rich well-bred fiancée and her chaperone, a bumboat girl who swoons at the sight of the captain and dresses up in sailor's uniform to get on board his ship, and the poor potboy from the inn who is pining for the girl. All ends happily and wittily, with the chaperone dressed up as Britannia, the captain promoted to admiral, and the potboy getting the captain's uniform and the girl! The dances include a hornpipe for the dashing captain, and an ingenious and amusing *pas de trois* in which the captain flirts with his fiancée while gossiping with the chaperone. *Pineapple Poll,* with its well-known melodies and simple, charming story, is always a hit with audiences. Several generations of British dancers have taken the leads, since they were created by Elaine Fifield, David Blair and David Poole. The music has become popular in its own right as a concert suite. The ballet has been in the repertoire of several foreign companies, including the Australian Ballet, the National Ballet of Canada and the Joffrey Ballet.

The Lady and the Fool was also made for the Sadler's Wells Theatre Ballet, in 1954. This time Charles Mackerras did for Verdi what he had earlier done for Sullivan, concocting an admirably danceable and tuneful score, with appropriate dramatic touches, from lesser-known Verdi operas. The ballet is similar to Balanchine's *Night Shadow*, both in subject matter and in its use of operatic music. It takes place at a party given by a rich man whose guests include various aristocrats and ambassadors, and La Capricciosa, a mysterious masked beauty. She arrives at the party with two clowns she has picked-up in the street outside, and they perform a touching little dance—squabbling over and then dividing a rose—for the entertainment of the guests. Finally La Capricciosa falls in love with the tall clown, who succeeds in removing her last mask. She is then rejected by all the society people at the party, becomes an outcast, and leaves the party with the two clowns. This sentimental little tale of a beautiful but lonely woman, rich but afraid of life, can also be taken as a comment on class, racial or any other social divisions and prejudices.

Cranko's choreography for *The Lady and the Fool* includes contrasting virtuoso solos for the three suitors and a *pas de quatre* in which the heroine dances with each of them in turn, in a dance inspired by the Rose Adagio in *The Sleeping Beauty*. (Instead of giving her roses, the suitors remove her masks.) The original Lady was the South African dancer Patricia Miller; subsequent distinguished dancers in this role included Beryl Grey and Svetlana Beriosova. Kenneth MacMillan, Cranko's contemporary and for many years his friendly rival as a choreographer, was the original tall clown. David Blair had one of his best created roles as the arrogant host of the party, Signor Midas.

Like *Pineapple Poll*, *The Lady and the Fool* has been frequently revived by the Royal Ballet. It has also been performed by various other companies, including Stuttgart, Berlin, the Royal Danish and the Houston Ballets.

During the time he lived and worked in London, Cranko also staged ballets for foreign companies, directed Britten's opera *A Midsummer Night's Dream,* and staged two original and highly successful intimate revues, *Cranks* and *New*

Cranks. His versatility and popularity made him a British equivalent of Jerome Robbins, and indeed his ballets have sometimes been criticized for the same reasons, for being too glib and theatrical and not sufficiently original choreographically.

Cranko's most important works in Stuttgart were his full-length ballets, *Eugene Onegin* and *The Taming of the Shrew,* and his new versions of *Swan Lake, The Nutcracker* and *Romeo and Juliet.* His *Romeo and Juliet* is still preferred by many people to either the Lavrovsky or MacMillan versions. He also made a large number of short ballets. The best-known of these are *Card Game* (1965), *Opus 1* (1965), *Présence* (1968), *Brouillards* (1970), *Poème de l'Extase* (1970), *Initials R.B.M.E.* (1972) and *Traces* (1973).

Card Game, to Stravinsky's music, was first choreographed by Balanchine in 1937. This version has not survived. Cranko's popular version has been performed by the Royal Danish Ballet and the British Royal Ballet as well as by the Stuttgart company. It has a dominating central male role, a malevolent Joker who puts on a tutu and hilariously parodies a ballerina. This role was brilliantly created by the Danish dancer Egon Madsen, and later done equally successfully in Copenhagen by another Dane, Niels Kehlet. Christopher Gable was the first British interpreter, but Stephen Jefferies was probably the most successful.

Opus 1, to music by Webern, is about a man striving to reach an ideal. It was frequently performed by the Stuttgart company, and was also staged by the companies in Berlin and Frankfurt, by the Royal Danish Ballet and the Joffrey Ballet. *Présence* to music by Zimmermann, treats Molly Bloom, Ubu Roi and Don Quixote—well-known literary figures—as symbols of sex, power and idealism. It was also performed by the Munich company.

Brouillards, to music by Debussy, is a series of enigmatic sketches, shadowy and transitory like its title. It is one of Cranko's most serious and elusive works. It has also been performed by the Joffrey Ballet.

Poème de l'Extase was created as a vehicle for Fonteyn when she was a guest with the Stuttgart company. Inspired by a Colette novel and with décor in the style of Gustav Klimt, it was set to Scriabin's symphonic poem. Fonteyn appeared as a lady recalling her past loves and rejecting the attentions of her latest young suitor. It was also given a few performances by the Royal Ballet.

Initials R.B.M.E. was Cranko's tribute to his four leading dancers—Richard Cragun, Birgit Keil, Marcia Haydée and Egon Madsen. It is an abstract ballet set to Brahms' second Piano Concerto. *Traces* was inspired by the struggle of the Panovs to escape from the Soviet Union and was dedicated to them. It is about a woman who does escape and has to forget the horrors of the past before she can start her new life. Danced to the adagio from Mahler's 10th symphony, it provided Marcia Haydée with a strong dramatic role.

In addition to these Stuttgart ballets, Cranko made *Brandenburg Nos. 2 and 4* (1966), to Bach's music, for the Royal Ballet. It was a display of virtuoso dancing, making very strong demands on the men. Although it was much liked by some critics, it did not remain long in the repertoire.

Cranko led the revival of classical ballet in Germany, and his influence there is immeasurable. John Neumeier, now the leading choreographer in Germany, got his first opportunities with Cranko and it was Cranko's success in building up an important and internationally accepted company in Stuttgart that encouraged other German cities to spend more money on their ballet troupes. Cranko died at the height of his creative power in a plane bringing him and his company back from a successful visit to the United States.

Kenneth MacMillan (b.1919)

For many years Cranko and MacMillan were friendly rivals regarded in Britain and Germany as the outstanding choreographers of their generation. Both were extremely versatile, making every sort of ballet from short 'abstracts' to three-act dramatic works. Where Cranko's work had a persistent streak of happy fantasy, MacMillan's often had a sadder quality, with a recurring theme of unhappy sex or of a frustrated 'outsider'.

While Cranko was an acknowledged and enormous success as director of the Stuttgart ballet, MacMillan's periods of directing companies, first in Berlin and then in London, were much more controversial. In 1978, when he gave up the direction of the Royal Ballet, he decided to concentrate on choreography.

Born in Dunfermline, Scotland, MacMillan studied at the Sadler's Wells School and joined the Sadler's Wells Theatre Ballet on its formation in 1946. His first ballets, *Somnambulism* and *Laiderette,* were made for the Sadler's Wells Choreographic Group in 1953 and 1954. Both of them immediately revealed him as a major new talent, and also showed his penchant for slightly bitter-sweet themes. *Somnambulism,* to music by Stan Kenton, was concerned with neurotic dancers; it was taken into the repertoire of the Sadler's Wells Theatre Ballet. *Laiderette,* to music by Frank Martin, was about an ugly, rich girl, rejected by society; it was for a time in the repertory of Ballet Rambert.

MacMillan then made three successful ballets for the Sadler's Wells Theatre Ballet: *Danses Concertantes* and *House of Birds* in 1955 and *Solitaire*

Kenneth MacMillan demonstrating to Nureyev at a rehearsal of Romeo and Juliet

in 1956. These have all been revived at regular intervals, and *Solitaire* has been especially frequently performed. *Danses* is an abstract work to Stravinsky's music, MacMillan's first essay in the Balanchine style, to which he brought his own individual touch. The ballet was later performed by the Royal Danish Ballet. *House of Birds,* to music by Mompou, is based on a Grimm fairy-tale, about a bird-woman who captures and cages children. It was also performed by the Stuttgart Ballet. Both these ballets were designed in a distinctive modern style by Nicholas Georgiadis, and started this designer's long association with MacMillan and with ballet.

Solitaire, to a suite of dances by Malcolm Arnold, is a semi-abstract work about a lonely girl who tries to join in various group dances and games but is constantly rejected and left alone. She shrugs off this fate, accepting it philosophically. The dances are vivacious and amusing, including some virtuoso work for the men, and a witty polka for one of the girls. *Solitaire* was originally designed by Desmond Heeley, in a setting vaguely but attractively suggesting a derelict site, and was re-designed in 1978 by Barry Kay.

MacMillan's first ballet for the main Sadler's Wells company at Covent Garden was *Noctambules* (1956), to music by Humphrey Searle. It was about a hypnotist whose performance goes wrong and antagonizes his audience; it did not remain long in the repertoire.

Further ballets for the main company followed in quick succession and were much more successful. *The Burrow* (1958) a dramatic work to the music of Humphrey Searle, based on *The Diary of*

Anne Frank, was also taken into the repertory of the Royal Danish Ballet. *Agon* (1958) was another abstract to Stravinsky music that had previously been choreographed by Balanchine. MacMillan's version, in which some critics found suggestions of a plot about a brothel, was not popular, and was later succeeded in the Royal Ballet's repertoire by Balanchine's original version.

Macmillan's version of Stravinsky's *Le Baiser de la Fée* (1960), however, was more popular. It followed the composer's original fairy-tale scenario and provided good contrasting roles for Beriosova as the mysterious fairy and Lynn Seymour as the girl under her spell.

The Invitation, also made in 1960, has proved one of MacMillan's most popular and enduring ballets. To music by Matyas Seiber, it tells a story—partly based on Colette—of innocent teenagers experiencing rude sexual awakenings. It provided Lynn Seymour with one of her most memorable created roles as the girl who is raped by an older man and emotionally crippled as a result. There are also good roles for the teenage boy (Christopher Gable) who enjoys his first experience with an older woman (Anne Heaton) and for the older woman's seedy husband, who commits the rape (Desmond Doyle). The ballet was also performed by the Berlin ballet, and has been frequently revived by the Royal Ballet, with different casts.

In 1961, MacMillan made *Diversions,* an abstract ballet to music by Bliss which was well received and performed for several seasons. His version of Stravinsky's *Rite of Spring* (1962), with its dynamic central female role, created by Monica Mason, has remained fairly constantly in the repertoire. It shows a barbaric primitive ritual and has great power.

Symphony, another abstract ballet, this time to music by Shostakovitch, followed in 1963. It too, was performed quite frequently, though not as much as MacMillan's later Shostakovitch abstract, *Concerto,* made in Berlin in 1966. This work, to the second Piano Concerto, is frequently revived and the *pas de deux* from the slow movement is often performed on its own.

Two ballets made by MacMillan in Stuttgart around this time also earned permanent places in the British repertoire. *Las Hermanas* (1963), to music by Frank Martin, is based on Lorca's *The House of Bernardo Alba,* a story about a repressive mother, her daughters and a suitor. It is a grim work, ending in suicide, and relying heavily on mime and natural acting rather than on dancing. It has also been performed by various other companies, including American Ballet Theatre and the Berlin Ballet.

Song of the Earth, to Mahler's song-cycle, was first performed in 1965. It was one of the first of many ballets set to Mahler and to orchestral song-cycles, which became a popular genre in the 1970s. It interprets the songs impressionistically, not literally; they are linked by a male angel of death, created by Egon Madsen and danced subsequently by many distinguished interpreters, including Christopher Gable and Anthony Dowell. Marcia Haydée and Lynn Seymour were especially notable in the chief ballerina role.

Two ballets made in London in 1964—the Shakespearian *Images of Love* and the comic setting of Milhaud's *La Création du Monde*—were interesting but only moderately successful and did not survive. In 1965, however, Ashton invited MacMillan to make his first full-length ballet, *Romeo and Juliet,* for the Royal Ballet at Covent Garden. It was an immediate success and has been frequently performed ever since, taking its place as a classic. (It is discussed in the chapter on full-length ballets.) It was MacMillan's last big success in London, before he left to take over the direction of the Berlin Ballet.

MacMillan made several ballets during his period in Berlin, 1966–69. Apart from *Concerto,* these included *Anastasia, Olympiad* and *Cain and Abel.* He also staged his own versions of *Sleeping Beauty* and *Swan Lake. Anastasia* (1967) was a one-act work set to electronic music and the Fantaisies Symphoniques by Martinu and based on the experience of Anna Anderson, a woman who claimed to be the Princess Anastasia, the youngest daughter of the last Tsar. She was shown in a hospital ward, having a nightmare full of memories of the Russian Revolution and her escape. This ballet later became the last act of MacMillan's three-act *Anastasia,* staged for the Royal Ballet at Covent Garden. (See chapter on full-length ballets.)

Olympiad (1968) is a series of athletic dances to music by Stravinsky. *Cain and Abel* (1968) is a version of the biblical story, to music by Panufnik. Both were highly regarded in Berlin but *Olympiad* was not a success when it was later staged at Covent Garden.

MacMillan returned to Covent Garden in 1970. Apart from his series of full-length ballets, he also made numerous short works for both Royal Ballet companies. Some of these disappeared rapidly from the repertoire. Those which survived include *Triad, Elite Syncopations* and *The Four Seasons.*

Triad (1972), to music by Prokofiev, is about the relationships between a girl and two men, described in the programme as brothers. *Elite Syncopations* (1974) is a series of humorous dances in a 1920s dance-hall, to rags by Scott Joplin and others. The musicians, in fancy costumes by Ian Spurling, are on the stage with the dancers. The

Members of the Royal Ballet in MacMillan's Song of the Earth, *considered by many to be his outstanding abstract ballet*

work is very popular and is in the repertoire of both Royal Ballet companies. *The Four Seasons* (1975), to Verdi's ballet music, had a detailed but ambiguous setting; the action took place in a town square, where the inhabitants included soldiers and what seemed to be the ladies of a brothel. It was not clear what this had to do with the seasons, and the ballet has since been redesigned and revised. It contains some interesting, inventive and difficult choreography.

In 1976, MacMillan returned to Stuttgart to make *Requiem,* to Fauré's oratorio, an abstract work expressing the religious feeling of the music. It was hailed as one of his best works, developing the style of *Song of the Earth.* Many people commented that it was ironic that MacMillan should have made both these works in Stuttgart, largely because the administration at Covent Garden did not think such big orchestral and vocal scores suitable for the ballet repertory there.

Two short ballets made in London in 1979 both proved controversial. *La Fin du Jour,* to music by Ravel, was a tribute or lament for the vanished age of the 1930s; it concentrated on the carefree sports and nightlife of that period, not on its social problems. *Playground,* to music by Gordon Crosse, made for the Sadler's Wells section of the Royal Ballet, was a grim, dramatic work about a man who is attracted by a girl in a lunatic asylum and tries to

join the strange games played by the inmates. Its purpose struck many critics as obscure.

Gloria, on the other hand, made at Covent Garden in 1980, was much more enthusiastically received. Set to Poulenc's Gloria in G Major, it was the third of MacMillan's semi-abstract works to vocal and orchestral music. Placed by some critics in the same class as *Song of the Earth* and *Requiem,* it worried others by its mixture of realism and abstraction in depicting the tragic effects of the First World War on the young generation.

Other choreographers

A number of other British choreographers have worked successfully at home and abroad. Walter Gore's small-scale but charming ballets were for many years in the repertoires of Rambert and his own company, while Andrée Howard's equally charming *La Fête Etrange* has remained one of the Royal Ballet's regular works. Jack Carter staged versions of the classics all over the world, and several new ballets for small British companies. His *Witch Boy* was for years one of the most popular dramatic works in Festival Ballet's repertoire.

In the 1960s, Norman Morrice of Ballet Rambert seemed one of the most promising new choreographers, making dramatic works using classical ballet technique. He turned to 'modern

215

dance', however, when Ballet Rambert changed its style, and has not so far gone back to classical choreography, though his duties as director of the Royal Ballet may tempt him to do so. Peter Darrell has made a substantial body of popular ballets, ranging from full-length neo-classics to short dramatic works, for his Scottish Ballet, and so has Ronald Hynd for Festival Ballet, and various companies overseas.

Turning to the younger generation, Jonathan Thorpe has done interesting works in neo-classical style for Northern Ballet, while the Royal Ballet now places high hopes on David Bintley, Jonathan Burrows and Michael Corder, young dancers who have all successfully seized their choreographic opportunities. Michael Pink, also a product of the Royal Ballet School and now a dancer in Festival Ballet, has had similar opportunities with his company. It is too early to say whether any of these young men will turn out to be a new Ashton, Cranko or MacMillan.

The American choreographer Glen Tetley has had a very successful career as a freelance, making numerous ballets for many different companies, including the Royal Ballet, Festival Ballet, American Ballet Theatre and Ballet Rambert. His reputation is controversial, being much higher in Britain and western Europe than in his native United States. His best-known work, *Voluntaries,* was made in Stuttgart in 1973 and later taken into other repertoires, including those of the Royal Ballet and American Ballet Theatre. It is abstract, with religious undertones, to Poulenc's Concerto for Organ, Strings and Timpani, and was made as a memorial to Cranko. Tetley's admirers praise his combination of classical and modern styles, and find his works innovative and exciting. Others complain of his somewhat arbitrary use of music and think his choreographic invention is limited and banal.

John Neumeier, another American choreographer, is equally controversial. He is hero-worshipped in Germany, where he lives and works, divides opinions in Britain, and is condemned by most critics in his native country. He is extremely musical and inventive, but his works are often burdened with dramatic, literary and psychological themes which some people find too complex for ballet.

The Americans who *do* find favour in their own country include Gerald Arpino, Eliot Feld, Robert Joffrey and Michael Smuin. Choo San Goh, though born in Singapore and mainly trained in Europe, has come to be regarded as an American choreographer and is hailed by many critics there as the most promising talent for the future. All these choreographers tend to work in a neo-classical, Balanchine-inspired style, rather than making the folksy, comic or dramatic story-ballets associated with their predecessors, Agnes de Mille, Eugene Loring and Ruthanna Boris.

A number of dancers in New York City Ballet have also been encouraged to attempt choreography, naturally tending to follow the company's prevailing abstract style. John Clifford, who moved on to form the Los Angeles Ballet and choreograph successfully for it in a wide variety of styles, and Jacques d'Amboise, whose works are still performed by the NYCB, were the first of these choreographers. Peter Martins, Jean-Pierre Bonnefous and Joseph Duell are among the most recent. Martins' *Calcium Light Night,* to music by Charles Ives, won a permanent place in the NYCB repertoire.

Among the leading present-day choreographers in western Europe are Rudi van Dantzig, Hans van Manen and Jiri Kylián, all working mainly in The Netherlands. Van Dantzig and van Manen both had works produced by the Royal Ballet and other major companies, as well as their own Dutch National Ballet. Kylián has so far preferred to concentrate on building up his repertoire for Netherlands Dance Theatre. He has been hailed in the United States as the most talented new choreographer to come from Europe for many years. Laszlo Seregi of Budapest and Heinz Spoerli, a Swiss choreographer who has also worked in Germany, France and Canada, are much admired by some discerning critics.

None of these choreographers, however, has yet achieved the status and general acclaim accorded to those discussed in greater detail in this chapter.

Ballet for a new age

It is a truism that art reflects or anticipates its age. Like our society, ballet has changed rapidly in recent years. This change will continue. Already 'élitism' has become a dirty word, a mass popular audience is more desirable than a small discriminating one, and the pejorative 'provincial' has been converted into the complimentary 'regional'. (Producing art in capital cities now almost seems to require apology or justification, despite the fact that people choose the expense and inconvenience of living in capital cities largely because they want easy access to the arts.) Products are made for immediate effect, not for long life. The arts—theatre, cinema, music and painting—have come to specialize in shock effects and visceral sensations rather than logical development or coherent structure. 'Well-made' when applied to a play, is a term of abuse. Finally, reticence and embarrassment about the human body and about sex have given way to nudity, near-nudity, and the realistic representation of every kind of sexual activity. The lines between male and female have become blurred, with open acceptance of homo- and bi-sexuality, with unisex fashions, and with both sexes competing in the same jobs and lifestyles.

Ballet grew up as an élitist art, intended primarily for court circles and rich patrons. Audiences were small and critical, quick to make comparisons and to apply accepted standards of taste. Dance was supposed to be pleasing to the eye and ear, with interesting steps well fitted to suitable music. Ballerinas were petite and ethereal or sexy; male dancers were strong and virile, or showy virtuosi. The two sexes were contrasted, in appearance and dancing styles, not equated. Costumes concealed as much as they revealed, and were pretty rather than functional. Love and sex were suggested by formal gestures and conventional dances, not depicted realistically. Ballet was stylized not naturalistic.

Although Diaghilev and his choreographers made ballets more realistic, they remained in many respects stylized. In some ways, Fokine made the rules for judging ballets more formal, demanding that they should be coherent works of art, with dance, music, drama and décor playing roughly equal roles. Even when this was not achieved, it remained an ideal and a standard of judgement for many years. If ballets contained drama or human relationships, these were supposed to make sense. Unities of time and place were to be observed.

Throughout those years, it was generally agreed that good choreography and dancing consisted of the art that conceals art. Technique was not supposed to be flaunted—that was the road to circus, music-hall and acrobatics. Great choreographers found ways of displaying their dancers' techniques without making it look as if that were an end in itself. Great dancers found ways of making the difficult look easy. Subtlety was preferred to blatancy.

Recently, however, it has become more and more popular to assert that dancers are athletes. This was a useful way of destroying their image as weak or effeminate. Then this assertion became transformed into the desire to make dancers *look* like athletes, a very different thing. Partly this is classical ballet's reaction to the threat of 'modern dance' with its emphasis on mood and drama and its more limited physical techniques. Partly it is a desire to show off the remarkable advances in ballet technique, though in some cases these 'advances' merely consist in kicking legs higher or holding balances longer than would previously have been thought aesthetic. Mostly it is the desire to make a quick impression on a new, unsophisticated, mass audience.

New audiences can certainly appreciate great classics, great performances and great art. But they are also susceptible to the flashy and the meretricious, because they are not yet able to make comparative judgements and cannot always know what they are missing. The temptation for choreographers and dancers to 'play down' to their audience, and reap a quick reward, is enormous.

Fortunately television and the jet-age are powerful factors against such lowering of standards. Everyone can now see great performances at home. Successful choreographers and star dancers constantly travel the world. Audiences everywhere want to see them, and the artists want worldwide exposure and the fame and rewards which accompany it. Fewer ballet companies now preserve distinctive styles and repertoires, and nurture their own stars. A great choreographer—an Ashton, a Balanchine or a Cranko—could still keep his dancers at home with the promise of new roles created for them. A company without such a choreographer cannot. Increasingly the same ballets turn up in every repertoire, and the same stars dance their favourite roles with every company. There is much to be said for this trend, although it is regretted by many ballet purists. It militates against mediocrity, provincialism and artistic isolation. It may be ballet's best hope of preserving high standards, and of raising them further.

Choreographers have found two principal ways of achieving popular appeal with comparatively little effort. One is the spectacular full-length ballet using music which is already familiar and popular from some other medium. Symphonic music, pop music, opera and operetta has all been utilized in this way. Dance replacing song in an opera or operetta is a particularly easy way to quick popularity, if not to lasting success. The choreography need not be original if the audience is carried along by well-known tunes and a well-known story, however absurd, with some pretty costumes and sets.

These danced spectacles, now popular in most of the world, have not yet caught on in the United States, though they may still do so. What has caught on there, and been exported to Europe, is the abstract display of technical virtuosity. Balanchine and Robbins used technical virtuosity in the service of music; they constantly invented new steps and combinations of steps. Many of their successors use virtuosity for its own sake, scarcely caring about the music; instead of inventing new steps, they string together standard classroom exercises in faster and more dazzling combinations. Sometimes they do invent steps, which may not be pleasing to the eye. Ugly lifts, awkward balances and contorted positions are displayed simply for audiences to marvel at their difficulty.

There are many practitioners of this kind of choreography. Gerald Arpino, Glen Tetley, Jiri Kylián and Choo San Goh are among the most successful. Opinions differ about their quality, and about which of them are the best—more musical, more 'artistic', more inventive than the others. Sometimes their search for musicality leads to another kind of emptiness, a literal marriage of dancing steps to notes of music which can be as tiresome and sterile as the dance which ignores music altogether, or uses it wilfully. When their work is good, these choreographers achieve a new kind of excitement, a new kind of beauty, and indeed a new kind of ballet. It is tempting to call these space-age ballets. They may be part of a new art for a new time. They demand to be judged by new standards, perhaps by new critics.

These critics will have different expectations about choreography and different ideas about what constitutes a good ballet. They will also have different expectations about dancers. Where critics used to want uniformity, of race, height and even hair-colour, they may prefer diversity. 'Equal opportunities' for all mean that there are now tall, strong girl dancers who would once have been thought suitable only for teaching or gymnastics. There are effeminate, pretty men who would once have been relegated to musical comedy. There are black and yellow dancers in predominantly white companies, and vice versa. As the world has become one, and societies have become variegated and multi-racial, so has ballet.

Choreographers meet these trends by devising steps and movements which can be done by everyone together—men and women, tall and short, fat and thin, white, yellow and black. A new kind of uniformity and new contrasts replace the old ones of classical ballet. Athleticism and vitality replace restraint and gentle grace. Physical movement, rather than the projection of personality or the expression of a mood or emotion, becomes the name of the game. At their worst, these new ballets can look like bland television commercials. At their best, they have an aesthetic impact of their own. The new can be as rewarding as the old. Can the old also be preserved, even if only as a nostalgic and escapist trip? The classics are much more than that, but even if not, they could and should still be treasured and performed. But ballet must move forward as well.

Index

220